WEAR YOUR CHAIR

❧ When *Fashion* Meets INTERIOR DESIGN ❧

WEAR YOUR CHAIR

When *Fashion* Meets INTERIOR DESIGN

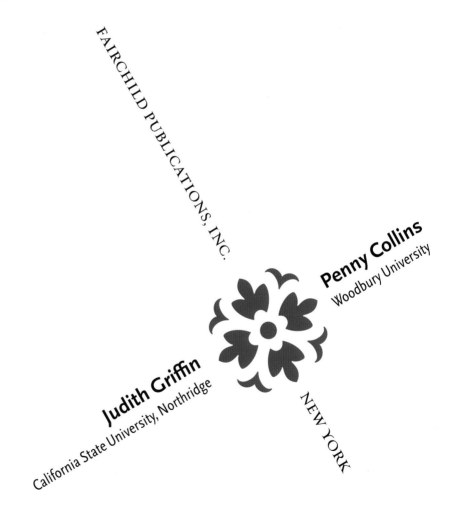

FAIRCHILD PUBLICATIONS, INC.

Penny Collins
Woodbury University

Judith Griffin
California State University, Northridge

NEW YORK

DIRECTOR OF SALES AND ACQUISITIONS: *Dana Meltzer Berkowitz*

EXECUTIVE EDITOR: *Olga T. Kontzias*

ASSISTANT ACQUISITIONS EDITOR: *Jaclyn Bergeron*

SENIOR DEVELOPMENT EDITOR: *Jennifer Crane*

DEVELOPMENT EDITOR: *Sylvia L. Weber*

PRODUCTION MANAGER: *Ginger Hillman*

SENIOR PRODUCTION EDITOR: *Elizabeth Marotta*

ART DIRECTOR: *Adam B. Bohannon*

PHOTO RESEARCHER: *Justine Brennan*

DEVELOPMENT EDITORIAL INTERN: *Claire Brennan*

DEVELOPMENT EDITORIAL INTERN: *David Shaiman*

PRODUCTION INTERN: *Michael Noto*

PRODUCTION HAZMAT SPECIALIST: *Anne Sanow*

COPY EDITOR: *Frances Koblin*

COVER AND INTERIOR DESIGN: *Adam B. Bohannon*

COVER ART: *Karl Lagerfeld's Chair Hat and Upholstered Dress*

FLIP-BOOK ANIMATION: *Bruce Cayard*

ADDITIONAL ILLUSTRATIONS: *Ron Carboni*

Library of Congress Catalog Card Number: 2006926684

ISBN: 978-1-56367- 581-2

GST R 133004424

Printed in China

TP15

We shared our ideas like sweaters, with easy exchange and lack of ownership. We gave over excess words, a single beautiful sentence that had to be cut but perhaps the other would like to have . . . we didn't so much discuss our work as volley ideas back and forth until neither of us was sure who belonged to what.

✿ Ann Patchett, *Truth and Beauty: A Friendship*

CONTENTS

PREFACE

This book is a celebration of imagination and an investigation of creativity and design. It is also a handbook intended to provide a framework for interdisciplinary courses and projects. In the view of many writers and educators, our educational system has given priority to fields based on the study of numbers and words and has neglected the arts, which are based on perception and the senses. Most of us are products of educational backgrounds that could be described in a similar way, yet we know that there is plenty of productive thinking that occurs in the pursuit of the arts and design.

Our book came into being when, as colleagues at American College for the Applied Arts, we became aware of the similarities among our students in the fields of fashion design and interior design, and we set out to provide a curriculum that could address and encourage these commonalities. We began to recognize that our interior design students have a broader perspective than walls, ceilings, and furnishings, that our fashion students stretch their imaginative pursuits far beyond apparel, that all of them move naturally across a seamless visual landscape, and that this landscape also contains elements of graphic design, animation, and architecture. It was the curriculum of the separate design programs that imposed limitations on them, so we began to

look at the broader concepts that would serve to unify the interests of our students.

It is perhaps a cliché of the field of education that one of the main benefits of teaching is learning; yet working across disciplines in this project made this observation especially true as we sought to understand the boundaries of the disciplines, trace them, and look for gaps. Just as geographical border areas take on a distinctive hybrid character where language, culture, and customs reflect a dynamic and often mutually enriching character, so do the areas where design disciplines collide, intersect, and overlap.

In this book, each chapter addresses an area important to the understanding of the collaborative process. The first three chapters serve as a foundation for understanding the concepts behind *Wear Your Chair*. Chapter 1, Wear Your *What?*, gives an overview of the development of the trend toward the blurring of distinctions between design disciplines, particularly fashion and interior design, and analyzes some of the reasons for this phenomenon, such as the popularization of material culture and its role in the achievement of status. We demonstrate how the overlap of the design disciplines can be traced through history and illustrated in current events, and we look at some of the material and technological developments that have contributed to this trend. Chapter 2, Where It All Starts: References and Influences, presents images from various artists and designers, demonstrating visual parallels over disciplines, media, and time, and suggesting the creative process that underpins the concept of *Wear Your Chair*. The images have been chosen to reflect a very broad range of design history in a framework to suggest relationships among the many design disciplines, with particular focus on fashion and interior design. Chapter 3, Sources of Design Inspiration, examines the role of inspiration in the design disciplines; it explores the origins of designers' ideas, using the model of the designer as inventor, and analyzes sources of the spark of inspiration that fuels a designer's imagination, guiding students through the process of inspiration and evolution of design ideas. The design development process is deciphered, translating the source of an idea into a new design.

The next four chapters are devoted to an in-depth look at the design process, including an overview of design theory. Chapter 4, The Vocabulary of Design, is an analysis of design from the perspective of the terminology of its formal elements and principles that design professionals use to articulate ideas about design, since it is important to have a common vocabulary to describe, discuss, and evaluate design projects. Chapter 5, More Than Meets the Eye: Surface Design, Pattern, and Motifs, takes an innovative approach to the ways in which surface and pattern designers visualize the world around them and interpret what they see in their designs. It also demonstrates how unusual sources of inspiration and new technological advances assist designers in the development of textiles and wall coverings. Chapter 6,

Furniture and Fashion: How to Wear Your Chair, analyzes current trends reflected in the fields of fashion and interior design; through the examination of various designers, projects, and exhibitions, it adds to the shared vocabulary of design concepts and reinforces our interdisciplinary approach to design. Chapter 7, Inspiration from Textiles: Everything Old Is New Again, is an overview of the qualities that textiles exhibit in their substance, structure, and surface pattern. The substance of a textile is the composition of its fiber content, the structure is the technique that is used to create it, and the surface is the application of design. This chapter further develops knowledge of textiles through consideration of historic fabrics and motifs and how they are incorporated into contemporary design.

The final three chapters of *Wear Your Chair* are devoted to the application of the design concepts that have been introduced. Chapter 8, Trend Forecasting: Seeing What's Not There . . . Yet, examines the role of the designer as a trend analyst, one of the most important functions of the designer. In this capacity, the designer functions as a historian, sociologist, psychologist, even as an archaeologist, making note of important events and developments that will influence society. This chapter introduces students to the methods utilized in trend forecasting and predictive services; it also examines the effectiveness of these services in contemporary design and how these services may contribute to the overlap of trends in design. Chapter 9, Design and the Shopping Experience, analyzes store design, visual merchandising, and changes in consumer demand and sales techniques in the evolution of shopping; it explores the activity of shopping from the perspective of the 21st-century consumer. This is a shopper for whom the media, including television networks and specialized cable programming, the Internet, and fashion and lifestyle periodicals have altered the traditional brick-and-mortar shopping experience and have enhanced the awareness of well-designed products. Chapter 10, When Life Became Style, examines the relationship between advertising and designer branding, and their influence in portraying lifestyle; it looks at future trends in branding and new approaches to advertising and the crossover of fashion and interior design.

Additional features of *Wear Your Chair* include copious images in each chapter, which serve to illustrate many of the concepts presented. Boxed features throughout the text include short articles and interviews with design professionals. The accompanying CD-ROM contains supplemental and updated materials to augment and encourage continued research and analysis. The Instructor's Guide contains suggestions for in-class activities, video presentations, case studies, and field trips, illustrating the usefulness of *Wear Your Chair* to a wide range of students.

ACKNOWLEDGMENTS

Starting this book was the result of many influences, some of which we may never be able to completely identify. Finishing it, though, is the consequence of having had assistance and advice from many people who were kind enough to lend their expertise and support to our venture.

We were constantly inspired by our current and former students, including those who participated in our first presentations of *Wear Your Chair* as a college course, and we want to thank our colleagues at Woodbury University and California State University, Northridge, for their understanding and encouragement. We are indebted to our professional colleagues who shared their insights in the interviews included in the text.

We thank the readers and reviewers for their helpful suggestions: Phyllis Borcherding, University of Cincinnati; Henry Dietrich Fernandez, Rhode Island School of Design; and Janet Hethorn, University of Delaware.

To the team at Fairchild we are full of appreciation: Olga Kontzias, executive editor, who with much enthusiasium and support understood our original concept; Sylvia Weber, development editor, who provided so much assistance with editing suggestions; Jennifer Crane, senior development editor, and Justine Brennan, assistant development editor, who assisted us with countless reviews of our images; Adam Bohannon, art director, who designed the cover and the text; Elizabeth Marotta, senior production editor; and Ginger Hillman, production manager.

We are extremely grateful to our families and friends who shared in the unfolding of *Wear Your Chair*, especially our husbands, Jerry Griffin and David Collins; for without their love and support, we could never have completed the manuscript. They seemed to develop a sixth sense to know when it was safe to ask, "So, how's the book going?"

WEAR YOUR CHAIR

❄ When *Fashion* Meets INTERIOR DESIGN ❄

CHAPTER ONE

Wear Your *What?*

Recent popular culture has focused on the importance of design. From Virginia Postrel's 2003 book, *The Substance of Style*, to the May 17, 2004, *Business Week* cover story, "The Power of Design," to the many museum exhibitions and to the various opportunities to participate in the process of design offered to cable television audiences, design has been in the spotlight. What is notable is not just that design is making news but the acknowledgment that design serves an important function. Over a long history, design has lived in the shadow of other endeavors and has often been considered frivolous in comparison. The erroneous idea that design is synonymous with surface adornment has put it in the category of being "fluff," not worthy of serious consideration. At the core of the recognition of the importance of design is an understanding of its meaning. Although the word *design* can be used either as a noun or as a verb, it is as a verb—denoting activity—that design becomes truly exciting. At its best, design is a process that involves many stages and many participants. Although the goal of design is the ultimate creation of a product, the basis of design is in research, thought, and analysis.

What's in Your Design Tool Kit?

Throughout *Wear Your Chair*, we use designers and their work to illustrate how design functions as process and product. A close examination of the work of influential designers reveals four key concepts in the process of design:

1. A respect for the past and an ability to integrate tradition and innovation
2. An understanding of technology
3. The pursuit of creative and collaborative solutions
4. A willingness to keep learning

Just as scales, rulers, and pens are design tools, these four concepts are tools to be used in the practice of design.

The *first tool, a respect for the past*, is seen in the ways in which all forms of history—design history, cultural history, and art history—inform the work of designers. The many historical references in *Wear Your Chair* will serve as examples of the continuing relevance of the past to contemporary life. Whether the quest is to understand the popularity of the retro Mini Cooper automobile, to appreciate the quality of a vintage couture gown, or to invent the next generation of flat-screen televisions, a knowledge of what has come before is essential.

The *second tool, an understanding of technology*, is an indispensable component of the designer's tool kit. The industrial revolution allowed workers in the 19th century to escape the drudgery of repetitive tasks, yet made some fear that their livelihoods were threatened by machine-made goods; computer technology has similar benefits and drawbacks. William Morris, who led the Arts and Crafts movement in England in the late 19th century and early 20th century, sought not to completely resist the industrial age but to gain a clear understanding of

the processes that could be best done by machine in order to free workers for more creative endeavors. Just as it did during the Arts and Crafts movement, respect for the unique and for the aesthetic value of the handmade continues to grow in our own computer age. Technologies can be liberating, especially if we can sufficiently address human concerns. The benefits that computer-assisted technologies offer to design, such as inexpensive modeling and rapid prototyping, promise to free designers from the constraints of time and energy that limit the creative process.

Our *third tool, the pursuit of creative and collaborative solutions,* is demonstrated in the work of our most influential designers. The lone genius individual designer is a myth; the best in design is achieved through team approaches, which draw talent from many sources. Karl Lagerfeld, in his prodigious work, not only under his own name but through collaborations with several fashion houses, including Fendi, Chanel, and Chloé, has been able to update signa-

1.1

4

1.2a

1.2b

ture labels and at the same time put his own mark on them. This concept of creative collaboration is important in an era of brand identification. The witty side of Karl Lagerfeld is seen in his chair hat and upholstered dress, from 1985 (Figure 1.1), which reflects a mix of the disciplines of fashion and interior design in a whimsical, tongue-in-cheek way. Not only is the bodice of the dress structured and tufted like the back of an upholstered chair, its skirt echoes the ruffle on the chair, and the ensemble's hat mimics the chair itself. This image captures the essence, both literally and figuratively, of our title, *Wear Your Chair.*

Our *fourth key tool, a willingness to keep learning,* has to do with bringing curiosity and a ravenous appetite for knowledge to all endeavors. The careers of our most interesting designers often demonstrate a wide range of pursuits—from architecture to fashion to photography and film—indicating how

these individuals make growing and learning a life-long pursuit. A recent trend in education is the interdisciplinary degree incorporating design and business—a reflection of the appreciation of aesthetic value. Not very long ago, a college degree was the respected symbol of academic achievement, and regardless of how often it was said at graduations, no one really believed that commencement was a beginning. It was, for most, including design professionals, the accomplishment of a goal that signified completion, "The End" on the last frame of a motion picture. But with the acceleration of change, the constant development of new materials and technologies, and the increasingly global nature of design and business, designers must continue to learn, grow, and develop new ideas to remain fresh and convey through their work an understanding of contemporary life to a wide audience.

FIG. 1.1 Chair hat and upholstered dress, a whimsical approach to interior and fashion design by Karl Lagerfeld (1985). FIG. 1.2 (a) Missoni patchwork vases by Stephen Burks of Mogu and (b) Missoni knits. [(a) Reprinted with permission of Stephen Burks. (b) Photo by Cristina Nunez/"Missoni's Golden Moment." *Women's Wear Daily,* September 2003. Courtesy, Fairchild Publications, Inc.]

5

Once you start to recognize these concepts or tools, you will see them in use in current popular culture and in the shared details of design history. They are apparent in the work of Yves Béhar, whose San Francisco-based group Fuseproject has designed everything from light fixtures to packaging to shoes. These concepts are at work in the collaboration between fashion designers, interior designers, and architects that has made fashion retail space the hottest property in cities around the world. The design alliance between the fashion house Missoni and the industrial designer Stephen Burks of Mogu, which produced the patchwork vases presented at the recent Salone de Mobile trade show in Italy, is a striking example of collaboration among designers. The vases shown in Figure 1.2a re-create the classic patchwork knits produced by Tai and Rosita Missoni in Figure 1.2b and illustrate the principle that good design works across a wide range of media. As we proceed to examine key moments in the history of design, current trends, and future possibilities with regard to ideas shared across the boundaries of design disciplines, the concepts of respect for the past, understanding of technology, collaborative approaches, and continuous learning will serve as valuable tools.

A Respect for the Past

From some vantage points, the past seems quaint and irrelevant. Who would wish to return to a time when using a telephone involved sharing a "party line" of several users on hardware that had to be connected to a system of wires in order to function? Would any

of us really want to live without the ease and comfort of our contemporary clothing fabrications, in a time when an entire day of the week was devoted to washing and ironing? Yet designers continually mine the past for ideas and inspiration, and our first design tool, *a respect for the past*, recognizes the importance of an appreciation of history in understanding the present and anticipating the future.

A Look Back

The late 20th century brought about an era of the mass marketing of design and a surge of popular interest in design. Style mavens such as Martha Stewart, Ralph Lauren, and Marc Jacobs have dominated the popular consciousness through their presence on the Internet and at mass retailers and in the mass media, advising us on not just what to wear and where to live, but how to live. Contemporary design

1.3

ALERY   PARIS

1.4

This interest in design is part of the general trend toward personal expression that became the hallmark of the 20th century and has continued into the 21st. In the fields of psychology and philosophy, the early part of the 20th century brought us Sigmund Freud and William James, whose work helped to define the individual. Since then, the 20th century has become known as "the century of the self" and as "the democratic century," indicating the widespread movement toward self-determination, individual expression, and personal freedom. This freedom of expression is evident in how we dress and how we interact with the built environment, leading to an atmosphere in which well-designed and aesthetically pleasing consumer goods begin to serve as the visible definition of personal identity.

has had an impact on consumers by providing the means to look and live well, and well-designed products have never been more available. Mainstream design publications, such as *Metropolis*, *Surface*, and *Wallpaper,** feature style updates and consumer products and focus on popular culture, fashion, and architecture. These publications blur the boundaries between design disciplines. Among the general population, there is a great deal of interest in dressing well and maintaining a well-designed home, and this trend has implications for those who study design and for those interested in the commercial viability of designs.

Images Communicate Across Disciplines

In his imaginative book *Style in Costume*, published in 1949, James Laver looked at images from architecture and the decorative arts, and commented, "The decorative unity of an age is manifest even in the most apparently insignificant details." This concept is shown in the geometric setting and streamlined clothing in the Hoyningen-Huene photograph, c. 1928 (Figure 1.3), illustrating the straight lines that dominated design in the 1920s. In contrast to the spare feeling of the image in Figure 1.3, the image in Figure 1.4 shows a softer shape in which the puffy details of the woman's Victorian sleeves are echoed in the poodle's grooming. Recognizing this type of visual similarity is essential in dissolving the strict boundaries between design disciplines.

FIG. 1.3 Model in two-piece Schiaparelli bathing suit (1928). [Copyright © by George Hoyningen-Huene/Corbis.] FIG. 1.4 Albumen print card showing woman with a black miniature poodle. [Copyright © Poodles Rock/ Corbis.]

1.5

1.6

Georges Lepape also recognized the similarity of line between clothing and architecture. This famous illustrator created the cover of an issue of *Vogue* magazine for 1928 in which the silhouette of a woman blends into the Manhattan skyline, with the name *Vogue* in the window of her apartment. This marvelous illustration, with the detailed pleats and tucks of the woman's suit, her elongated figure and posture, and the architectural details of the buildings behind her, is shown in Figure 1.5. *Vogue* has, of course, been an ongoing visual record of changing tastes not only in clothing but also in furniture, interior environments, and lifestyle. Figure 1.6 shows two women in 1945

fashions with distinctly different clothing, chairs, and even pets. It is tempting to think that in our contemporary brand-conscious society we have somehow invented the concepts of style and image, but these vintage illustrations are evidence to the contrary.

These examples demonstrate that many of the trends that we might feel are unique to our age have actually been recurring over time. The branding of designer fragrances, for example, which we might assume to be a unique development of the designer consciousness of our era, was first introduced by Paul Poiret in 1910 and advanced by Coco Chanel in 1921. Figure 1.7 features an advertisement from a

1945 issue of *Vogue* magazine for an Adrían fragrance, showing a woman in a column dress posed next to an Ionic column in a wonderful mingling of architectural and fashion detail.

An Understanding of Technology

Our second tool, *an understanding of technology*, conjures up for most of us a suggestion of the importance of computers. But technical pursuits related to industry and science were certainly very much in evidence prior to our digital age. In fact, the *Oxford English Dictionary*, which traces the earliest known uses of words, dates the word *technology* to 1615, to mean the scientific study of practical or industrial arts. It is important to realize that mastery of the technical aspects of the skills used in production has long played an important role for designers. While the emphasis of 21st-century technology is indeed on computers, and this advent has been termed by some "the digital revolution," the entire focus of the last century was on machines and the effects of the industrial revolution.

1.7

Machines Versus Handicraft in the 20th Century

The question that plagued William Morris and his followers in the Arts and Crafts movement—whether we lose our humanity and personal expression in the process of mass production—seems to have been answered with a resounding *no*. Mass-produced items are being marketed to an increasingly large population for a lower cost, arguably improving the standard of living for large groups of people. Moreover, since the industrial revolution, for most of the 20th century and up to the present, design has existed in a constant flux, stretched between the progress offered by the machine and the artistic promise of handcrafted products. The history of design for this period can be read as a journal of the ebb and flow of respect for mass production versus individual making. One of the questions implicit in the current embrace of technology is whether computer assistance will enable designers and artists to achieve new accomplishments in creativity because of the freedom from the drudgery of manual labor, or whether the handcrafted product possesses a spirit that is absent if the work is done by computer.

FIG. 1.5 Georges Lepape's May 1928 cover for *Vogue* magazine. [Copyright © 1928 Condé Nast Publications. Reprinted with permission. All rights reserved.] FIG. 1.6 1945 *Vogue* magazine cover showing furniture, fashion, and pets of its day. [Original artwork by John Rawlings. Copyright © 1945 Condé Nast Publications. Reprinted with permission. All rights reserved.] FIG. 1.7 An Adrían fragrance ad from a 1945 issue of *Vogue*.

The Modern design movement emerged in the early 20th century, perhaps in reaction to the overly ornamental features of the Victorian era, in which interior and architectural details were limited by the masonry techniques and materials available. For example, when the Eiffel Tower was created for the Paris International Exhibition of 1889, it was the tallest structure ever built. At one thousand feet tall, it stood as a monument to that feat of engineering until after World War I (Pevsner, p. 140). The idea that it is little more than a century since materials such as steel revolutionized building is remarkable.

A parallel feature of the tension between technology and the handmade has been illustrated in changing attitudes toward ornamentation. The Austrian architect Adolf Loos (1870–1933) presented a summary of his ideas in "Ornament and Crime," his 1908 lecture that was published as an essay in 1910 and led the way toward the spare and industrial-looking design genre that became known as Modernism (Trilling, p. 186).

The architect Louis Sullivan (1856–1924), a leader of the Modernist movement, coined the phrase "form follows function," which became short-hand for practical simplicity in design and architecture. Instead of imitating the past, this new philosophy looked to the future, and embraced the 20th century as the "machine age." These new ideas, evident in all aspects of the arts, music, painting, and sculpture as well as in architecture and design, were greeted with trepidation by the public. It was revolutionary for designers to be thinking about how something was used and not designing with only aesthetics in mind. Awareness of the new Modernist

1.8

1.9

style was spread through publications that were available to the growing middle classes. Figures 1.8 and 1.9 show the contrasting styles that emerged in this remarkably short time.

Computers: The 21st-Century Machines

The 20th century was shaped by developments in production and distribution that made a wide assortment of goods almost universally available. The current "new economy" enjoyed in developed parts of the world is based on the premise that the machine age has given way to a postindustrial era in which the major "products" are service and

information. There is every indication that the technological revolution is the 21st-century counterpart of the industrial revolution. The computers and microchips that are embedded in every aspect of our lives are causing fundamental changes in the way that people approach life and work. In the industrial revolution many tasks that were previously performed by hand were augmented if not entirely executed by machine; in the current technological revolution the machine is a computer. These changes are apparent in the design fields, where computer-aided design (CAD) is replacing manual drawing and drafting. In architecture and interior design, 3-D virtual tours are assisting end users in understanding new environments. Computerized pattern making is becoming the standard in apparel design. Computer-generated animation and computerized simulations of mock-ups for graphic projects merge the worlds of fantasy and reality so seamlessly that only professionals can determine the processes used.

Additionally, computer-generated imagery, whether used for advertising or entertainment, is available on such a mass level that visual literacy involves recognition of popular cultural icons and brand logos. We may not be able to identify past presidents or current world leaders, but present an image of Donald Trump and *The Apprentice* is the overwhelming response. The Nike "swoosh" logo no longer needs to be accompanied by the brand name. On its own it communicates all of the strength and potential in the phrase "Just do it." Nor does the iPod advertising silhouette need any verbalization. With one image of dancing movement the suggestion is made: iPod = cool.

FIG. 1.8 Eiffel Tower in Paris, France. [Copyright © by Louie Psihoyos/Corbis.] FIG. 1.9 The Larkin Building in Buffalo, NY (1904) by Frank Lloyd Wright. [Reprinted with the permission of the Lake Erie County Historical Society.]

11

Technological Changes

Technology, with advances in "smart" textiles, appliances, and built environments, is showing potential to change our lives as wireless capabilities lead to the development of technology that can be worn and lived in. These advances challenge some of our assumptions about our relationship with objects. Susanne Küchler, in her article "Rethinking Textile: The Advent of the 'Smart' Fiber Surface," states that we are "arguably at the threshold of a new age—not just of intellectual economy and of new ways of managing knowledge—but also of materiality in which not objects, but images reign" (p. 264). She describes the current state of the art of "I-wear," or intelligent clothing, that creates a local network around the wearer. Cloth is becoming an avant-garde tool of design and technology, in which it is no longer the cover for electronic equipment, it *is* the electronic equipment. These wearable electronics offer promising collaborations among artists, scientists, computer programmers, and engineers as functional devices such as blood pressure sensors

---

BOX 1.1

Smart Skin
A Sixth Sense, and a Seventh, and an Eighth . . .
By Cade Metz

One day, your baby monitor will alert you to a great deal more than a crying fit down the hall. Thanks to hundreds of tiny wireless sensors laced into your baby's clothing, you'll be alerted to the slightest changes in temperature, pulse, or movement. Whether your baby develops a fever or has trouble breathing, you'll know about it—in a matter of seconds.

At the University of Texas at Arlington, Zeynep Celik-Butler and Donald Butler are well on their way to creating that sort of all-knowing baby monitor. Just as other scientists are building flexible computer chips and displays, this husband-and-wife team is working to build flexible microsensors, tiny devices supple enough to sit inside a window curtain or an ordinary piece of clothing yet smart enough to detect changes in their immediate surroundings.

"We were watching all the work being done to build transistors and light-emitting diodes on flexible substrates," says Donald Butler, "and we thought, 'Why not put sensors on a flexible substrate as well?'"

They call their project Smart Skin, and they've already demonstrated a prototype that monitors infrared radiation, which means it's also capable of tracking changes in body temperature. In the near future, they hope to build devices that respond to all sorts of other stimuli. "We plan to duplicate another sensing ability of the skin," says Zeynep Celik-Butler, "creating devices that detect touch and pressure." Her husband envisions sensors that monitor changes in air flow, alerting you to, say, an open window or a gas leak.

Their prototype begins with a flexible polymer substrate that can withstand temperatures as high as 752 degrees Fahrenheit. The higher the temperature, the easier it is to deposit the sensing materials on the substrate. In this case, the microsensors are made of yttrium barium copper oxide, a material that responds to infrared radiation.

The project, funded by the National Science Foundation, still has another five years to run, so we may be well into the next decade before such devices are commercialized. There are any number of places these sensors could reside, and any number of things they could monitor.

Woven into the uniform of a combat soldier, the sensors might detect toxic chemicals or bacterial agents floating through the air. Worn by a diabetic—just under the skin—they could track insulin and glucose levels. Donald Butler suggests they might soon find a home in the world of robotics. A NASA machine, for instance, could carefully track its surroundings as it moves across Mars or the moon. And then, of course, there's the baby monitor—with a capital M.

1.10

and thermostats are incorporated into the fabric. The article in Box 1.1, "Smart Skin," describes a futuristic baby monitor that is woven into the fabric of a child's clothing, alerting parents to the details of the baby's temperature and condition.

Technology is beginning to serve as a medium in its own right in addition to enabling designers to construct computer-generated models for garments, furniture, or structures that might not other-

wise be possible to create because of time and financial limitations. The detail in the work of the famous architect Santiago Calatrava would probably not have been possible in the days before computer-generated modeling. The fusion that he has created between architecture and engineering is innovative and dynamic, as seen in his double bow-stringed arches designed for the velodrome at the 2004 Olympic Games at Athens (Figure 1.10).

FIG. 1.10 Double bow-stringed arches of the velodrome for the 2004 Olympics in Athens. [Copyright © by Milos Bicanski/Getty Images.]

Stretching Design Boundaries: The Pursuit of Creative and Collaborative Solutions

This book is dedicated to the proposition that all design disciplines are created equal, and all of them should be fun. Relatively speaking, of course, the one essential element in design success is to enjoy exercising your imagination. Part of the fun of *Wear Your Chair* is looking at the world without strict design definitions, and this attitude is underscored by our third design tool, *the pursuit of creative and collaborative solutions* in design. Take shoes, for instance. We all wear them. Some of us collect them and are obsessed by them, and in this context they become sought-after works of art. If there is any doubt about this, visit eBay and witness a bidding war over a pair of vintage Charles Jourdan pumps or observe block-long lines at sport stores when a new style of limited edition Air Jordan sneakers is introduced. But aside from the product sense, shoes have made their way into our consciousness as forms of art and sculpture: On a pure

design level, a shoe becomes an example of structured unit, in which its construction and materials are considered. As designers, we become aware of the many perspectives from which an object can be viewed. Figure 1.11, "Miss Goodnight" by Ronny Saint Claire, presents the very recognizable form of a pump, which turned upside down forms a light fixture.

Designers from various disciplines use similar vocabulary but have distinct points of view. The "abstract" or "four-leaf clover" section drawing of a gown designed by Charles James in Figure 1.12 presents a cutaway view of the many layers of construction present in a couture gown. The exposure of the garment's foundation in this way has much in common with an architectural rendering. An interior designer looking at this illustration might focus on the many tiers of different fabrics and how they might be suspended, what materials might be used, and how those materials would retain their shape. A fashion designer might look more closely at the surface qualities of the fabrics used and the effect of the gown in movement, but both designers would consider concepts of shape, surface interest, size and proportion, methods of joining and linking, and relationships of materials with form and function.

Another example of construction in fashion echoing concepts in architecture and interior design is seen in the work of Belgian designer Martin Margiela. His explorations of the deconstruction of tailored garments and further experi-

1.11

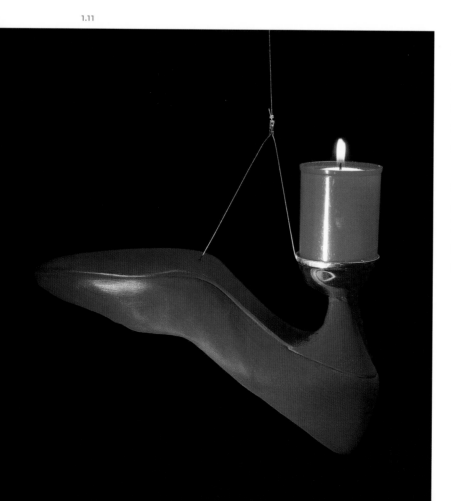

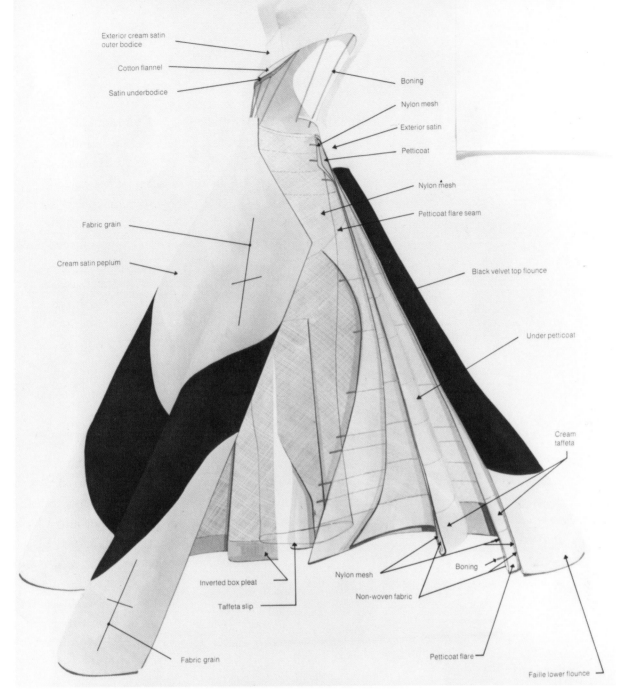

Exterior cream satin
outer bodice

Cotton flannel

Satin underbodice

Boning

Nylon mesh

Exterior satin

Petticoat

Nylon mesh

Petticoat flare seam

Fabric grain

Cream satin peplum

Black velvet top flounce

Under petticoat

Cream
taffeta

Inverted box pleat

Nylon mesh

Boning

Taffeta slip

Non-woven fabric

Fabric grain

Petticoat flare

Faille lower flounce

1.12

mentation with the devolution of textiles served to strengthen the trends of deconstruction that were so apparent in the 1980s and 1990s, when the interior structures of building systems were exposed. Figure 1.13a shows Martin Margiela's pinstripe skirt, in which the waistband is partially deconstructed from the garment, exposing the lining. Figure 1.13b shows this in detail. Similar interior-exterior exploration is seen in the work of Los Angeles designers Stefan Loy and Frank Ford. Their line, LoyandFord,

FIG. 1.11 Ronny Saint Claire's "Miss Goodnight" (1993). [Reprinted with the permission of Ronny Saint Claire and Samuele Mazza.] FIG. 1.12 The garment's foundation is exposed in Charles James's "Four-Leaf Clover" gown. [Illustration by Bill Wilkinson. Reprinted with permission of the Brooklyn Museum.]

1.13a

1.13b

1.14a

1.14b

1.14c

features garments that are constructed inside out, seams exposed, with unusual juxtapositions of fabrics that create asymmetrical transformations (see Figure 1.14a–c).

Taking apart or exposing the technological and structural elements in interiors and architecture creates tension and excitement within a space or structure that is typically whole or concealed. The architecture of Frank Gehry is an excellent example of this dynamic deconstructionist architecture, where joists, beams, and ductwork are left exposed; walls slope, overlap, and curve; and different materials merge. This dynamic organization is evident in Gehry's design for the Guggenheim Museum in Bilbao, Spain (Figure 1.15).

Flexibility and Functionality

In recent years, functionality in the end use of products has increased across all parts of the design spectrum. This trend toward functionality and the overlap of uses is additional evidence of the merging of

1.15

FIG. 1.13 (a) Martin Margiela's design reveals the deconstruction of a pinstripe skirt and (b) waistband detail. [Photos by Amanda Michaels. Skirt provided by Nikki Krysak.] FIG. 1.14 Stefan Loy and Frank Ford, Loyand-Ford (Garments 2001) reveal the inside-out construction of (a) "Sunburn and Inside" (b) "Lining Too Long" and (c) "Front on Back Jacket." [Photos by Marc Lecureuil. Reprinted with permission of Cooper-Hewitt National Design Museum, Smithsonian Institution.] FIG. 1.15 Guggenheim Museum in Bilbao, Spain. [Copyright © Eberhard Streichan/zefa/Corbis.]

17

design disciplines, in which designers share expertise, ignoring strict professional designations. Perhaps creativity is taking on an aspect of reality in the engineering of functional and changeable products. Figure 1.16 shows Michael Solis's "Four Forty, 2000," a coffee table designed in two sections that can be pulled apart to expose an interior drawer. Similar efficiency of design is seen in the dual-dressing concept shown by Karl Lagerfeld in the fall 2004 couture collections pictured in Figure 1.17a

and b, in which a suit can be worn over a dress to create many different outfits.

Comparable flexibility is seen in Figure 1.18, "Lighting and Seating," showing chair seats constructed of translucent plastic containing fluorescent elements, so that when hanging, these chairs can double as lamps. The "Cabriolet," in Figure 1.19, features a tabletop constructed of a flexible piece of wood that can be raised to form the back of a seat, transforming the table into a bench.

Duality also exists in open-office planning, where modular furniture components are designed for multifunctional use. The components can perform as space dividers, computer workstations, desks, conference tables, and storage and filing systems. A single workstation can be adapted to different users with adjustable ergonomic features, such as work surfaces, chair seats, and chair backs that can be raised or lowered. In a similar way, recreational and marine vehicles also incorporate design features that serve multiple functions. Touted as "homes away from home," these vehicles provide maximum comfort and storage space in a very limited area, as seen in Figure 1.20. Tables can be lowered to convert to sleeping accommodations, and seat cushions can be removed to expose drawers and storage compartments.

1.16

1.17a   1.17b

1.18

1.19

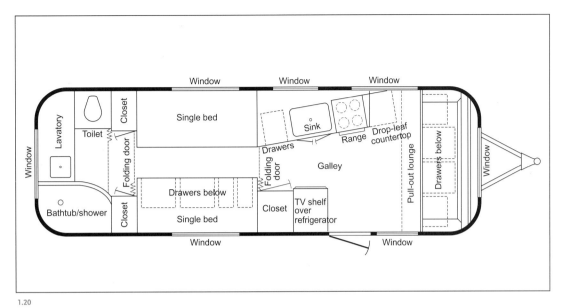

1.20

Changing Attitudes About Materials

One of the striking aspects of materials as they have developed since the industrial revolution is the transformation of their inherent distinguishing features. An opposition has gradually occurred as new materials have been developed. There was a time when materials, like people and institutions, fell neatly into categories. Building materials were normally rigid and hard, clothing was soft, and furnishings were combinations of hard structures covered by soft surfaces. With the development of new materials, perhaps since the development of nylon, fiberglass, and plastics, traditionally soft materials such as woven fabrics have become hard. With the application of substances such as carbon fiber, which is extremely lightweight and soft, soft materials can be molded into sturdy structural elements. Colombian fashion designer Miguel Caballero has designed stylish bulletproof T-shirts and suits that are lightweight and more breathable than Kevlar.

He jokes that these gabardine-like suits can go "from the boardroom to the shootout" (Glasse).

The concept of rigidity and flexibility has also changed as materials such as plywood, fiberglass, resins, and polymers have revolutionized furniture design. While there used to be a huge distinction between interior and exterior space and use, this distinction has undergone considerable change. As materials allow the outdoors to come inside and the interiors of clothing and furnishings to be exposed as more transparent and translucent, materials play with our concepts of inside and outside. Designers of retail stores, conventions, and special events are using translucent materials for dressing rooms, exhibit kiosks, and even tents for wedding parties. An advertisement for Eventscape, a manufacturer specializing in these ethereal custom fabric environments, is shown in Figure 1.21. Even the concept of temporary and permanent has undergone a shift, as temporary housing options are explored.

FIG. 1.16 "Four Forty, 2000," a coffee table designed by Michael Solis. [Photo by Nick Vaccaro. Reprinted with permission of the Cooper-Hewitt National Design Museum, Smithsonian Institution.] FIG. 1.17 Dual dressing by Karl Lagerfeld (fall 2004 couture): (a) suit over dress and (b) jacket with dress. [Photos by Jean-Luce Huré/the *New York Times*.] FIG. 1.18 Chairs doubling as lamps by Horgen-Glarus and N2 Seat/Lighting. [Photo by Wouter Vandebrink. Reprinted with permission of N2.] FIG. 1.19 Table/bench designed by Paolo Ulian. [Reprinted with permission of Paolo Ulian. Photo by Amendolaggine e Barracchia.] FIG. 1.20 The versatility of a recreational vehicle is shown in this floor plan based on a design by Airstream.

**Experimentation, Imagination, and Innovation:
A Willingness to Keep Learning**

Many of the projects considered in this volume challenge the accepted notions of "appropriate" materials, and exist in the undefinable boundaries between design and art. But part of the exercise of

1.21

20

the imagination is the exploration of these boundaries. This attitude of constant experimentation is suggested by our fourth tool, *a willingness to keep learning.*

The armchair shown in Figure 1.22 is at first glance an upholstered chintz chair, but the "Eudora Chair," designed by Critz Campbell, eventually reveals itself to be constructed of fiberglass with the floral pattern captured in acrylic resin. What's going on when designers of "upholstered" furniture work in acrylic resin? Design can be considered as existing in a balance between longing for the past and desire for innovation. This concept is illustrated clearly in Critz Campbell's chair. The chintz pattern suggests a cozy retro armchair, one that might be seen next to a large radio in a 1930s parlor, yet the translucent resin gives this chair a futuristic materiality, which is emphasized by the sharp corners and slightly streamlined shape.

1.22

Wear Your Chair examines design history, design trends, and ideas about creativity. It also asks some philosophical questions that underpin the concepts presented: Does mass production devalue or benefit the individual? Do we have better opportunities if we can take care of our needs with modest means by using cheap consumer goods, or are we all devalued by the low wages and environmental impact that accompanies mass production and disposable products? Why is the fading of the boundaries among the design disciplines happening now? When has it happened before, and what is the relationship with emerging technologies? Is our current dependence upon computer-assisted design likely to cause an opposite reaction in which people once again embrace the skills of handcrafting? What is the relationship between creativity and good design? Does the definition of accomplishment in design include commercial success?

Think of this chapter as a tasting menu for the feast that follows. We examine the visual parallels among disciplines, media, and time as well as the role of inspiration in interior design, fashion design, graphic design, and other design disciplines. We explore the origins of designers' ideas, using the model of a designer as inventor, and we examine sources of the spark of inspiration that fuel a designer's imagination. We analyze the formal elements and principles of the vocabulary of design used by design professionals to articulate the qualities of designs. We discuss the importance of textiles and the qualities that textiles exhibit in their composition, structure, and detail as well as in their pattern and surface design. We look specifically at the relationship between furniture and fashion. We consider the role of the designer as a historian, sociologist, and trend forecaster, and we explore the activity of shopping from the perspective of the 21st-century consumer, for whom the media, including specialized cable programming and the Internet, have altered the traditional shopping experience. We look at the role of design in advertising, brand creation, and lifestyle and consider some implications for the future. In the chapters that follow, there will be many opportunities to examine the work of designers in various fields, always with the view to understanding not only what a designer makes but how a designer thinks.

FIG. 1.21 The play of light and shadow is visible in this Eventscape Custom Fabric Environment designed by Giorgio Borruso. [Reprinted with permission of the designer, Giorgio Borruso, and manufacturer, Eventscape Inc. Copyright © Benny Chang/Photoworks.] FIG. 1.22 The floral-patterned "Eudora Chair" with fiberglass, designed by Critz Campbell, reveals an unusual use for fabric and resin. [Reprinted with the permission of B9 Design. Photo by Critz Campbell.]

CHAPTER TWO

Where
It
All
Starts

References and Influences

This chapter presents selected images from design history in a framework to suggest relationships among the many design disciplines, with particular focus on fashion and interior design. A look at history reveals a past rich in examples of cross-fertilization among design fields; it also reveals a large number of designers and artists whose work transcends any given discipline. Design is influenced by external conditions that affect designers in various disciplines who are working at the same time. In different periods and places when similar conditions prevail, design may be similarly affected. The influence of political, psychosocial, economic, and technological developments on material culture and design is well documented. These influences may be manifested in conscious or unconscious decisions made by the designer. Also, designers may deliberately refer to design solutions from the past in either their own or other design disciplines.

Most of the images in this chapter are paired to demonstrate visual relationships. Sometimes the designer's point of reference is a theme or motif taken from nature; sometimes a form or silhouette or a surface detail is borrowed from designs of an earlier era or a different design discipline to produce a similar mood. The images are drawn from different branches of design—art, architecture, interiors, fashion, and graphics. They relate to nature, structure and the built environment, the personal environment, surface embellishment, and the decorative arts.

Before it becomes an advertising poster, dress, table, room, or building, a design idea has a starting point. For most designers, that starting point is images. Images of clouds and leaves and trees and city streets; of microscopic views and long-range views; of Grandma's handkerchief; of books, photo albums, and tourist postcards; of babies and bald heads and skin and hair; in short, of all the things that in the designer's imagination are related to the project at hand. Nearly every design project begins with a collection of images arranged on a board, and this becomes the reference point as an idea develops. Visual imagery is used as inspiration throughout the design process, assisting designers in articulating their final outcomes.

Of course, artists and designers do not exist in a vacuum. For example, during the 18th-century industrial revolution, the spinning jenny increased yarn production and the flying shuttle accelerated the rate of woven fabric production. These inventions created opportunities that led to the development of a middle class with some disposable income. Newly affluent people began to show an interest in how design affected their daily lives, and mass production made designed products affordable to a larger market. Eventually something of a backlash against low-quality machine-made items occurred, culminating in the Arts and Crafts movement in the late 19th century and early 20th century, which had the goal of reestablishing the primacy of the handmade product.

Similarly, developments in politics and international events can change the way we relate to the world around us. Wars have had an influence on fashion and material culture, sometimes due to such factors as large numbers of women joining the workforce to perform jobs previously held by men. Created in 1942 by artist J. Howard Miller, the character Rosie the Riveter was a young woman in factory

24

2.1

clothing (Figure 2.1). Her name and image came to symbolize the wartime accomplishments of millions of women on the home front. Fashion design was influenced by the need for more practical and comfortable apparel for those female factory workers.

Additionally, a decrease in the availability of consumer materials in wartime often has resulted in the development of new trends in style. In 1942 the U.S. government introduced L-85 guidelines that restricted the amount of cloth that could be used in clothing design. These guidelines, coupled with wartime fabric shortages, resulted in shorter skirts and the use of synthetic materials in apparel design. Nylon, which was developed by the DuPont Corporation in the 1930s, was used for the fabrication of nylon stockings. But during World War II, DuPont's nylon production was used for parachutes and aircraft tires, and the manufacturing of stockings ceased until the end of the war.

Regardless of the specific conditions leading to design innovations, one constant is that these innovations remain as a source of influence on design for future generations.

Flora and Fauna

Influences from nature are apparent in interior design, architecture, and town planning. Landscape as an art form is evident in Japan, where rocks, gravel, sand, and moss are used to create subtle Zen gardens (Figure 2.2a), and in France, where flowers, plants, and trees are arranged with a lush informality in Provençal gardens (Figure 2.2b). Designers and artists have borrowed color from gardens for

2.2a+b

FIG. 2.1 Rosie the Riveter symbolized the accomplishments of women on the home front during World War II. [Copyright © J. Howard Miller/Corbis.] FIG. 2.2 (a) Rocks, gravel, and sand in a Japanese Zen garden and (b) a Provençal garden. [(a) Copyright © Charles and Josette Lenars/Corbis. (b) Copyright © Corbis.]

hundreds of years. The names of fabric swatches and paint colors are often borrowed from nature. Colors such as forest green, sky blue, or dandelion yellow are common in a designer's vocabulary.

Fashion and furniture can also be inspired by nature, sharing similar floral silhouettes and design elements. The complete metamorphosis of the shape of a flower into the anthropomorphic form of an upholstered chair is achieved in the "Petal Chair"

(Figure 2.3a). In Thierry Mugler's "Flora Begonia" (Figure 2.3b), realistic but oversized flower petals create the contours of the dress.

Charles James's dress mimics the shell of a lobster, with the model posed on a sofa with the same curve as that of a lobster shell (Figure 2.4a). The influence of design interpreted from nature is also shown in the fabric of Elsa Schiaparelli's "Lobster Dress" (Figure 2.4b), a painted textile.

2.3a

2.3b

2.4a

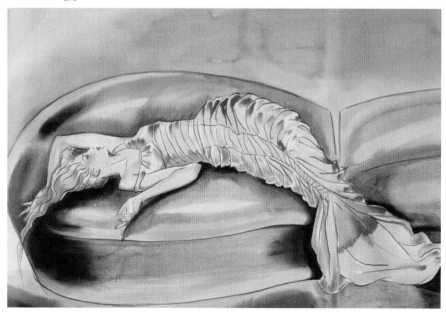

2.4b

Art Movements and Design Styles

Surrealism

The influences of early-20th-century art movements are apparent in design. Surrealism was an art movement that was based on challenging our perceptions and visual expectations. It prepared the way for the design developments of the late 20th century. Its followers explored images that were connected with the subconscious mind, dreams, and symbols (Figure 2.5a and b). Salvador Dalí, one of the most prolific of the surrealist artists, was responsible for some of the more challenging images that came out of that art movement. In a unique interpretation of the Aphrodite of Melos, also known as the "Venus de Milo" (Figure 2.6a), a masterpiece of sculpture from the Hellenistic period in Greece, Dalí created the sculpture "Venus de Milo with Drawers" (Figure 2.6b) in 1936. In the same year, Elsa Schiaparelli, an artist, fashion designer, and friend of Dalí, created the "Desk Suit" (Figure 2.6c). With the advent of computer graphics, we have become accustomed to seeing a car morph into an animal, but when the surrealist movement was developing in the 1920s and 1930s, images that relied on intuition rather than reason for understanding were rare. Perhaps we owe to the surreal-

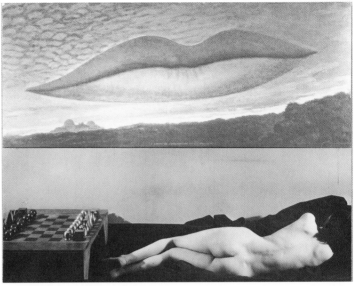

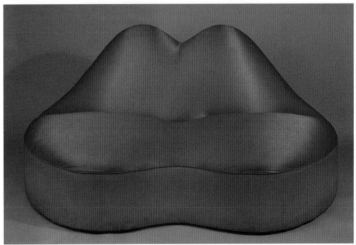

2.5a+b

2.6a   2.6b   2.6c

FIG. 2.3 (a) The shape of flower petals transforms a chair; (b) oversize flower petals create the contours of this dress designed by Thierry Mugler in 1981–82. [(a) Photo by Judith Griffin. (b) Reprinted with permission of the Montreal Museum of Decorative Arts.] FIG. 2.4 (a) Antonio's illustration of the siren-crustacean dress by designer Charles James. It emulates Dali's famous lip design and the (b) Schiaparelli organza dress with a painted lobster (1937).[(b) Photo by Taisha Hirokawa. Courtesy, The Museum at the Fashion Institute of Technology, New York.] FIG. 2.5 (a) "Observatory Time" by Man Ray (1934) and (b) Mae West sofa by Salvador Dalí, 1936–37. [(a) Copyright © CNAC/MNAM/Dist. Réunion des Musées Nationaux/Art Resource, NY, and © ARS, NY. (b) Reprinted with the permission of ARS/Bridgeman Art Gallery.] FIG. 2.6 (a) The seconnd-century B.C.E. Greek sculpture of "Venus de Milo." (b) "Venus de Milo with Drawers" by Salvador Dalí (1936). (c) "Desk Suit" by Elsa Schiaparelli. [(a) Photo by Hirmer Fotoarchiv. (b) Reprinted with the permission of ARS/Bridgeman Art Gallery. (c) Reprinted with permission of Musée des Arts decoratifs, Paris, France.]

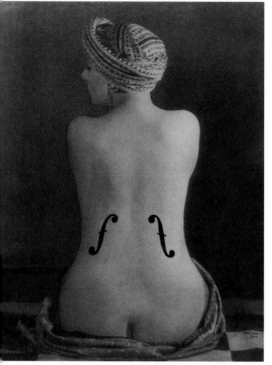

2.7   2.8

Gropius in Germany, was a melding of design disciplines. The main purpose of the Bauhaus was to bring designers, artists, craftspeople, and architects together for the purpose of interdisciplinary studies. During this period, there was much exploration and collaboration, particularly in applications of textile design. Evidence of similar techniques of tapestry weaving can be seen in Sonia Delaunay's 1923 woven overcoat for the actress Gloria Swanson (Figure 2.9a), which envelops the body, and the design of the 1922–1923 tapestry (Figure 2.9b). This similarity of pattern design indicates that a similar thought process was being used in apparel and in the design of interior furnishings during the same time period.

ists our ability to accept human violins (Figure 2.7), chests of drawers that emerge from the body (Figure 2.6b), and corset hats (Figure 2.8). A lack of technical restrictions on hat design, unlike some forms of apparel that must be functional, allows hats to be very decorative and creative, but this hat really pushes tolerance to an extreme. After surrealism, with its somewhat bizarre images, later surreal images such as a building wrapped in fabric (see Figure 2.28a later in this chapter) or a sofa in the shape of lips (see Figure 2.5b) seem almost commonplace.

A model for an interdisciplinary design approach, the Bauhaus made it possible for many disciplines to be taught under one roof and encouraged artists with many different talents to collaborate. Roy Lichtenstein paid homage to the Bauhaus in his painting "Bauhaus Stairway" (Figure 2.10a), which he based on T. Lux Feineger's famous photograph "Weavers on the Stairs" (Figure 2.10b). The reinterpretation of this photographic image on canvas is another example of the transference of ideas between periods and across design media.

The Bauhaus School
Another influential period in design was the 1920s, when the Bauhaus School, led by Walter

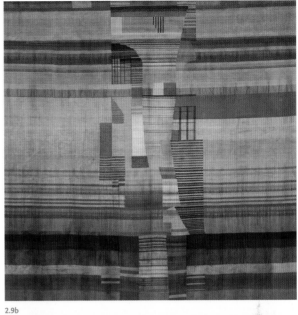

2.9a 2.9b

2.10a 2.10b

FIG. 2.7 "Le Violin d'Ingres" by Man Ray (1924). [Reprinted with permission of CNAC/MNAM/Dist. Réunion des Musées Nationaux/Art Resource, NY, and © ARS, NY.] FIG. 2.8 Corset hat by Karl Lagerfeld, 1985. [Photo by Roxanne Lowit.] FIG. 2.9 (a) "Woven Coat" by Sonia Delaunay and (b) tapestry with cotton, wool, and linen fibers by Gunta Stölzl (1922-23). [(a) Copyright © L&M Services B.V. Amsterdam 20040308. (b) Reprinted with permission of Busch-Reisinger Museum, Association Fund, BR49.669.] FIG. 2.10 (a) "Bauhaus Stairway" by Roy Lichtenstein (1988) and (b) "Weavers on the Stairs," Bauhaus (1927). [(a) Digital Image © The Museum of Modern Art/Licensed by SCALA/Art Resource, NY. (b) Reprinted with the permission of T. Lux Feineger.]

29

Line and Silhouette

Line and silhouette represent the contour or outline of an object. Lines can be angular and dynamic, as in a zigzag pattern, or they can be soft and fluid, as in the curvilinear silhouette of an elegant ball gown. Designers interpret line and silhouette in their architectural plans or in patterns for their garments. A shapely human form is suggested in the Gaultier corset for a Piper-Heidsieck Champagne bottle (Figure 2.11a), and the understructure of the Mainbocher corset (Figure 2.11b) molds the body's silhouette.

Corset-like apparel dates from the late Minoan period, approximately 1800 B.C.E., when the Snake Goddess (Figure 2.12a) is seen adorned in a garment supported by a metal understructure. The corset took many forms throughout history, being worn as undergarments and outergarments, in shapes and materials ranging from wide elastic bands to whalebone-supported bodices. An example from the 1800s is shown in Figure 2.12b. The corset, once considered necessary, was often a controversial garment since it molds the human body into somewhat of an unnatural shape. Napoleon expressed his opinion of the corset to his personal physician, Corvisart: "The corset is the murderer of the human race" (Boucher, p. 347).

Similar stylistic details can be found in different eras. Whether deliberate or not, designs seem to reemerge throughout

30

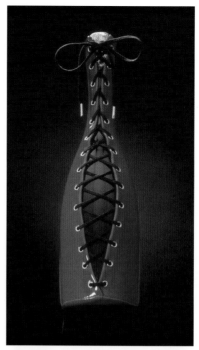

2.11a

2.11b

2.12a

2.12b

2.13a

2.13b

history and to be somewhat cyclical. For example, in comparing the silhouettes of the Empire style, we can observe that the simplicity of the silhouette is evident in both furniture and fashion. The Rouget portrait of the "Mesdemoiselles Molien" (Figure 2.13a) captures the essence of the high-waisted, delicate quality of the Empire style. The dress and chaise shown in Figure 2.13b are a reinterpretation of the Empire style in the early 20th century.

Paul Poiret's studio produced furniture, fashion, fabrics, and tableware. Poiret is considered as the primary design force in liberating women from the heavy corsetry of the Victorian period. He looked to the Directoire and Empire periods and, as they had, to the ancient Greeks for his design influences. Poiret's work is rich in many of the themes covered in this chapter, and hence, several examples of his designs appear in this chapter.

The intricacy of the pattern and line in the wicker chair (Figure 2.14a) and the iron tracery of the Bradbury Building's atrium (Figure 2.14b), although different in scale, convey a similar feeling of airiness.

In the chair (Figure 2.15a) that British fashion designer Bruce Oldfield created for the vignette shown at the Decoration Haute Couture Exhibition in Paris in 1992, clothes and fashion become interior appointments. The draped vanity chair has a quality similar to the silhouette of William Travil-

FIG. 2.11 (a) Gaultier corset for Piper-Heidsieck Champagne and (b) Mainbocher corset (1939). [(a) Copyright © Steve Azzara/Corbis/Sygma. (b) Photo by Horst P. Horst/Art + Commerce. Reprinted with permission of Condé Nast Publications. All rights reserved.] FIG. 2.12 Corsetry mid-1800s: (a) Minoan snake goddess and (b) Dr. Strong's Tampico corset trade card. [(a) Copyright © Archivo Iconografico, S.A./Corbis. (b) Copyright © Swim Ink 2, LLC/Corbis.] FIG. 2.13 (a) "Mesdemoiselles Molien" by Georges Rouget. (b) Empire revival dress and chaise by Georges Lepape (1911). [(a) Reprinted with permission of Erich Lessing/Art Resource, NY. (b) Copyright © Phillip de Bay/Historical Picture Archive/Corbis.]

2.14a

2.14b

2.15a

2.15b

la's halter dress designed for Marilyn Monroe's famous manhole cover scene in *The Seven Year Itch* (Figure 2.15b).

Cross-discipline similarities in design are evident in the line and linear movement of the full-skirted, striped silk evening dress by Tiziani (Figure 2.16a) and the striped deck chairs shown in Figure 2.16b. The tension between the shape of the curve and the verticality of the stripe creates dynamic linear movement. The scale of the stripe in the dress is more typical of furniture design. Normally, the scale of the pattern for textiles used in apparel is much smaller than the scale in textiles used for interiors, but in these two examples, they are similar.

Just as the wicker and metal detail in Figure 2.14a and b relate to each other, so do the iron and wood detail in the fireplace screen (Figure 2.17a) and bentwood rocker (Figure 2.17b). The curvilinear

movement of the spiral shapes takes on the quality of a line drawing.

In the silhouettes of Isamu Noguchi's paper lamp shades (Figure 2.18a) and the "Flying Saucer" dress of Issey Miyake (Figure 2.18b), we see evidence of similarities in the creativity of the disciplines of fashion and lighting design. British designer and entrepreneur Terence Conran, the founder of London's Design Museum, has drawn attention to the relationship among these disciplines, as his multifaceted career demonstrates. He is responsible for Gatwick Airport's North Terminal, the first Mary Quant Shop, and the Discovery Range Rover. In writing about design, he states, "Fashion is proverbially fickle, a playful means of reinvention and expressing joie de vivre." He also refers to this playfulness in the designs of Issey Miyake, "whose work reminds me of the springy organic shapes of Noguchi lights" (Conran, p. 102).

2.17a

32

2.16a

2.16b

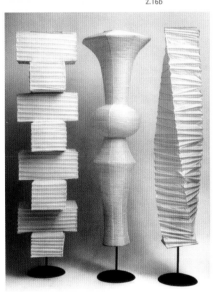

2.17b

2.18a

2.18b

FIG. 2.14 (a) Wicker chair and (b) the atrium of the Bradbury Building by George H. Wyman. [(a) Copyright © Mark Hamel/Alamy. (b) Copyright © Nik Wheeler/Corbis.] FIG. 2.15 (a) Manuel Canovas chair (1992). (b) William Travilla's design for Marilyn Monroe in *The Seven Year Itch* (1955), 20th Century Fox. [(a) Photo courtesy Bruce Oldfield, Inc. (b) Copyright © The Kobal Collection.] FIG. 2.16 (a) Model wearing a striped dress by Tiziani (1966). (b) Striped deck chairs. [(a) Photo by Henry Clark. Reprinted with the permission of Condé Nast Publications. All rights reserved. (b) Copyright © Parque/zefa/Corbis.] FIG. 2.17 (a) Wrought iron fireplace screen by Edgar Brandt (1923) and (b) Thonet rocker. [(a) Reprinted with the permission of the Minneapolis Institute of Arts, the Modernism Collection, gift of Norwest Bank Minnesota. (b) Copyright © The Art Archive/Dagli Orti.] FIG. 2.18 (a) Paper lampshades by Isamu Noguchi (c.1950). (b) Colorful "Flying Saucer" dress by Issey Miyake. [(a) Copyright © 2006 The Isamu Noguchi Foundation and Garden Museum, NY, Artists Rights Society (ARS). (b) Photo by Irving Penn/Issey Miyake Ltd.]

Architecture, Structure, and Detail

Referencing architectural structure and detail in other design media seems to be a recurring theme. The incorporation of the concept of architectural structure within clothing design is apparent in the famous photo of New York architect William Van Alen dressed as his favorite building for the 1931 Beaux Arts Ball (Figure 2.19a). Whitney Warren, an architect whose firm Warren & Wetmore designed the Grand Central Terminal in New York, founded this event. In a similar vein, costumes with silhouettes and details influenced by buildings (Figure 2.19b) were designed and constructed by Sonia Delaunay for a masquerade party in 1923.

Adele Lutz's surrealistic interpretations of wearing apparel (Figure 2.20a and b) further demonstrate this creative use of architectural detail. In the same way that a building exterior provides shelter but portrays a style, clothing can be viewed as an expression of style that also provides protection. Conceptually, we can think of architecture as a protective covering serving a purpose similar to that of clothing on the body.

In another take on architectural detail, the angular pattern and embellishment on Bauhaus student Dörte Helm's appliquéd quilt (Figure 2.21a) picks up the same diagonal linear design qualities as the building exterior created by Sonia Delaunay for her "Costume for a Fancy Dress Ball" (Figure 2.21b).

2.20a

2.19a

34

2.19b

2.21a+b

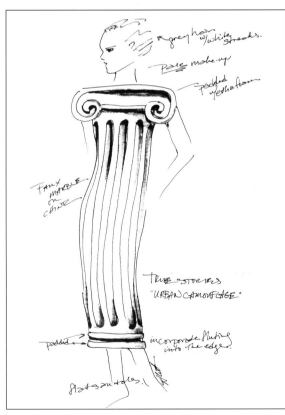

2.20b

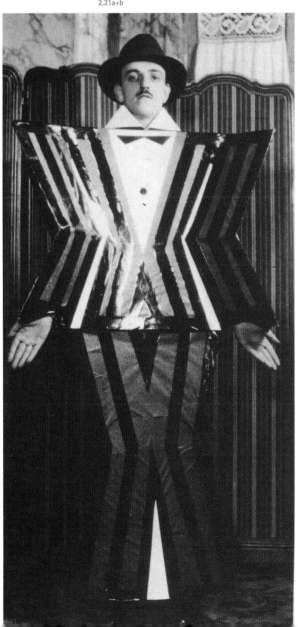

FIG. 2.19 (a) William Van Alen in Chrysler Building costume at the Beaux Arts Ball (1931) and (b) India ink drawing by Sonia Delaunay. [(a) Copyright © Bettmann/Corbis. (b) Copyright © L&M Services B.V. Amsterdam 20040308.] **FIG. 2.20** (a) "Urban Camouflage Clothing" by Adele Lutz (1986) and (b) "Woman Column" by Adele Lutz (1986). **FIG. 2.21** (a) Embroidered Afghan quilt by Dörte Helm (1921–22) and (b) "Costume for a Fancy Dress Ball" by Sonia Delaunay (1923). [(a) Copyright © Christine Osbourne Pictures/Alamy. (b) Copyright © L&M Services B.V. Amsterdam 20040308.]

Adorning oneself with a facade that suggests features not normally found in apparel gives a person a larger-than-life image. Features of masquerade can come from numerous sources, such as a typical window treatment using drapery with a swag (Figure 2.22a).

In the 1939 film *Gone with the Wind,* Scarlett O'Hara's desire to go to Atlanta "looking like a queen" leads her to design a gown from the only textile resource available to her—the draperies from her home, Tara. Known as "the drapery dress," this costume (Figure 2.22b) is used by Scarlett in her famous pretension of wealth. This dress was obviously the reference point of Peter Steiner's *New Yorker* cartoon (Figure 2.22c).

Michael Graves's Portland Building (Figure 2.23a) is a prime example of postmodernism in architecture. Some qualities of postmodernism are symmetry, use of color, creative application of decorative details, and references to the past (Pile, p. 359). Although it predates the Portland Building by more than 50 years, the linear and geometric qualities of architecture are apparent in Sonia Delaunay's "Building Costume" (Figure 2.23b).

Graves's body of work, like that of Sonia Delaunay, has shown that boundaries between design disciplines can be artificial. He has designed everything from kitchen appliances and tools to interiors and buildings.

Commonplace objects such as those designed by Graves become the obvious source for the creative design process in programmatic architecture, also known as *kitsch.* Doughnuts and hats (Figure 2.24a), hot dogs (Figure 2.24b), teapots, paper lanterns,

2.22a

2.22b+c

2.23a

2.23b

"You know what? I'm sick of clothes. I decided to go for a window treatment instead."

2.24a

2.24b

FIG. 2.22 (a) Drapery with swag. (b) Drapery dress from *Gone with the Wind* (1939), Plunkett. (c) the *New Yorker* cartoon "You know what? I'm sick of clothes. I decided to go for a window treatment instead," by P. Steiner. [(a) Copyright © Stewart Ferebee/Getty Images. (b) Reprinted with the permission of the Harry Ransom Humanities Research Center, The University of Texas at Austin, David O. Selznick Collection. (c) Reprinted with permission of the *New Yorker* Collection 1999/Peter Steiner/cartoonbank.com.] FIG. 2.23 (a) The Portland Building, Portland, OR, by Michael Graves (1982). (b) "Building Costume" by Sonia Delaunay (c. 1925). [(a) Copyright © Peter Aaron/Esto Photographics, Inc. (b) Copyright © L&M Services B.V. Amsterdam 20040308.] FIG. 2.24 (a) Brown Derby Restaurant in Los Angeles and (b) Tail o' the Pup Hotdog Stand in Los Angeles. [(a) Copyright © John Margolies Collection/Getty Images. (b) Reprinted with permission of Google Art.]

2.25a

2.25b

2.26a+b

slinky toys, and fountains, although mundane, are among the sources of inspiration for some very imaginative buildings, costumes, products, and apparel.

In the coffee shop facade (Figure 2.25a) and the Mad Tea Party ride at Disneyland in Anaheim, California (Figure 2.25b), the disciplines of architecture, set design, costume design, and graphic design merge.

In architecture, what is universal is how weight is distributed by the use of post-and-beam construction. Using this structural methodology, the load is transferred from the horizontal (beam) to the vertical (post or column). These same principles seem to apply in the structure of the chaise lounge (Figure 2.26a) and in the Japanese clogs in Figure 2.26b. In both of these images, the vertical support element, although it appears to be delicate, is a very strong structure, as both the chaise and the clog support the weight of the body, although in different ways.

38

2.27a

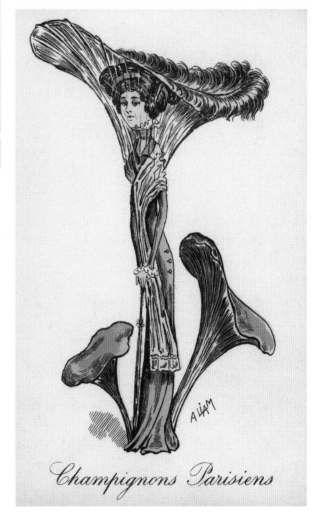

2.27b

Champignons Parisiens

The stylized concrete structural columns in the administration offices of Frank Lloyd Wright's famous Johnson Wax Building (Figure 2.27a) also appear to be delicate and have been described as "mushroom shaped" (Pile, p. 318), but Figure 2.27b uses a similar stylistic shape for a whimsical costume. This unusual approach for an advertisement for mushrooms demonstrates that inspiration is drawn from many sources.

In Christo and Jeanne-Claude's "Wrapped Reichstag" (Figure 2.28a), the identifying features of the government building in Berlin have been disguised. The hard surfaces that we normally associate with architectural structures are draped with diaphanous fabric, and the form of the building is concealed and softened. Conversely, the hard surface and structure of Carolyn Broadhead's

FIG. 2.25 (a) Grand's restaurant by Robert Venturi. (b) Mad Tea Party ride at Disneyland in Anaheim, CA (1994). [(a) Reprinted with the permission of Venturi, Scott Brown and Associates, Inc. Photo by Laurence S. Williams. (b) Copyright © Robert Holmes/Corbis.] FIG. 2.26 The structures of (a) chaise lounges and (b) Japanese clogs. [(a) Copyright © Colin Paterson/SuperStock. (b) Copyright © Corbis.] FIG. 2.27 (a) Johnson Wax Building, Research Tower in Racine, WI, by Frank Lloyd Wright (1936–39). (b) "Champignons Parisiens" postcard advertisement for Parisian mushrooms by A. Liam (1914). [(a) Copyright © Farrell Grehan/Esto Photographics. (b) Copyright © Swim Ink 2, LLC/Corbis.]

39

2.28a

2.28b

2.29a

2.29b

"Wobbly Dress" (Figure 2.28b) give it an architectural quality due to the rigidity of the materials. Where we would expect to see a garment that is soft and fluid, we are startled because we see the reverse.

Architectural detail and symbolism have been widely used as a source of inspiration for textile design. This is evident in the geometric farmhouse patchwork quilt (Figure 2.29a), which references a shape similar to the Irish thatched roof cottage (Figure 2.29b).

John Storrs, son of an architect, reveals his roots in "Forms in Space" (Figure 2.30a), which at first glance is a high-rise building, but in reality is part of

2.30a

2.30b

his body of work as a sculptor. "Storrs was naturally drawn to geometric shapes, the order and permanence of the skyscraper form" (www.sheldon.unl .edu). The dynamic geometric design of Georges Lepape's "Woman with an Automobile" (Figure 2.30b) reflects the streamlined detail in the Storrs sculpture.

Pattern, Trims, and Embellishment

Textile pattern, color, embellishment, and silhouette enhance the similarity of the images in Figure 2.31a and b. The images emphasize curves rather than hard edges. We can surmise that Luttrell was a man of importance from his regal, fur-trimmed cloak, striped silk shirt, and majestic hat, and the fact that his portrait was painted. The armchairs (Figure 2.31b) with their rolled arms echo the overstuffed comfort of the portly gentleman, while the fabric on the chairs augments the feeling of elegance. Although from different eras, we can observe that elaborate, detailed design emerges again and again.

In addition to textile surface design, trims are used as ornamentation in both fashion and interiors, whether embroi-

FIG. 2.28 (a) "Wrapped Reichstag" in Berlin by Christo and Jeanne-Claude (1995). (b) "Wobbly Dress" by Carolyn Broadhead (1992). [(a) Photo by Wolfgang Volz. (b) Copyright © Caroline Broadhead/Crafts Council Photostore.] FIG. 2.29 (a) Farmhouse patchwork quilt from the Los Angeles County Fair (2002). (b) Thatched roof house in Spiddal, Ireland. [(a) Photo by John Sohm. Copyright © Visions of America, LLC/Alamy. (b) Copyright © Joey Nigh/Corbis.] FIG. 2.30 (a) "Forms in Space" by John Storrs (c. 1924). (b) "Woman with an Automobile" from *Vogue* by Georges Lepape (1925). [(a) Reprinted with permission of Munson-Williams-Proctor Arts Institute. (b) Copyright © Snark/Art Resource and © 2007 Artists Rights Society (ARS), NY/ADAGP, Paris.] FIG. 2.31 (a) "Simon Luttrell of Luttrellstown" by Jean-Etienne Liotard (ca. 1754). (b) Damask upholstered armchairs. [(a) Reprinted with permission of Kunstmuseum Bern. (b) Photo by Dennis Stone. Copyright © Elizabeth Whiting & Associates/Corbis.]

2.31a

2.31b

dered directly on the fabric or added as an architectural border. The style lines of the dress and hat in Figure 2.32a are accentuated by ornate trim detail. Figure 2.32b illustrates samples of trim by the British interior design firm Colefax and Fowler. These are typical of embellishments used in the design and fabrication of drapery, wallpaper, and upholstery, where trim is the element that highlights the piece, much as it emphasizes the lines of the dress and hat.

Gilded detail was a favored form of 17th-century embellishment, evident in both the costume of the Earl of Holland and the ornate fireplace mantle in the Tredegar House (Figure 2.33a and b). These images reflect the elegance and splendor enjoyed by the ruling classes during the colonial past of northern Europe.

The 18th century, with its many advancements in industrialization, has been described as an "Age of Elegance" in design. By the late 1700s in France,

2.32a

2.32b

2.33a

2.33b

the French Revolution had ushered in a move toward simplicity in dress and furniture that began with the Directoire period and extended into the reign of Emperor Napoleon I, the Empire period. Part of the reason for the shift in taste was that the social and political reorganization brought about by the revolution swiftly changed attitudes toward apparel and objects that symbolized the wealth of the past. People looked toward ancient Greece for aesthetic inspiration, and these influences can be seen in both fashion and furniture.

This chapter has presented examples of artists and designers whose work has been influenced by other eras, disciplines, and media and by other artists and designers. Sharing their innate love of the principles and elements of design, artists and designers constantly strive to discover and reinvent methods of using materials while preserving the distinct character of their viewpoint. In so doing, their individual expression leads to the creation of a broader, more varied body of work that represents the collaborative process.

The images in this chapter, representing a wide range of ideas, are intended to stimulate the imagination and provide a backdrop for the creative process. The act of designing is the communication of a visual thought process, and designers constantly refresh their visual vocabulary with new images and new combinations of images. Where it all begins is in the margins between the old and the new, and in the intersections between design disciplines.

FIG. 2.32 (a) Embroidered dress and hat. (b) Trim samples from Colefax and Fowler (2005). [(a) Copyright ©Philadelphia Museum of Art/Corbis. (b) Photo by Oberto Gili. Copyright © Beateworks.] FIG. 2.33 (a) Henry Rich, Earl of Holland by Daniel Mytens, (1640). (b) Fireplace at the Tredegar House in Newport, Wales (17th century). [(a) Reprinted with the permission of the National Portrait Gallery, London. (b) Reprinted with permission of Tredegar House.]

CHAPTER THREE

Sources of Design Inspiration

The role of the designer has traditionally been to formulate ideas for projects or products. Much has been said about the distinctions between the artist and the designer, and normally the differences revolve around the product that is created and the subtleties of function and aesthetics. For our purposes, whether in interior design, fashion design, graphic design, or other design disciplines, a product is the end result of the efforts of the designer. But where do the designer's ideas originate? What is the source of the spark of inspiration that fuels a designer's imagination? How does a successful designer manage to invent timely products that appeal to the desires and fulfill the needs of consumers? How does it happen that occasionally a design so captures the essence of an idea that it becomes a memorable aspect of the history of design itself? How does a designer imagine the new while existing in the present?

When you look around, do you see sources of inspiration? When you look outside, is there evidence in the natural world that provokes thoughts about design? In your conversations do you hear stories that fuel your thought processes and imagination? What is happening in the world today that will become memorable in the future? What effect will the events of today have upon our lives?

In psychology, the Rorschach inkblot test is used to reveal aspects of the personality of the subject, the idea being that each person brings to the picture a unique perspective that becomes part of the interpretation. In a similar way, designers bring a unique point of view to each project, and as a designer achieves recognition, that point of view can become identifiable. For example, architect Frank Gehry has become known in recent years for constructions featuring creative uses of materials in which hard surfaces appear to be windswept and undulating, such as the exterior shapes of the Walt Disney Concert Hall in Los Angeles (Figure 3.1a). These novel uses of materials have become a Frank Gehry signature in spite of the fact that many projects by the architect do not utilize these design features. In fact, his earlier work includes furniture constructed from corrugated cardboard (Figure 3.1b) and the use of chain link fencing as a building material. From a recent perspective Gehry's work might be seen as all curves and waves, yet from a wider perspective the overall ongoing theme might be considered the creative use of materials. The images featured in Figure 3.1a and b show just two of the wide range of creative design solutions that Gehry has explored.

Part of a design education is the development and communication of a unique perspective, the discovery of the distinctive "something" that you will bring to each project.

Designers Interpret History

In considering sources of inspiration, successful designers rely heavily on a knowledge of history and on historical research to create a setting in which to develop new designs. Yet when asked to name a favorite subject in school, relatively few designers would choose history, and even fewer would consider history to be a source of inspiration. However, if we look at history with the help of some contemporary terminology, rather than viewing it as a tedious catalog of events and dates, we can begin to appreciate how some type of

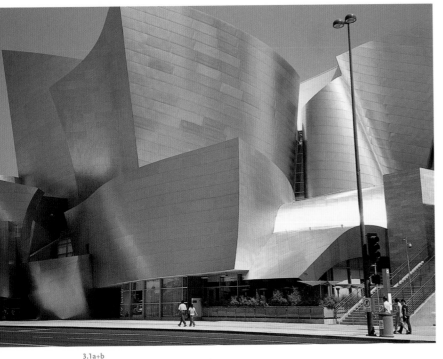

3.1a+b

3.2

history informs almost every design process. If instead of "history" we refer to "backstory," "background," or "the story behind . . . ," we can begin to understand the design process and the way that inspiration is generated for this process.

Now that history has been released from its stodgy image, we can proceed to examine the many different sources of inspiration that emerge from the story behind an idea. In many instances, especially as students, we are encouraged to look to sources of pleasure for inspiration. The picturesque sunset, the exquisite flower, or the joy of life becomes the theme for a design process. But most designers find that inspiration can come from both the beautiful and the terrible, and from a wide variety of places in between. The determining factor seems to be the designer's relationship to the source of inspiration and the answer to the questions "Why is this important?" and "What is it about this that I want to communicate?" In many ways, all of design is based on a personal interaction between the designer and the source of inspiration for the project. In analyzing interiors, the designer must become aware of the feelings provoked by arrangements of space and use of materials. The successful designer of apparel has a similar involvement in exploring the comfort, sensation, and movement of clothing.

Personal History Inspires Design

Designers frequently utilize personal history—events or acquaintances from their own lives—as sources of inspiration. Over time, designers often examine and reexamine their personal, cultural, or ethnic heritage, mining their own backgrounds for starting points of inspiration. For a designer this may be a method of coming to terms with events of the past, honoring a cultural legacy, or exploring personal issues. From the perspective of the consumer, however, successful designs transcend the designer's personal history. They are accepted and appreciated regardless of any specific awareness of background details.

For example, fashion designer Issey Miyake, who spent his childhood in Japan during World War II, based some of his early work on his personal experiences there and on traditional Japanese folk wear, as shown in Figure 3.2. In doing so, he honored his country's strong textile traditions. While knowledge of Japanese textiles might augment a viewer's appreciation of Miyake's work, the strength of the designer's approach to color, texture, line, and proportion is evident without regard to background knowledge.

FIG. 3.1 Frank Gehry's (a) Walt Disney Concert Hall in Los Angeles and (b) "Experimental Easy Chair" made from layers of corrugated cardboard. [(a) Photo by Penny Collins. (b) Reprinted with the permission of Gehry Partners, LLC.] FIG. 3.2 Traditional Japanese folk wear by Issey Miyake. [Courtesy, Fairchild Publications, Inc.]

For some designers, inspiration is found in the process of making things. One such person is Christina Kim, whose Dosa line includes clothing, accessories, and designs for the home, all of which demonstrate her respect for traditional techniques and sustainable manufacturing practices. Many of the products she creates are handcrafted by artisans in various parts of the world. The article in Box 3.1 describes the work of Christina Kim in more detail.

BOX 3.1

Style: A Handmaiden's Tale
By Lisa Eisner and Román Alonso

In Los Angeles, you don't expect to find someone like Christina Kim—New York maybe, or Paris. She designs clothing, accessories, and housewares under her label, Dosa, but her process is different from that of other designers. "In my dictionary, fashion means moment," she explains with a hint of Korean still in her voice. "The women I know don't really wear fashion as much as they think they do. They wear clothes." Christina isn't looking for the newest or the most unique—her quest is for "the essence, the most unadorned simple form of something."

Dosa makes its home on two floors high above downtown Los Angeles across from the Eastern Building, a historic turquoise tile monument built in 1930. One floor is used as a gallery and retail space. The other is the office, showroom and factory that ships to 100 stores in 20 countries. It is not what you would expect in the middle of L.A.'s garment district. There are huge floor-to-ceiling windows, no receptionist, no offices or cubicles; there are no interior walls at all—a bit like one of those ant farms where you can see the inner workings. There are rows of sewing machines with seamstresses in matching smocks and an open kitchen where everyone brings things to cook for lunch. "I didn't like the idea of people thinking that the clothing industry equals 'sweatshop,'" Kim says, "so I decided to create a working place that is enjoyable."

She continues: "What I love about the West is we have space. You can see the horizon—it's a horizontal way of looking at things. The East Coast is more vertical; you have to look up. The whole democratic ideal of what I do comes from the horizon, so we had to be in L.A."

These spaces are her laboratories—repositories for volumes of meticulously handwritten travel journals as well as tables filled with photographs, fabrics, yarns, beads, feathers, and embroideries from Mexico, China, Chile, Turkey, Myanmar, and on and on. Christina is sort of like Margaret Mead. She travels around the world working with indigenous people and artisans—learning, cross-pollinating ideas, and adapting traditional crafts to her modern needs.

In the last 20 years she has built a devoted clientele that appreciates not only her bohemian aesthetic and beautiful fabrics in simple comfortable shapes but also her gestalt.

For Christina there's more to it than just making products. As a child in Korea she'd spend hours with her grandmother, hemstitching linens that they would then dampen, spread over a hot piece of marble and beat with a couple of sticks to arrive at a shiny finish. She fell in love with the process of artfully making things that are labor intensive rather than resource intensive. "I'm always conscious of how we use natural resources," she explains. "I hate waste, and there's this incredible growth of human population. So if I use little resources and use a lot of human hands, maybe I'm balancing things a bit."

Kim walks her talk. Home is a small Richard Neutra building in Silver Lake that is perfect in design and function. Everything she needs fits perfectly in this tiny space—there is no excess—no walk-in closets filled with shoes and handbags here. Out of a small kitchen filled with jars of herbs and spices collected in her travels, she cooks exotic vegetables she gets from her friend James Birch, an organic farmer. The food is all color and texture, and it's delicious—seriously, like nothing you've ever tasted.

It's all about the hands for Kim. She's the connoisseur of handmade—whether it's food, or jewelry, or sheets, or rugs, or clothing—it's that one-on-one, on-site experience with the people growing it or making it that turns her on. "It's important for me to gracefully be the conduit between design and indigenous people," she says. "Keeping what they do alive. Ultimately it's the time you spend and relationships you create that make the projects successful. It isn't the speed of doing things, it is doing things with care and love."

Reprinted with permission of the *New York Times*, October 31, 2004, pgs. 54–59.

Designers Are Inspired by Nature and the Sciences

Nature is frequently a point of reference for design. The forms, processes, and events occurring in nature are very often used as sources of inspiration by designers seeking to interpret the world around them in new ways. Nature can include the objects of astronomy, physics, chemistry, biology, botany, anthropology, and the environmental sciences. Color, used in all areas of design, is largely influenced by nature. Colors occurring in nature generally form the basis of the design palette, with deep browns and rusts normally finding their way into fall and winter color schemes, and light, bright colors into spring and summer. Forms and shapes occurring in nature are often the starting point for interior furnishings and details.

In architecture, inspiration from the natural world can be seen in the work of Antoni Gaudí, the designer of the Cathedral of the Sagrada Familia (Figure 3.3a) and many other buildings in Barcelona. Beginning in 1883 and until his death in 1926, Gaudí supervised the construction of the cathedral, which to this day remains unfinished. The organic forms of the spires and arches of the cathedral are inspired by nature. "'Do you want to know where I found my model?' he once asked a visitor to his workshop. 'An upright tree; it bears its branches and these, in turn, their twigs, and these, in turn, the leaves. And every individual part has been growing harmoniously, magnificently, ever since God the artist created it'" (Zerbst, p. 30).

Another architect whose work shows extensive reference to and respect for nature is Frank Lloyd Wright. He understood how buildings could

3.3a+b

FIG. 3.3 (a) The Cathedral of the Sagrada Familia in Barcelona by Antoni Gaudí. (b) "Falling Water" in Bear Run, PA, by Frank Lloyd Wright (1935-39). [(a) Copyright © Gaudi Images/Superstock. (b) Copyright © Peter Cook/Superstock.]

become extensions of their natural environments and used forms and construction materials that reflected the surrounding landscape in an organic way. Probably his most renowned project is "Falling Water" in Bear Run, Pennsylvania, built between 1935 and 1939 as a vacation residence (Figure 3.3b). Rather than locating the house opposite the stream and waterfall that are the focal point of the property, Wright chose to perch the house above the falls, where an ingenious construction method lets the house blend into the woods and become part of the natural terrain.

Certain technological discoveries in the sciences can influence designers in very specific ways. Just as some designers find inspiration in the unspoiled outdoor environment, others celebrate scientific developments that suggest a more synthetic approach. During the 1960s the United States and what was then the Soviet Union were engaged in the "space race," and some designers thrived on imagining new looks for what was bound to be a new world. For example, fashion and furniture in the era of space exploration yielded to the look of *The Jetsons*, which first appeared as a television animation produced by Hanna-Barbera in 1962, set in the then-distant 21st century. Concurrent scientific developments in knits, synthetics, and plastics made sleek, futuristic looks technically possible. French fashion designer André Courrèges captured the aesthetic of that era in spare, unadorned clothing such as the minidress shown in Figure 3.4a. Similar visual references to the atomic age and space travel appeared in interior furnishings, with designs such as George James's "Starburst" (Figure 3.4b), which enjoys a retro popularity now with col-

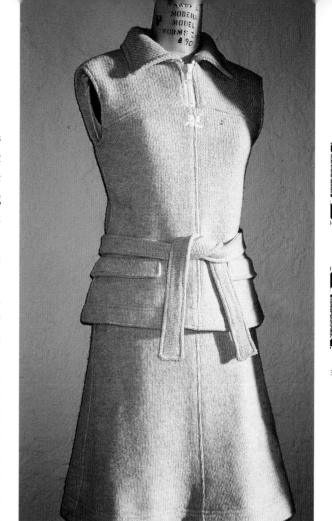

3.5

3.4a+b

lectors, becoming a best-selling dinnerware pattern.

The influence of nature on design is particularly noticeable in relation to textile design, in the many examples of motifs from nature for fabric prints, as well as woven and knit patterns. When you look at the leaf of a fern or a slide through a microscope, do you imagine incorporating what you see into patterns on fabric? Textile and fashion designer Jhane Barnes utilizes miniscule images of plant life as the basis for some of her designs. These are based on the mathematical theory of fractal geometry (Figure 3.5), which is the origin of organic growth. Jhane Barnes utilizes computer technology to advance her creative process by employing mathematicians to write programs that can translate these concepts into patterns for woven textiles (Jennings).

Cultural History Is a Source of Inspiration

Cultural history is another source of inspiration for designers, who often travel the world in search of a starting point for new ideas. World cultures, especially those in transition, are often magnets for designers. For example, Asian cultures have long been considered exotic by European designers. This fascination stretches back to the Silk Route which extended from Rome to China, approximately six thousand miles, as long ago as 100 B.C.E. (see Figure 7.3). During the 18th century, goods from China were imported into Europe, leading to a trend known as "Chinese Madness" (Batterberry, p. 160). Motifs considered to be Asian, such as pagodas, parasols, and temples, appeared on walls, textiles, and furniture, such as the chairs pictured in Figure 3.6. Again at the beginning of the 20th century, after exotic articles from Russia and the East had been featured at the Salon d'Automne in Paris, textile, furniture, and fashion designer Paul Poiret showed Oriental motifs and Eastern materials in his collections (Mulvagh, p. 6). When President Richard Nixon visited China in 1972 after it had been essentially closed to Westerners since the cultural revolution of Mao Tse-Tung, interest in China was once again aroused, and fashion and textile designs again showed an Asian influence.

This exotic influence was a source of inspiration for the work of designer Tony Duquette. His

3.6

FIG. 3.4 (a) Minidress by André Courrèges. (b) George James's Franciscanware starburst pattern (1953). [(a) Photo by Penny Collins, Woodbury University Fashion Study Collection. (b) Reprinted with permission of the Dallas Museum of Art, Visual Resource Center.] FIG. 3.5 The Halley Map is an example of fractal geometry, in which small elements repeat and connect to form a complicated pattern. [Copyright © Corbis.] FIG. 3.6 The texture and color of these bamboo chairs suggest an Asian influence. [Copyright © Beateworks, Inc./Alamy Images.]

credits include a Tony Award for the costumes of the Broadway production of *Camelot*, but he is equally well known for his set, jewelry, and furniture designs, and for Dawnridge, his estate in Beverly Hills, California. The landscape includes pagodas, bridges, terraces, sculpture, and pavilions in a dreamlike Asian garden. Tony Duquette's creative energy often focused on Asian-inspired themes, as in one of his earliest furniture pieces, shown in Figure 3.7, which he made for Elsie de Wolfe, Lady Mendl, the first "interior decorator" (Columbia, p. 3).

Social History Fuels Inspiration

Like cultural history, social history often serves as background to an idea that fuels a designer's inspiration. In this context, *social history* refers to the influence of events, conflicts, or changes in political structures or governments. Political upheavals, even though they often leave disastrous results, can spark inspiration in creative individuals. During the occupation of Paris by the German military during World War II, with only sparse resources at hand, creativity abounded, particularly in millinery. Hats, especially turban styles, made of newspaper and scraps of fabric and ribbon were proudly worn by Frenchwomen, such as those pictured in Figure 3.8, who were determined to remain stylish during a difficult time.

During the late 1960s in American society many changes began to occur as a large group of "baby boom" women entered adulthood freed from the rigid role expectations of previous generations. Many women chose to pursue careers and climb the corporate ladder. Clothing designers of this era found inspiration in adapting traditional men's style details such as tailored suits and ties for a new audience. Figure 3.9 shows an example of the type of professional dress favored by women entering the workforce in the 1970s.

Just as they are now, changes in society were reflected in communication channels and the media. Thanks to the proliferation of cable and satellite broadcasting, television programs that doc-

3.7

3.8

3.9

ument social history are readily available for viewing today. *Three's Company* (1977–1984), a situation comedy that featured three single people sharing an apartment, was revolutionary for an era in which most programs portrayed households with more "traditional" family structures. Similar changes in society have been reflected in residential interior design, where the single-family house has been modified to include a bedroom suite for each family member, a great room combining aspects of what

previously would have been separate kitchen, dining, and living areas, plus a large garage for multiple vehicles.

An instance of design influence from events in social and political history can be seen in relation to the consequences of the attacks of September 11, 2001. In the designer collections for the fall 2002 season, presented in February 2002, Jeremy Scott showed a long, straight, sheath dress with a geometric pattern of insets that was thought to resemble a

FIG. 3.7 An elaborate, Asian-inspired desk designed by Tony Duquette for Elsie de Wolfe. [Reprinted with permission of the Duquette Estate.] FIG. 3.8 Parisian women during the German occupation of France during World War II. [Copyright © Hulton-Deutsch Collection/Corbis.] FIG. 3.9 A woman's professional dress suit from the 1970s. [Copyright © Hulton Archive/Getty Images.]

53

high-rise building (Figure 3.10). In a *Los Angeles Times* article describing that season's collections, fashion writer Michael Quintanilla noted that the dress evoked the World Trade Center towers for some audience members.

Similarly, trends in economics can be seen as social history. During the 1990s and into the 21st century, although some professionals have become increasingly wealthy, a majority of middle-class workers have seen incomes stand still or decline; however, well-designed yet affordable products have become available on a mass-market level that has encouraged everyone's enjoyment of what has come to be known as "good taste." As John Leland put it, "Just look at your toothbrush, designed by Philippe Starck for Alessi. . . . Here was a distinctively American perspective on democratic design: If you couldn't afford to make your home look like Buckingham Palace, you could get some of the snob appeal of an Ian Schrager boutique hotel" (p. 90). Discount retailers such as Target and Kmart have capitalized on this growing trend, taking inspiration from high-end products but translating them for the mass market by hiring designers from exclusive lines to work in budget categories. Martha Stewart's home products and linens for Kmart and both Michael Graves's houseware designs and Isaac Mizrahi's clothing line for Target are examples of this phenomenon. According to A. O. Scott, the "wide availability of a variety of beautiful, unusual things . . . increases the pressure, the sense of responsibility, that attends every purchase" (p. 19). Even mass-produced home accessories carry a certain charm when they are called "antiques" or carry the brand of an upscale designer.

3.10

Art Influences Design

Art—and in this context *art* is taken to include cinema, literature, and music—is yet another source of inspiration for designers. The histories of art and design are interdependent, and the process of inspiration for artists and for designers is similar. But design is normally focused on a functional product or process as the end result. The influence of major art movements and art exhibitions on design is well documented, whether in a subtle suggestion of line, color, or material, or in an outright borrowing of whole motifs. Inspiration from art is seen clearly in some of the work of fashion designer Yves St. Laurent, in his pieces featuring motifs recognizable from the color-block geometric paintings of Dutch artist Piet Mondrian. The Rietveld armchair, dated 1918 (Figure 3.11a), the Mondrian painting, dated 1930 (Figure 3.11b), and the St. Laurent dress, dated 1966 (Figure 3.11c) each show an interpretation of the color-block abstract style initiated in the Dutch de Stijl movement. St. Laurent's shift dress with geometric shapes of white and primary colors separated by a grid of black bands captured the modern mood of the mid-1960s and was widely imitated in the popular fashion of the time (Mendes and de la Haye).

An example of the cross-fertilization of art, film, and fashion is seen in the contemporaneous nature of several exhibitions of the work of artists Diego Rivera and Frida Kahlo (Figure 3.12), coinciding with the approach of the fiftieth anniversary of her death in 1954. In the film *Frida* (2001), Salma Hayek plays the surrealist artist whose personal style influenced fashion, leading to the short-lived "unibrow" trend (after Frida Kahlo's full eyebrows that seemed to make one

3.11a

3.11b+c

FIG. 3.10 Jeremy Scott's slender sheath gown, which resembles a high-rise building. [Copyright © George De Sota/Getty Images.] FIG. 3.11 (a) De Stijl influence is evident in the geometric blocks of color in "Armchair Red and Blue" by Gerrit Rietveld (1918). (b) "Composition with Red, Blue, and Yellow" by Piet Mondrian (1930).(c) Geometric color blocking finds its way to fashion in the Yves St. Laurent Mondrian Dress, (1966). [(a) Copyright © ARS, NY, and Erich Lessing/Art Resource, NY. (b) Copyright © HCR International and Erich Lessing/Art Resource, NY. (c) Reprinted with permission of V&A Images/Victoria and Albert Museum.]

continuous line across her forehead) and the popularity of folkloric skirts and huipiles, the handmade blouses that Kahlo wore in many of her self-portraits (Theis).

Designers Are Inspired by the Design Past

Finally, each branch of design has its own history that is continually mined for new inspiration. Writing about costume history, Ulrich Lehmann states, "Nothing . . . is ever lost, and fashion as a phenomenon always advances its

3.12

own life span through constant citations from its historical sourcebook." A rich example of this recycling is in the way vintage clothing and furniture reveal the past. It is the part of design history that is accessible and wearable, and as such it becomes a kind of living history. Of course, a large proportion of antique and quality vintage items are housed in museums, where they receive special care, but thanks to a wide interest in period clothing and domestic items, pieces from the past several decades remain in circulation and reveal not only the history of the development of the design industries but something about the social history of the user or wearer. In the spring of 2003, Abercrombie and Fitch debuted the "Abercrombie Vintage" line, featuring "aged" clothing for men and women. Of course, the aging processes were manu-

factured, but the look, nonetheless, was there, and the inspiration was definitely vintage.

For some, much of the interest in vintage items can be traced to the increasing simplification and cheapening of sewing and construction details. Anne Rubin, describing a long and successful career as a designer of high-end knitted garments that are increasingly sought after as vintage pieces, says, "These are classics . . . the women knitting in their back rooms are gone . . . and this is all that's left of them." "History comes in many forms," she says. "Sometimes you can wear it" (Hirschberg, p. 108). In terms of value for money, where $20 might purchase a mass-produced garment lacking in design originality, the same money invested in vintage might buy a garment whose fabric and design provide a glimpse of history. And it isn't difficult to appreciate the comment of Austin Bunn in his analysis of worldwide interest in vintage denim, such as that pictured in Figure 3.13: "Woven up in this appreciation of old clothes is not only an envy for an older

3.13

way of life but also a nostalgia for hard, damaging work" (p. 65).

Similarly, in furniture design, changes come about as designers react and adapt to changing conditions in social history. In an analysis of the success of IKEA, John Leland notes that "market research in the mid-1990s found that many Americans were frozen by decor fear, holding onto sofas longer than to cars. IKEA's new ad campaign can be seen as a kind of curriculum by which to teach a more commitment-free approach to furniture" (p. 88). According to Leland, the boundary between "things like refrigerators and furnaces, which are expected to last forever," and "things that turn over at the speed of fashion" is less distinct than it once was (p. 90).

Roy McMakin is an artist who, although difficult to classify, makes furniture. McMakin, referring to his approach to furniture design, says that his goal "is sometimes to make life easier, other times to make it more fun" (Freudenheim, p. 52). While one trend in furniture seems to be in the direction of very low-cost, mass-produced items with "some assembly required" and built-in obsolescence, another growing trend is increased interest in one-of-a-kind pieces (see McMakin's "Benedek House Model" in Figure 3.14, one of his signature treatments). Realizing that in the construction of furniture there is a great deal of defective wood that is wasted, he works patches into his designs in order to extend the amount of usable wood. The artist tells the story of how he first developed this technique: His dog had chewed some wood, and in order to be able to forgive his pet, he invented a patch technique (Freudenheim).

Architecture is yet another branch of design that

3.14

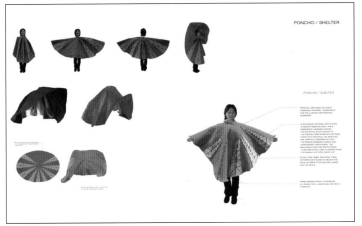

3.15

often takes inspiration from its own history, developments, and issues. One issue that architects contend with is the need for temporary housing for people in emergency situations such as armed conflict or natural disasters. One solution, which combines apparel and architecture, is the poncho that converts to a tent. It was designed in a class called Weaving Material and Habitation, taught by Toshiko Mori, chair of the department of architecture at Harvard's Graduate School of Design. The

FIG. 3.12 The distinctive look of artist Frida Kahlo is evident in the "The Frame, Self-Portrait" (c. 1937–38). [Reprinted with permission of CNAC/MNAM/Dist. Réunion des Musées Nationaux/Art Resource, NY.] FIG. 3.13 Interest in vintage and "faux" denim continues to grow, and it also reflects nostalgia. [Copyright © Alamy Ltd.] FIG. 3.14 The "Benedek House Model" by Roy McMakin (1991) shows the labor-intensive handmade quality of his work. [Photo by Mark Woods/the *Los Angeles Times*.] FIG. 3.15 Architecture and fashion merge in the "Poncho Tent" developed in a course taught by Toshiko Mori at Harvard's Graduate School of Design. [Reprinted with permission of Aziza Chaouni/the *New York Times*.]

project, illustrated in Figure 3.15, is an interesting example of the kind of design inspiration that can arise out of extremely unpleasant situations, and if developed on a large scale, could perhaps provide a timely response in many parts of the world where portable emergency shelter is needed.

Box 3.2 relates the development of a project of low-cost housing built from recycled cardboard. Architect Sonny Ward was inspired by the stacks of discarded cardboard boxes he encountered in urban commercial alleyways, and he invented a process by which this cardboard is converted into building material.

Graphic design is another of the design disciplines that presents a multitude of examples of crossover into other areas. For instance, a notable graphic style known as Russian constructivism developed following the Russian Revolution of 1917. During the 1920s artists and designers looked for ways to pay respect to working people by incorporating images of machinery and work into graphic designs for posters, books, and textiles (Yasinskaya, p. 16). These designs were striking in their use of color-blocked patterns and stylized lettering (Figure 3.16). Fashion designer Jean Paul Gaultier's collection of Autumn–Winter 1986–1987 included graphic applications reminiscent of the style of Russian constructivism (Figure 3.17). It is interesting to note that the Berlin Wall speech given by then U.S. President Ronald Reagan was in June of 1987, when the Soviet Union was on the verge of disbanding, so possibly the nod to Russian constructivism was inspired by the focus on Russia and the former Soviet Union in the late 1980s.

BOX 3.2
Sonny Ward: Cardboard Cabins

WEAR YOUR CHAIR: *Describe the completed project.*
SONNY WARD: The cabin is a small 12 feet by 12 feet in Ovett, Mississippi, at Camp Sister Spirit, a nonprofit lesbian and feminist education center. The cabin is made mostly of used cardboard with a construction technique I developed, in which used corrugated board, or cardboard, is stacked and compressed using threaded rods and plywood compression plates. The cardboard is protected from weather by cardboard shingles that have been dipped in latex. The shingles are varying shades of green to blend with the surrounding forest. The flat roof extends out past the thick cardboard walls to protect the structure from the weather.

WYC: *What inspired you to do a project such as this?*
SW: During a break from a fourth-year urban design architecture studio at Woodbury University, in which we were exploring low-cost solutions for housing units, I took a stroll around the building on Hollywood Boulevard. While walking through an alley, I saw mounds of trash behind each of the stores. A common element to almost every mound was discarded cardboard. I had the idea that I would actually propose building units out of discarded cardboard. I spoke to my adviser, Jeanine Centouri. I fully expected Jeanine to say that I should get another idea or that I should explore a more pragmatic approach. Instead, she simply asked why not. She then quickly told me that if I chose to proceed with this project, I would need to be able to show the jury exactly how I planned on building low-cost housing out of cardboard.

I decided that I wanted to explore this building technique as part of my senior project. I also knew that I wanted to move the project outside of the Los Angeles area, preferably for a "client" in my home state of Mississippi, which would both have the need for low-cost housing and appreciate the environmentally friendly aspects of the project. It was while talking with a friend from Mississippi that I realized Camp Sister Spirit would be the perfect client for such a project.

WYC: *Describe translating the concept into reality.*
SW: During the final month of completing my thesis project, my adviser told me about a foundation grant that might be available. The Arcus Foundation, which is

based in Kalamazoo, Michigan, had announced a competition for grants that further critical study of the relationship between sexuality and the built environment. In June 2002, I was awarded a grant for $3,000. In theory, this could have been enough to build a cardboard house. I had been fairly unequivocal at my project review and had speculated in my grant request that a prototype, complete with solar lighting and built-in furniture, could be built for a mere $2,150.63.

After the initial joy of being awarded the grant wore off, I began to realize what a task I had ahead. Organizing the construction of a cardboard cabin in rural Mississippi, more than 2,000 miles away, would be quite an undertaking. Money, time, and distance all seemed to present formidable problems, but I proceeded nevertheless. Many here in Los Angeles actually said they would very much like to go and take part in such a project, and I took a trip to the Summit, a convention of gay and lesbian student organizations from Mississippi universities, to drum up support. I was overwhelmed by the positive response and the pledges people made to help me build the house.

It was challenging to coordinate all of the volunteers. On top of organizing volunteers, I would also need to create a budget, plan for materials to be purchased, and coordinate their delivery. This was enough to worry about without the political realities of building at a socially ostracized community in a relatively hostile environment. Many potential suppliers were simply unwilling to deliver materials or provide services at Camp Sister Spirit. The task ahead felt Herculean, particularly when having to fit it in after I returned home from my job around six or seven every evening.

WYC: *Describe the process of completion of the project, the time frame, stages of development, and changes or alterations to the original concept.*
SW: I decided the house could be built in two

phases over two separate weekends. I was overly optimistic. The first construction weekend, phase one, took place in November 2003. After I flew on a Thursday, purchased material early on a Friday, and arrived at the site to organize volunteers, there wasn't much time left in the day for construction. Work finally began late that evening, and miraculously we had created the form for the concrete slab by midnight. We woke early to add the finishing touches and the concrete truck arrived mid-morning. After cleaning up the construction site, I realized that the next critical step was to educate my volunteers about the tasks ahead.

I thought that I had designed this house to be builder friendly, but many of the volunteers had only rudimentary construction experience. More significantly, I had designed building techniques for many aspects of the house that were entirely new. I later found that articulating the techniques to the volunteers took more time than actually building the house.

The advent of winter weather delayed further building until spring. In the interim, I began the search for cardboard to meet the needs for the building. Fortunately, an owner of a recycling plant in southern Mississippi had heard about my project and contacted me to donate the cardboard. I returned to Ovett in April of 2003, after keeping in touch with my newly recruited group of volunteers. I knew that their continued support was critical. During the second trip, we built the frame for the roof, trimmed the cardboard for wall thickness, and began the laborious process of crafting the individual shingles. I returned in June and, joined by a smaller group of volunteers, dipped the shingles in latex and built the windows and doors. In November of 2003, I was joined by the same group of dedicated volunteers to complete all structural elements, with all interior finishes completed during a final trip in February of 2004. The cabin survived its first hurricane season and continues to be used regularly by people visiting Camp Sister Spirit.

WYC: *What are the most memorable aspects of working on this project?*
SW: By far, the most memorable aspect of this endeavor has been meeting a dedicated and hard working group of volunteers. Without them, this project simply could not have happened for the allotted funds within any reasonable schedule. These volunteers were excited both by the idea of helping the client and by the prospect of working on an experimental construction technique.

3.16

3.18

3.17

In Figure 3.18, the lines between fashion, graphic design, and architecture are blurred. Buildings are anthropomorphized, taking on fluid forms, with silhouettes and design details echoed in clothing and forms of transportation, incorporating all of these disciplines into one witty illustration.

Images of the Future Inspire Design

Although the future is unknown, it has been and is a huge source of inspiration for designers. Throughout history, creative people have looked ahead and invented future realities. From a broad perspective, these imagined futures have presented two alternative visions, the optimistic view and the pessimistic

60

view. Visions of utopia and dystopia have long been seen in literature and film. The films *Frankenstein*, *Metropolis*, *1984*, *2001*, and *The Matrix* present glimpses of the future from differing vantage points. In 1971, the designer Rudi Gernreich, whose plastic armor suit is shown in Figure 3.19, was notoriously focused on the future. He predicted, "Once the sewing machine has been replaced or sophisticated, once a designer can spray on clothes or transmigrate fabrics to the body, new things will happen. The designer will be less artist, more technician" (Moffitt, p. 31).

As the world shrinks through the ease of communication of images and information using electronic media, perhaps one effect is the further assimilation of diverse cultural influences. Only a click away on the Internet is a seemingly limitless supply of details, facts, records, and illustrations. But although the Internet can provide a gateway to vast resources of knowledge, the creative activity of design often relates to direct experience. The textile and graphic designer Anni Albers (1899–1994), in her texture studies, took inspiration from the graphic arrangement of rows of repetitively typed letters on paper, kernels of corn, and twisted paper. She interpreted these with various yarns and weaves, yet the graphic quality of her work remains. Anni Albers was one of the group of artists and designers who were part of the Bauhaus in Germany during the 1920s and brought a new appreciation for the design of utilitarian objects, working across all design disciplines. Almost 40 years ago, in *On Weaving*, she wrote, "Modern industry saves us endless labor and drudgery; but . . . it also bars us from taking part in the forming of material and leaves idle our sense of

3.19

touch and with it those formative faculties that are stimulated by it" (p. 62). For her work she found inspiration in the smallest details and related the design process to acute use of the senses. She spoke of an "attitude of attentive passiveness" (p. 74) and said, when considering the necessity for designers to look ahead, "We must learn to detect, in particular occasions, manifestations of general developments; that is, we must learn to foresee. And to foresee we need a contemplative state of mind" (p. 77).

CHAPTER FOUR

The Vocabulary of Design

Design is everywhere. It is difficult to find any milieu that has not been touched by human ideas of design, and whether it can be judged "good" design or not, there is hardly any argument that everywhere we turn, there is evidence of some form of design. Most of us, even with little or no professional training, have intuitive feelings about what constitutes a successful or pleasing design. But it is in courses related to design education that we begin to discover the intentional or intellectual aspects of the design process. This chapter is devoted to an analysis of the formal elements and principles of the vocabulary of design used by design professionals to articulate the qualities of designs. For designers, it is important to have a common vocabulary to describe, discuss, and evaluate design projects, whether in interiors, fashion, architecture, graphics, or another design discipline.

Starting from our nearest environment—the clothing and accessories that we wear, the appliances and furniture we use in the rooms we inhabit, the buildings that enclose those spaces and the grounds surrounding the buildings—and ranging to the cities and towns in which they are located, at some phase of development, each of these has undergone a process of design. Designers are in the unique position of affecting their surroundings as skilled professionals in the fields of fashion design, graphic design, interior design, industrial design, and architecture, and it is crucial that they have a shared language of design with which to communicate. Over time, there have been disagreements on what is recognized as aesthetically pleasing, depending upon shifts in the popularity of and taste for certain styles. But over the course of design history, whether we are looking at classical architecture, Russian Constructivist poster art, Art Deco interiors, or clothing of the 1960s, analysis of designs from varied media will reveal that certain components are recognized as "good" design. The common features that successful designs share are generally articulated in terms of the "principles and elements of design." These function as the laws that govern the organization of visual expression.

Although it was founded in the early 20th century and flourished only briefly, design studies from the Bauhaus school (see Chapter 2)

have had a remarkable impact on design education and continue to be used as a basis for the analysis of design. Johannes Itten, who was connected with the Bauhaus and went on to found his own art college in Berlin in 1926, developed theories about design and color that are still in use today. One of the fundamental methodologies of his approach to design education was the strengthening of the imagination. His "Representation of Contrasts" shown in Figure 4.1 remains a standard used to illustrate essential ideas about design. In it he visually represented concepts that are basic to the analysis of design but are sometimes difficult to define. This chart is particularly effective in representing the four most basic concepts of design—point, line, plane, and volume— and how they relate. These four concepts make up the foundation of the study of design.

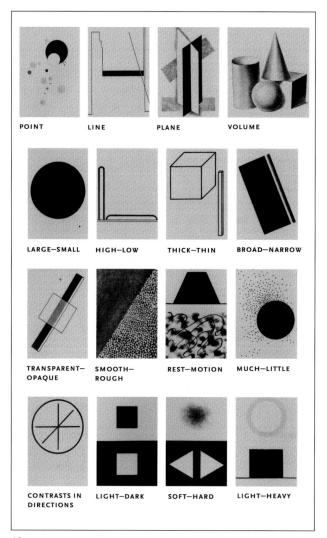

POINT   LINE   PLANE   VOLUME

LARGE–SMALL   HIGH–LOW   THICK–THIN   BROAD–NARROW

TRANSPARENT–OPAQUE   SMOOTH–ROUGH   REST–MOTION   MUCH–LITTLE

CONTRASTS IN DIRECTIONS   LIGHT–DARK   SOFT–HARD   LIGHT–HEAVY

4.1

Elements and Principles of Design

Numerous writers, theorists, and teachers have explored the nature of the elements and the principles of design and how they are to be differentiated. The elements of design refer to properties that are visible and inherent in aspects of the design; the principles of design describe how these formal elements relate to one another. This distinction between the elements and the principles will be further clarified in the discussion that follows.

Elements of Design

Generally speaking, the elements of design can be arranged into the four categories of point, line, plane, and volume, represented visually in Figure 4.1. In addition to these conceptual elements, design educator Wucius Wong has identified the relational elements—position, direction, space, and gravity—and the practical elements—representation, meaning, and function—and finally the visual elements. His illustration of the concepts of point, line, plane, and volume shown in Figure 4.2 is a classic visual communication of abstract ideas, as he demonstrates the steps in the process of a point becoming line, plane, and finally taking on volume (Wong, pp. 42–44).

For our purposes, in order to achieve a working vocabulary of design, we will concentrate on the visual elements of design, which are identified as line, shape, form, space, color, and texture. The elements of design refer to the overall visible structure of a design and the parts it is composed of. Briefly defined, these elements provide a structure for

understanding the process of design. Starting with a point, which denotes a position in space, a point extended in any direction turns into a line, and a line expanded to form the outline of a shape becomes a plane. Shape is the outline of a design and the main classification of its silhouette, for example, circle, square, or triangle. Form describes an object, whether a familiar form such as a cube, cylinder, or sphere, or something more irregular, and includes qualities like size and surface appearance. Form can be two-dimensional or three-dimensional. Space is a description of the area around a plane or a form. A form can also be referred to as a figure, so in design vocabulary, description of the connection between

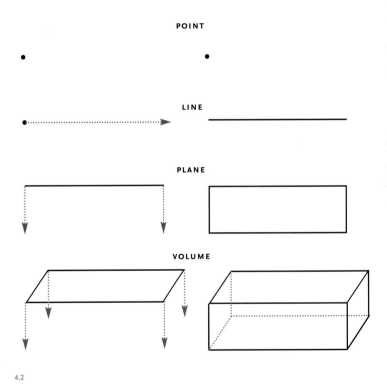

4.2

FIG. 4.1 Examples of Itten's "Representation of Contrasts." [Based on *Design and Form* by Johannes Itten, New York: Reinhold Publishing Corp., 1964, pp. 10–11.] FIG. 4.2 Wong's demonstration of the progression from point to line to plane to volume. [Based on *Principles of Form and Design* by Wucius Wong, New York: John Wiley & Sons, Inc., 1993, p. 42.]

the figure and the space around it can be called the figure-ground relationship, and this is the relationship that enables us to perceive pattern in design. Optical illusions are based on the confusion of figure and ground, and the eye's inability to distinguish which is which. Figure 4.3 shows a common optical illusion, that of a vase, or two profiles in silhouette facing each other.

The design element color, which will be considered in more detail later in this chapter, is further described by its properties: hue, value, and intensity or chroma. There are six hue families, yellow, orange, red, violet, blue, and green. Technically, objects appear to be different colors depending on the quality of the light reflected from their surfaces. Value refers to the lightness or darkness of color, including black and white. The relative values of light and shade between figure and ground allow us to perceive dimension. Intensity or chroma (also referred to as saturation) indicates the purity of a color, its relative vividness or dullness. Texture

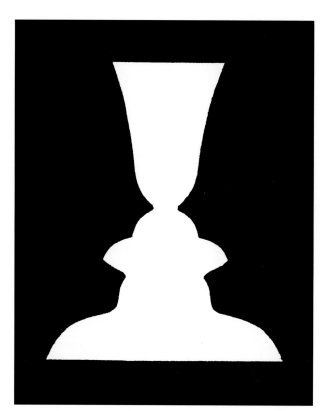

4.3

refers to the surface characteristics of the material used in the design, and can be both visual and tactile. Normally we think of texture as an uneven surface, but in terms of design, even the smooth, luminous surface of a car can be described as texture.

The elements of design, taken together, refer to characteristics that can be identified within a design, and the language of design allows us to isolate each of them, analyze it, and evaluate its contribution to the design as a whole. In order for a design to succeed, whether it is for a lamp, a road sign, a sweater, or a patio, all of the elements must work in harmony. If they do—and equally if they don't—it is important to go beyond statements such as "That looks nice," or "That's ugly," and to be able to discover, understand, and explain why, using language that a designer will understand. Skill in this ability to look at a design idea and articulate options for improvement in the combination of factors that make up the whole is one mark of a seasoned designer.

Principles of Design

Each of us already possesses an instinct about design. We know what "looks good," and we know what we like. In the observation of nature, we can see certain principles at work, such as the way branches spread out to balance each other all around a tree, and we take that for granted, as a kind of natural order. In natural disasters that order is upset, so in the aftermath of earthquakes, hurricanes, or floods, we have a sense of disorientation seeing branches broken, tree roots exposed, or a forest of trees flattened. There is a similar sense of order in design, expressed in the principles of design, and as we gain knowledge and experience in design, we can sense when something is off-kilter, in the same way that we perceive something out of order when we see an uprooted tree.

4.4

The basic principles of design, which are used to describe how the elements of design relate to each other, are harmony, balance, rhythm, repetition, contrast, transformation, proportion, and scale. Whenever we look critically at a design, we are taking into account the principles of design that help us to determine whether the design is a cohesive statement. Whether we are looking at a design for product packaging, drapery fabric, or stiletto heels, these principles of design are in evidence. Normally all of the principles are evident in a design, although one or two may appear to be predominant. For example, in Figure 4.4, balance is most in evidence since the structure of the design includes symmetrical forms evenly spaced, yet analysis will confirm that the other design principles are also at work.

Harmony refers to the manner in which the parts of a design function as a whole. Sometimes the term unity is used to describe this quality of wholeness in a design. Balance refers to the manner in which, probably because of the force of gravity, the human eye looks for stability. Balance includes symmetry, which is a mirror image, and asymmetry, in which different parts of the design equalize each other without being identical. Rhythm refers to the visual movement that leads the eye through a design. Rhythm can be created by the direction of motion through a design, in the same way that the eye can follow the motion of waves radiating out from a pebble tossed into still water. Repetition is the reiteration of certain components of the design, such as lines, shapes, or forms. Both rhythm and repetition

FIG. 4.3 Ambiguous figure-ground relationships are sometimes the source of optical illusions. [Based on *Creative Color* by Faber Birren, Atglen, PA: Schiffer Publishing Ltd., 1987, p. 61.] FIG. 4.4 Design principles applied to landscape architecture in a formal garden. [Copyright © Michael Boys/Corbis.]

are important to the perception of the organizational structure of a design. Figure 4.5, a simple treatment of a leaf form, shows the development of a border pattern illustrating the design principles of rhythm and repetition. In it, the eye travels along a path suggested by the placement, shape, and direction of the leaves.

4.5

Another of the principles of design, contrast, can occur in many different ways: the contrast of textures, shapes, sizes, colors, or any aspects that can be placed in juxtaposition. It is created when a design consists of opposing factors, such as thick versus thin, transparent versus opaque, and soft versus hard, to name a few. These are most effectively demonstrated visually referring back to Figure 4.1, as that chart categorizes many types of contrast, giving an illustration of each. Transformation refers to the manipulation of elements and how they are changed or altered to produce a whole design. Transformation can be achieved, for example, by a gradual alteration of angles that results in a change in the perception of advancing and receding elements. In Figure 4.6 a gradual variation of the shapes of triangles results in the perception that the center of the triangle has a point, and the shape transforms from a triangle to a pyramid.

4.6

68

Proportion denotes the visual relationship of parts of the design in terms of size, and whether those size relationships fit with the overall concept of the design. The idea of proportion is easily understood if we compare Figure 4.7a, a fashion illustration, with Figure 4.7b, a figure drawing. An adult human's height is normally seven times the length of the head. But figures used in fashion drawing are often shown at a height of "ten heads." The fashion figure, like a Barbie doll, is out of proportion when compared with a person. But because this lengthened proportion fits within the somewhat eccentric world of fashion, the proportion works.

Scale refers to the perception of the different sizes of parts of the design in relation to each other. The scale of a section of the design in relation to the whole can determine whether it is perceived as a single shape, a repeating pattern, or an overall texture. For example, the use of a bear first as a central

4.7a+b

image, then as a recurring image in Figure 4.8 illustrates the ways in which scale can be used. The scale of the pattern determines whether the design is seen as a single motif or as an overall repeating pattern. All of these principles are considered in analyzing what is happening in a design and how successful the design is.

Like the elements of design, the principles of design must work in harmony to create the whole. While the elements are qualities that exist within the design, the principles illustrate the relationships that those features have with each other. In analyzing any design, we must be able to recognize how these principles function, and to use the vocabulary of design to communicate our ideas about changes or alterations that might contribute to an improved design.

4.8

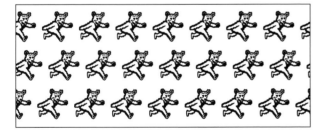

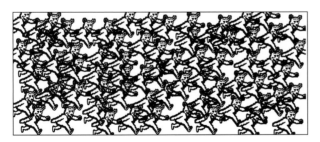

Color

If you have recently attempted to purchase a roll of film for black and white photography or have searched the telephone directory for a lab to have black and white film professionally developed on equipment other than that intended for color use, you know that color photography has become the standard, with the possible exception of art photography. Color print film, now widely available and able to be developed in 30 minutes, will eventually become outmoded as digital cameras become smaller, more convenient to use, and less expensive. It is probably safe to say that advances in technology have had an impact on the availability of color media of all types. Computer and printer technology are making reasonably priced color reproduction available to all. Daily newspapers, once typeset by hand with moveable letters and printed in black ink, now feature color news photos and advertisements. But has the wide availability of color media made color experts of us all? To the contrary, this trend has opened new opportunities for design professionals who understand the theory, philosophy, and psychology of color and can apply these principles to contemporary design projects.

Color Theory

Color, as we have seen, is considered to be one of the elements of design, but because of its complexity, it is often treated as a separate topic. In many design programs, an entire foundation class is devoted just to the study of color, with others to follow exploring uses of color in specific fine art or design disciplines. Obviously, color has long been a topic of study for philosophers, artists, designers, and scientists, who

FIG. 4.5 A repeated design motif produces a rhythm. [Based on *Text Books of Art Education* by Hugo B. Froehlich and Bonnie E. Snow, New York: The Prang Educational Company, 1905, p. 74.] FIG. 4.6 The transformation of a triangle into a pyramid. [Based on *Principles of Form and Design* by Wucius Wong, New York: John Wiley & Sons, Inc., 1993, p. 42.] FIG. 4.7 (a) Stylized fashion illustration showing elongation of a figure. (b) Illustration showing more realistic human proportions. [Illustrations courtesy of Jemi Armstrong.] FIG. 4.8 Scale is demonstrated in the use of the bear as image, pattern, and texture.

have sought to articulate the essence of the human experience of color. Many different approaches to the study of color have yielded as many different lists of colors considered the "basic" colors.

There are two main types of color that we perceive. One is light color, also called additive color, and the other is pigment color, or subtractive color. The primary colors of light are red, blue, and green. While the mixing of light color is important for understanding the appearance of color on a video screen, computer monitor, or television screen and for understanding theatrical lighting and lighting effects in interiors, our focus here is on pigment, or subtractive, color. Pigment color is the type of color we see on objects, whether organic or static. Pigment color is used in dyes, pigments, and inks for photography,

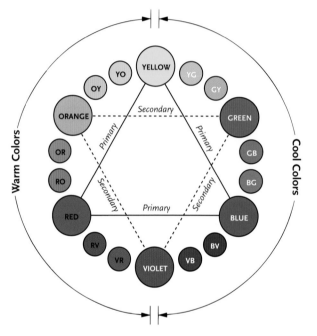

4.9

printing, and painting. The color on fabric, tile, and painted surfaces is pigment color, and so is the color we see on the leaves of a tree, pictures in a book, or a painting in a museum.

During the early 20th century, Albert Munsell, an American painter, identified red, green, blue, yellow, and violet as "main" colors, and categorized them in terms of intensity. In the middle of the century, the

European art educator Johannes Itten developed the "color circle" based on three major colors: red, yellow, and blue (Jerstorp, p. 144). The primary colors red, yellow, and blue are now the basis of most studies of subtractive color. Figure 4.9 shows the color wheel based on the pigment colors red, yellow, and blue, expanded to show the gradations of hue that occur between these colors as they are mixed.

An analysis of the progression of the color wheel shows the three primary hues of pigment color, red, yellow, and blue. The secondary hues, which are made by combinations of the primaries, are orange (between red and yellow), green (between yellow and blue), and violet (between blue and red). The tertiary hues are created alternately between the primaries and secondaries. The tertiary hues are yellow-orange, red-orange, red-violet, blue-violet, blue-green, and yellow-green. These twelve colors form a spectrum, an arrangement of hues placed in a continuum. The wheel is further divided into categories based on their sense impression: warm colors, from yellow through red-violet, and cool colors, from violet through chartreuse. A term used to describe the relative lightness or darkness of color

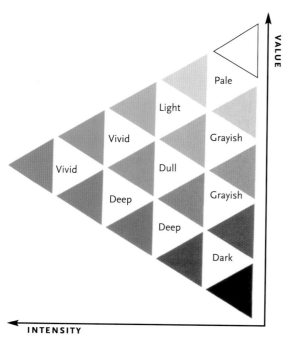

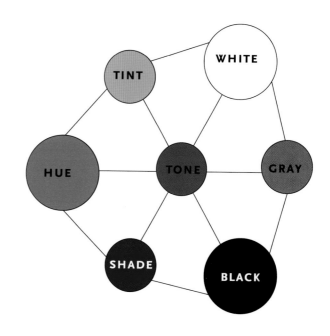

4.10a+b

is *value*, and the descriptive terms used to refer to the brightness of a color are *intensity, saturation,* and *chroma.*

Another geometric device utilized in the study of color is the triangle. At the points of the triangle are white, black, and a hue. Between white and the hue, there is tint; between black and the hue, there is shade; between white and black, there is gray, which is formed by the mixture of white and black. And in the center, there is tone, which is formed by the mixture of the hue and gray. These relationships are represented visually in Figure 4.10a, the color triangle, which locates these terms on a diagram. This concept is further analyzed by Faber Birren in Figure 4.10b, which expands on this model using the color red.

Color Is Relative

Because the selection of color and the process of specifying combinations of colors in various environments are so much a part of the world of design, it is important for designers to understand color according to its position in relation to other colors on the spectrum and to be able to detect tints, shades, and tones of color. Because the perception of color involves the transmission of impulses from the eye to the brain, the position of one color in relation

FIG. 4.9 The color wheel. [Courtesy, Fairchild Publications, Inc.] FIG. 4.10 The color triangle as conceptualized by (a) Ogawa, Yamamoto, and Kondo and (b) Birren. [(a) Based on *Color in Fashion* by Yoko Ogawa, Junko Yamamoto, and Ei Kondo, Rockport, MA: Rockport Publishers, 1990, p. 17. (b) Based on *Creative Color* by Faber Birren, Atglen, PA: Schiffer Publishing Ltd., 1987, p. 12.]

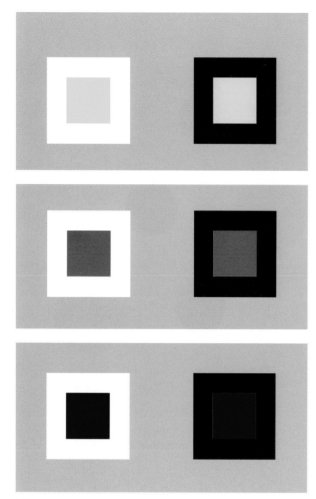

4.11

colors, when placed next to each other, appear to be more concentrated than when viewed separately. This occurs because each color in a complementary pair does not contain any of the hue of the other; in other words, these colors are as far from each other as possible, which is visually evident when viewing the color wheel. When placed next to each other, a color that contains some of the hue of the other will be perceived as closer to that color. For example, in Figure 4.12, against a turquoise background, magenta looks bright and pink; against an orange background, it looks less bright and blends with the background color.

The effect of one color in proximity to another must be understood in order for a designer to create a color palette, or a color scheme for a project. Color palettes refer to the group of colors used in a design. This concept can be illustrated by studying color combinations used in any design medium such as

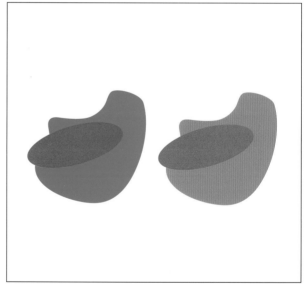

4.12

to another can cause changes in the way the colors are perceived. Figure 4.11 illustrates how the perception of colors can change when placed against different color backgrounds, and also how even the perception of the relative size of a figure can change depending on the color of the ground.

Another important aspect of the perception of color is that the intensity of colors that are directly across from each other on the color wheel is heightened. These hues, referred to as complementary

paintings, textiles, wallpaper, or interiors. Harmony, when used in relation to color, indicates that certain colors go well together. There are many types of color harmonies. Colors adjacent to each other on the color wheel are known as analogous colors, and generally speaking, analogous colors are harmonious, and form the basis of well-balanced color palettes. Looking at the color wheel, it is easy to identify analogous or adjacent colors; for example, orange, red-orange, and yellow-orange are adjacent colors. Analogous combinations of colors are often found in nature: for example, flowers in which the color of a single petal may range from magenta through red to red-orange, and fields of pasture in which the greens range from yellow-green through blue-green. We tend to think of grass as being green and sky as blue, but these natural surroundings actually contain a variety of analogous color palettes.

Another basis for the development of a color palette or a color scheme is the use of colors that are opposite each other on the color wheel, which, as we have seen, are known as complementary colors. Perhaps the most commonly used example of a complementary color combination is red and green, which demonstrates the brightening effect that complementary colors have on each other. Perhaps the reason that red and green are designated signals for "stop" and "go" is that the brightening effect calls attention to these colors on a traffic light.

But complementary color schemes are not limited to primary colors and their secondary complements. Any two colors directly opposite each other on the color wheel are complementary, and have a brightening effect. The mixing of two complementary colors results in a drab tone that is referred to as neutral, or achromatic. The explanation for this is that two complementary colors actually contain all three of the primary colors, so in effect the colors cancel, or neutralize, each other. Neutral, or achromatic, colors are the basis of another type of color palette.

The color scheme based on split-complementary colors is one in which colors adjacent to a color's complement are used together. The colors used in a split-complementary palette have no colors in common. For example, because the complement of blue is orange, the split-complements of blue are red-orange and yellow-orange. Color schemes can also be based on triadic relationship, in which colors at the points of an equilateral triangle placed on the color wheel are used together. Another type of color combination is the monochromatic palette, which is based on using different tints, shades, or tones of one hue.

Cultural and Psychological Aspects of Design and Color

Now that we have established a fundamental vocabulary of design and color, we can look at some of their cultural and psychological aspects. Over time, certain design motifs have become associated with regions or cultures. Many of these have to do with plants and animals indigenous to a geographical area or with mythology and religious symbols and icons. Mass communications, media, and international trade have made once regionally specific symbols familiar around the world, but designs based on these forms are still recognizable and meaningful. For example, Figure 4.13a shows familiar motifs in

FIG. 4.11 Different perceptions of color with background changes. [Based on "Color Agent and Color Effect" in *Design and Form: The Basic Course at the Bauhaus* by Johannes Itten, New York: Reinhold Publishing Corp., 1964, p. 87.] FIG. 4.12 The perceived hue or contrast depends on the adjacent color. [Based on *The Textile Design Book: Understanding and Creating Patterns Using Texture, Shape, and Color*, by Karin Jerstorp and Eva Köhlmark, Asheville, NC: Lark Books, 1986, p. 131.]

Chinese design, which include symmetrical floral patterns superimposed on a geometric border, in bright contrasting colors. Designs from India often represent stylized flowers in repeating patterns, in paisley or ogee shapes, in which the ground color is strong and relatively dark, as shown in Figure 4.13b. Figure 4.13c shows traditional design from Arab cultures featuring interlocking and repeating geometric shapes, often interconnected and transforming

from triangles to stars to hexagons. The earth tones in these designs suggest that they were for tile work.

Around the world and over time, colors have taken on different symbolic meanings, and for each of us, colors can also have personal connotations. In our work with color and design, it is important to be aware of these cultural and personal differences and be sensitive to them. However, there are some associations that seem to be

4.13a

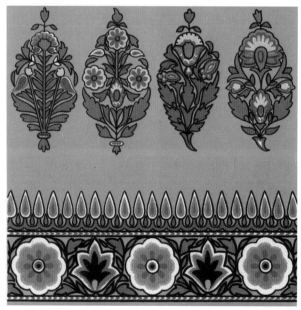

4.13b

4.13c

74

fairly universal. Red, orange, and strong yellow are generally associated with fire and energy, and gold with wealth and luxury. Blue relates to the sky and water, and to restfulness; and green is connected with forest and plant life and with hope and renewal. Violet and purple, because dyes to make these colors were so expensive that they were only available to monarchs, are usually associated with royalty, but these colors can also suggest mystery, and in some cultures, mourning. The browns and umbers that are referred to as "earth colors" invoke images of home, hearth, and security. In addition to these associations, colors can have specific meanings when used in flags and banners. For example, in the design of the American flag, red was chosen to represent courage, white to symbolize purity, and blue to signify loyalty (Fehrman, pp. 45–52).

The cultural and psychological aspects of color are taken into account when color selection decisions are made. Box 4.1, an interview with Margaret Walch, the president of the Color Association of the United States, describes some of the ideas that are considered when large-scale color trends are analyzed.

Application of the Vocabulary of Design

Now that we have constructed a foundation, we can build. In the pages that follow, we will look at several different types of design projects and demonstrate how knowledge of design and color fundamentals can serve the designer. The images in this section illustrate the elements and principles of design drawn from the different design disciplines—

BOX 4.1

A Conversation with Margaret Walch

WEAR YOUR CHAIR: *From your books on color to your involvement with the Color Association of the United States, it is apparent that much of your career has been devoted to working with color. How did you become interested in the study of color?*

MARGARET WALCH: As a college student at Swarthmore College, I majored in art history. Then, married to an art historian at Yale University, which has an excellent color library, as a young mother, I was looking for a career that would enable me to be independent. The color expert Faber Birren was at Yale at that time, and I was able to work with him, and this led to my writing *Color Source Book*, which was later expanded into *Living Colors: The Definitive Guide to Color Palettes through the Ages.*

WYC: *In that book, you analyze color palettes from the ancient Greeks to the 1980s. If you were to add palettes for the 1990s and early 2000s, what combinations of colors would be featured?*

MW: The two great sources of inspiration for color in design are art and nature. Living in a big city and as an urban person by nature, art is the most important source for me. Right now I am very interested in color palettes that come from food. In a way, these are the urban person's nature palette. An update of *Living Colors: The Definitive Guide to Color Palettes through the Ages* would include a high-tech palette with colored light, a technical-architectural palette, and an art palette around the colors of contemporary painter Paul Henry Ramirez (paulhenryramirez.com).

WYC: *Our book is geared toward a multidisciplinary audience. Do you have insights to share about the similarities and differences in the use of color in, for example, fashion versus interior design?*

MW: There is definitely a blurring of boundaries and extensive borrowing now, but one influence in the use of color is economic. It is more costly to produce automobile and interior colors, so these are somewhat more conservative because of the expense. Fashion apparel color can be produced relatively inexpensively so can be more

FIG. 4.13 Traditional (a) Chinese, (b) Indian, and (c) Arabian design motifs. [From *The Grammar of Ornament* by Owen Jones, New York: Dover Publications, Inc., 1987, (a) Plate LXI, (b) Plate LII, and (c) Plate XXXV.]

daring and change more frequently.

WYC : *What are some of the factors that influence the popularity of certain colors at certain times? Is there a cycle for the re-emergence of color palettes?*

MW: Color is definitely cyclical, and right now there is a return to the psychological comfort of the mid-20th century, the 1950s, 1960s, 1970s. Also, we are in a politically active, vocal time, and we are seeing more color, with a return to the bright colors of the political activism of the 1960s, and a return to the earth tones of the 1970s.

WYC : *You have been involved in CAUS [Color Association of the United States] for quite some time. Can you give us some insight into the association and the benefits of membership?*

MW: The Color Association is an active color organization of roughly a thousand people. The Association's forecasting process operates on two principles: color cycles and consensus. Both of these seem especially necessary for the working colorist, who needs to meet tastes of many individuals. Because color is so abstract and so intuitive, it is useful, I think, for those working in color design to be a part of a larger group. Interior color cycles normally last about 10 years and recur about every 30 years, and fashion cycles have a shorter duration. The second principle, consensus, refers to the interest and involvement of professionals. My role is to be a reporter. There is a point of saturation that is reached, and then newness is needed. For example, the current interest in crafts reflects the saturation with technology and longing to use our hands and touch something real. The comfort level of color is regional. For example, California is more open to change and to color intensity; New York is more conservative, less open to change. But because the colors are selected for the entire United States, one needs to tweak them for the various regions within our country. This involves the application of a forecast, and a good designer needs to be adept at this.

WYC : *What advice would you give to those just entering the design professions?*

MW: Figure out where you are comfortable. Are you comfortable in a big city? Do you enjoy travel? To really predict color, you have to be out there doing it, making a color line. Color forecasting is a very commercial & practical endeavor, yet choosing colors for a future time is an intuitive & abstract one. As a colorist, one needs to operate in these two very different ways.

fashion design and illustration, textile design, interior and landscape design, and architecture. We will analyze an advertising vignette, a patio design, a sarong fabric, a design for a library, a fashion illustration, and a design for a swimming pool, each from the perspective of its use of the elements and principles of design.

An Advertising Vignette

The focal point of the image shown in Figure 4.14, a ball gown from 1958, is an excellent example of an evening dress of that era. From a design perspective it shows clearly the elements of form and texture. The large and extremely full skirt, enhanced by the panniers and a train, accentuates the narrow fitted

4.14

with its subtle lighting, gauzy drapes, and velvety carpet accentuates the perception of softness. From a design perspective, the elegance of the gown lends elegance to the mundane image of the product it is promoting.

A Patio Design

Color is the first element that is apparent in the patio and garden in Figure 4.15. The analogous hues of blues and greens blend with the shady foliage of the garden to create a very tranquil setting. The few touches of bright color are emphasized by their contrast with the overall cool color palette. The neutral colors of the structural support and the concrete

bodice and sleeves by contrasting the slim top with the full, floor-length skirt. The light pink floral and ribbon trim that cascades down the back complements the mint green of the dress fabric, and the fabric's smooth texture enhances the elegance of the gown. The exaggerated detail of the dress, although not out of character for its time, is humorous from the vantage point of the early 21st century in that this photograph was used by the Scott Paper Company to advertise its new shade of mint green toilet tissue. The design details of the dress are replicated on the dressing table, which features a skirt and draped swag, and the setting for the photograph

4.15

FIG. 4.14 A pastel gown by Sarmi added an elegant touch to a 1958 advertisement for bathroom tissue. [Reprinted with permission of Horst P. Horst/Art and Commerce.] FIG. 4.15 Interior and exterior merge in this tranquil outdoor living room. [Photo by Marion Brenner © 2003.]

steps and stone paving further enhance this peaceful quality. The proportion of the natural to the constructed setting is emphasized as the delicate frames of the lattice that supports a climbing vine do not obstruct the view. The scale of the low furniture opens the view to the trees and shrubbery beyond, and the horizontal rhythm of the platform tables and sofa leads the eye out toward the garden. There is contrast between the smooth, solid shapes in the interior and the texture of the leaves and shadows outside. This "outdoor living room" is a relaxing and inviting space.

A Sarong Fabric

Design and color details abound in the sarong textile pictured in Figure 4.16. The design of the sarong, the Indonesian batik skirt, has a long and intriguing history. The process of creating batik involves waxing parts of the design and applying dye, which is resisted by the wax, and then repeating until the desired effect is achieved. According to tradition, the patterns and their placement have specific meanings. The borders serve to protect the wearer from the intrusion of anything harmful. The flowers, animals, birds, and insects can represent a garden, which is seen as a refuge from everyday concerns. The patterns are abstract and possibly symbolic, and yet they are recognizable.

The detail of the textile pictured in Figure 4.16 demonstrates an exceptional use of design elements, from the line of the flower stems through the figure-ground relationships produced by the forms in space, distinguished by the use of color and emphasized as the patterns create texture. As only a few

colors are used in batik, color gradations are created by the use of texture. Principles of design are equally apparent in this example. The animal and floral motifs balance one another and create a rhythm of movement through the piece. The undulating vine or snake motif near the lower edge and the repetition of small flowers creates a frame and background for the design. There is color contrast in the dark blues and reds against the yellow ground, and also between the lightness and heaviness of parts of the design. Transformation occurs as abstract shapes are combined to form the floral motifs. Looking at the large size of the floral patterns in relation to the animals, which appear small, the principle of proportion is apparent, and the effect is to emphasize the flowers. Scale is seen in the use of different sizes of animals in different parts of the design. For example, in the border area, below the wavy blue line, the animals and flowers are in a smaller scale than the ones in the main part of the design. This smaller scale is very effective in creating a border at the edge of the fabric. Design of textiles is further explored in Chapters 5 and 7.

4.16

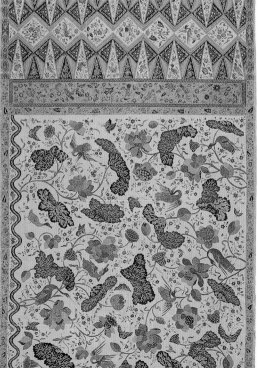

78

A Design for a Library

Looking first at the color palette in Figure 4.17, a library, we see warm hues of the earth colors. These tones of rust, brown, and taupe, used in an analogous color scheme, create a sense of contentment, security, and well-being. The feeling of stability is further emphasized in the design of the room's features. The vignette shows a very balanced plan, with the hearth as a central feature, and chairs and bookshelves symmetrically placed. The symmetry is echoed even in the placement of the painting above the fireplace and objects on the mantle below it, and the matching horses on the bookshelves. The chairs, with their comfortable, oversized scale, add to the cozy atmosphere with plush upholstery in an inviting shade of deep blue. The scale of the floor-to-ceiling bookshelves compared with the relatively low furnishings and the detail of the floor and rug calls attention to the books and emphasizes the use of the room: This is indeed a library.

4.17

A Fashion Illustration

The drawing in Figure 4.18, "Unpleasant Occurrences," shows a fashionable woman in an oversize hat, obviously from a past era. This illustration is a study in the use of proportion to emphasize a point. The woman is approached by her dresser, who is attempting to tie an apron around her waist, but his access is completely blocked by the extreme width of the brim of her hat! This satirical cartoon is from early 19th century Europe, a time remembered for fashion excess. The brim of the hat is so out of proportion that we hardly notice the very large puffed sleeves.

4.18

FIG. 4.16 The surface design on this 19th century woman's hip wrapper from Indonesia is a hand-drawn batik (wax-resistant). [Photo © 2005 Museum Associates/Los Angeles County Museum of Art, Inger McCabe Elliott Collection.] FIG. 4.17 Color and design principles help to create an atmosphere of contentment, security, and well-being in this plush library. [Copyright © Remi Benali/Corbis.] FIG. 4.18 "Unpleasant Occurrences" (c. 1825). [Copyright © Gianni Dagli Orti/Corbis.]

A Swimming Pool

Overlooking the Pacific Ocean on the central coast of California, San Simeon, the Hearst Castle, is the location of the estate of William Randolph Hearst, who made his fortune in publishing and media. The design of the estate, by architect Julia Morgan, was begun in 1919, and the construction was not entirely completed until 1948. The Roman Pool at the Hearst Castle is an indoor swimming pool lined with mosaic tile made from handmade Venetian glass and 22-carat gold. The tile covers every surface, including the walls and ceiling. From a design perspective, this creates a startling effect, shown in Figure 4.19a. The blue and gold tile not only reflects from the surface of the water but is also seen below the water. The balance and symmetry of the ceiling and wall details create a new symmetry when seen in reflection. The perception of scale in the beams and columns is intensified in comparison to the size of the sculptures and lamps. Observing the features of surface patterns, for example the borders around

4.19c

4.19a

4.19b

ladder, shown in Figure 4.19b, includes spiral and shell-like carvings. In Figure 4.19c, the motifs of the mosaic patterns include mermaids, fish, dolphins, and Neptune, the mythological Roman god of the sea, swimming along with his scepter.

Using the Language of Design

As is the case with any language, our design vocabulary increases with use. The concepts presented here are similar to the rules of grammar, which seem cumbersome at first, but become second-nature as the language becomes more familiar. The terminology used to describe the elements and principles of design may seem awkward, and some terms may be easier to grasp than others. But with practice, it will become routine to look with a critical eye and analyze the designed environments that surround us and to consider alternative solutions. As we have seen in this chapter, successful design solutions are as varied as they are numerous. Ultimately, the key to a successful design is in the harmonization of the design with its intended use.

the arched windows, the principles of rhythm and repetition are apparent as the eye is drawn through the space. In closer views, the details of the pool further develop the nautical theme. The marble pool

FIG. 4.19 Julia Morgan's design for (a) the Roman Pool at Hearst Castle, San Simeon, (b) the marble pool ladder, and (c) the mosaic in the Roman Pool. [Copyright © Hearst Castle®/CA State Parks.]

CHAPTER FIVE

More Than Meets the Eye

Surface Design, Pattern, and Motifs

Surface design, pattern, and motifs take on many forms and over thousands of years have been inspired by innumerable sources of visual material. Designers work with surface embellishment and pattern every day. But did you ever stop to wonder where these patterns and motifs come from? Architects and designers working in fashion, interiors, and textiles draw inspiration from many sources, both conventional and unconventional. In this chapter we'll focus on what's behind all those patterns and motifs. This chapter does not take a traditional approach to surface design, hence the title "More Than Meets the Eye." Rather, it discusses the evolution of fashion and interior design from numerous perspectives, including how the development of technology has affected design, how designers physically see things, how designers' attitudes are shaped by what they see, how their vision of our world has changed, and finally, how designers have produced patterns and motifs reflective of more than merely superficial influences. We will look at historical writings and textiles, nature, traditional native designs, city maps, and the technology that assists us in our quest for new and uncharted inspirational sources.

Ancient Sources

The cave paintings at Lascaux in southwestern France, painted more than 22,000 years ago, were among the first images created by humans (Figure 5.1). "These cave paintings were used to convey simple messages using drawings, signs, or pictures," since a formal system of signs and symbols did not yet exist (Jean, p. 11). These signs or pictures were not actually writings, which would not be developed for another 17 millennia, but they were still a form of communication used to express the creator's thoughts and feelings (p. 11).

Early Forms of Writing

Some of the earliest examples of writing have been found in Uruk, an ancient Mesopotamian settlement in what is now Iraq. One example, dating from the end of the fourth millennium B.C.E., is a tablet inscribed with a special vocabulary arranged in columns. It appears to be an accounting record of sacks of grain and heads of cattle (Jean, p. 13). Other ancient forms of writing consisted of pictograms, a picture or drawing that represents words or objects (Figure 5.2), which when combined began to express ideas, record social histories, and communicate information about agricultural and commercial development.

5.2

5.1

84

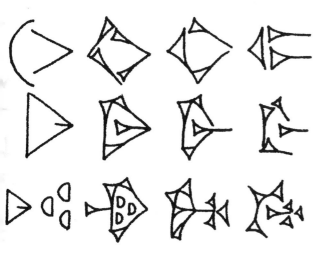

signs: pictograms, phonograms—forms used to represent sounds as in a phonetic alphabet—and, finally, determinatives—signs used to indicate which category or group the object or being belongs to (Jean).

Cuneiform and hieroglyphics had a common thread, and that was the need to understand and master a very large number of signs and characters in order to read and write. The invention of the alphabet by the Phoenicians in 1200 B.C.E. made it possible to read and write using only about 30 signs. The Phoenician merchants and sailors traveled throughout the Mediterranean and their alphabet traveled with them.

Several books of the Old Testament were written in Aramaic, another alphabet developed in Syria in about 800 B.C.E. Hebrew, dating back to 1000 B.C.E., was also used in the Old Testament. When the biblical texts of the Dead Sea Scrolls were found in 1949, it was discovered that they were written in Hebrew and in Aramaic.

The Greeks spoke and transcribed a totally different language but borrowed some signs from the Aramaic alphabet to transcribe their vowel sounds. The Greek alphabet, consisting of 24 signs or letters, was being used in the fifth century B.C.E. The Greeks wrote on tablets made of slate covered with a layer of wax. Using a narrow stick, scholars could erase their letters by rubbing over the soft waxy surface. Greek was also the source of the Latin alphabet, which was the basis of the alphabet we use today.

Utilizing the new technology of the time, reeds were formed into a triangular wedge or stylus that was used to create the inscriptions on clay tablets. The name of this writing, cuneiform, comes from the Latin *cuneus*, meaning "wedge," from which evolved the ability to record an alternative method for communication.

During the same time period, other writing styles were being developed in Egypt and China. In Egypt, the writing was more stylized, depicting human heads, birds, animals, plants, and flowers. These Egyptian characters, or hieroglyphics, "writing of the gods" (from the Greek *hieros*, meaning "holy," and *gluphein*, "to engrave"), were a more evolved form of writing, capable of expressing everything the Egyptians wanted to record (Figure 5.3). These inscriptions, dating back to the third millennium B.C.E., underwent no major changes until 390 C.E., when approximately five thousand signs were in use. This more developed form of communication consisted of three categories of

5.3

FIG. 5.1 Cave paintings at Lascaux in Dordogne, France. [Copyright © Paleolithic/Bridgeman Art Library/Getty Images.] FIG. 5.2 Early pictograms. [Based on *Writing: The Story of Alphabets and Scripts* by Georges Jean, New York: Harry N. Abrams, 1992, p. 13.] FIG. 5.3 Egyptian hieroglyphics. [Copyright © Jochem D. Wijnands/Taxi/Getty Images.]

Illuminated Manuscripts

In the Middle Ages a form of sacred writing became established in the monasteries. For more than a thousand years, only monks were trained as copyists and taught calligraphy. This calligraphic art form created by monks consisted of a beautifully drawn alphabet with elaborate ornamentation and illustration. These illuminated manuscripts (Figure 5.4), which took years to complete, were to become the first books (Jean).

Early Printing

The Chinese were an extremely advanced society when it came to writing, printing, and paper. It is believed that they invented paper in the second century C.E., but it was kept a well-guarded secret until the eighth century C.E. and not brought to Europe until the 13th century. The Chinese had also been using movable characters since the 11th century C.E. The German printer Johannes Gutenberg was the first to mechanize printing, in about 1440, and with that he revolutionized book production and communication. However, the screw press was also used for centuries before Gutenberg's time for pressing grapes and impressing patterns on textiles.

Writing as Design in Logos

Methods of communication using pictures, hieroglyphics, and ancient alphabets, once created out of necessity, have emerged in modern history as a design phenomenon. We use calligraphic computer fonts for stationery, invitations, and announcements (Figure 5.5); illuminated illustrations are used as ornamentation. While design schools have traditionally offered calligraphy and typography in their curriculum, those courses have evolved into highly advanced and complex computer-driven multimedia programs.

Top fashion design houses have incorporated lettering into their distinctive logos for many years. These much-sought-after logos are printed on belt buckles, scarves, T-shirts, shoes, bed and bath linens, and handbags. The logos often become the largest and most visually prominent element of the article's design.

The Louis Vuitton logo, designed by Takashi Murakami, is an excellent example of this trend. Rap star Eve was pho-

5.4

WEAR

Wear Yo

We

Wear Y

We

5.5

86

tographed carrying the bag with the brightly printed logo across the white canvas background, and soon after, everyone wanted the Murakami bag (Figure 5.6). The Louis Vuitton manufacturing facility could not keep up with the demand, and a wait list of 2,500 names was started with no guarantees of actually obtaining one of these sought-after $300 bags. Murakami also designed several other prints for Vuitton in the same Japanese anime style (pop art animation or cartoon drawing). Each was a piece of art, made by hand with 12 to 15 silk screens used for each print. "Onion-head" and "Flower Hat Man," each incorporating the LV logo, were in great demand (Moore).

Gucci, Yves St. Laurent, Fendi, Louis Vuitton, and Coach handbags are in such demand for the mass market that knockoffs are selling in record numbers in cities like Los Angeles and New York. But, buyers beware: The Bureau of Immigration and Customs Enforcement is constantly on the lookout for these counterfeit designer leather goods (see Chamberlin; *WWD*, August 5, 2003, p. 2).

Begun as a family-run business more than half a century ago, the Coach leather company modeled its first handbags after the distinct markings and suppleness of a base-ball glove. Coach still maintains these high standards of workmanship throughout their entire product line. But, in order to maintain competition with other designers, Coach has now joined this logo trend by producing shoes, handbags, and accessories with an emphasis on the Coach logo. In Figure 5.7, the Coach logo is printed across the vamp of a high-heeled clog.

In addition to apparel and fashion accessories, designers are utilizing their logos for home decor. Missoni, like other designer labels, introduced a line of home furnishings and accessories in 2005. The collection consists of seating; pillows; cushions; rugs; curtain panels; tableware; and bed, bath, and table linens patterned with broad stripes, variegated zigzags, and bold prints (Figure 5.8). To complete its home decor line, Missoni has plans to open a

5.6

5.7

UR CHAIR

Chair

our Chair

Chair

our Chair

FIG. 5.4 Illuminated manuscript. [Reprinted with permission of The J. Paul Getty Museum.] FIG. 5.5 Various showings of a typeface called Poetica, an example of a calligraphic font. FIG. 5.6 Louis Vuitton Murakami handbag. [Reprinted with permission of Louis Vuitton, Inc. Photo courtesy, Fairchild Publications, Inc.] FIG. 5.7 Coach high-heeled clog.

lifestyle hotel, which will incorporate its designer label collection.

Monograms (initials of a name presented in a sim-

5.8

ple design format) are not new to linens, as they have been used for centuries depicting family crests and initials. Flea markets and estate sales feature handkerchiefs, napkins, sheets, and towels with simple monograms or intricate embroidered details.

Monogramming is still used today, with many department stores offering custom on-site initials for linens and men's shirts. Catalogs such as *Martha Stewart Living* and Frontgate offer single or three-letter monograms in

custom colors at no extra charge or for a small additional fee when purchasing their featured linens (Figure 5.9). Requests for monogrammed linens are featured on many bridal shower and wedding registry lists.

Inspiration from Nature and Natural Patterns

As cave painters, hieroglyphists, and ancient artists and craftspeople drew their inspiration from nature, so too do modern designers look to nature's vast yet effortless forms for creative stimuli. Japanese designers have meditated upon the inward lessons of nature for centuries. The Japanese culture "believes that man and nature are indivisible," and that this man–nature harmony is represented in their entire lifestyle (McHarg, p. 27). The ancient Greeks believed that connecting to nature is innately calming, and the Chinese believe that plants, flowers, and animals improve the energy, or *qi*, in built environments. In this next section we'll focus on how this omnipresent man–nature harmony becomes inspiration for our design process.

"In nature all is useful, all is beautiful." This quotation from Ralph Waldo Emerson seems to say it all, especially for designers and artists whose inspiration is derived from the simplest of nature's forms. Tree bark, leaves, flowers, mountains, rocky landscape, sandy beaches, soil, shells, fossils, stones, water reflection, grasses, reeds, the sunrise and sunset, animals, insects, and birds are among nature's most inspirational sources.

5.9

88

In turning to nature, we notice that all surface patterns appear to be random, not planned or contrived, and that these patterns have always served as the basis for the form in designs.

Animal Prints

Animal skins and fur have been around since prehistoric man first slaughtered animals for food and used their pelts for protection. In costume remnants found dating from the Iron Age, fur was used to line a young girl's cape. Hunting civilizations used animal skins as foot protection. The Steppe nomads from the plains of the Ukraine wore tunics, trousers, and boots made of fur and leather for protection from the elements. The Greeks and Romans used animal felt as padding under their heavy armor. Later, in more technologically advanced societies, animal skins and fur were worn as a symbol of wealth and class. Artists such as Rubens and Van Eyck painted their subjects wearing fur muffs and collars. But it wasn't until early Hollywood movies associated fur with the feminine erotic that animal skins and furs were truly "in vogue." The designer furs worn by Madonna in the 1996 movie *Evita* and by Glenn Close as Cruella De Ville in *101 Dalmatians* have popularized fake spotted furs.

A 2001 issue of *Metropolitan Home* magazine, in a feature titled "Metro," juxtaposes an article about a Rudi Gernreich fashion retrospective with a model dressed in a giraffe print with a real giraffe. So authentic are Gernreich's animal print designs that it is difficult to determine that the cat suits modeled in Figure 5.10 are not real tiger, giraffe, and leopard skins.

5.10

5.11

FIG. 5.8 Missoni linens. [Courtesy, Fairchild Publications, Inc.] FIG. 5.9 Monogram detail on handkerchief. [Photo by Judith Griffin.] FIG. 5.10 Animal print outfits designed by Rudi Gernreich for his fall 1967 collection. [From a scene in William Claxton's 1967 fashion film *Basic Black*. Photo by William Claxton/Demont Photo LLC.] FIG. 5.11 Woman in leopard cape. [Copyright © Horst P. Horst. Reprinted with permission of Condé Nast Publications. All rights reserved.]

89

The very popular *New York Times* feature "On the Street" by Bill Cunningham has featured photographs of women, children, and even dogs on the streets of New York in coats, jackets, gloves, hats, and handbags made of real and faux furs.

Vintage animal prints are so popular that they are sought after in resale shops and on eBay. The leopard-skin cape featured in this 1940 Horst photograph (Figure 5.11) would probably command a high price.

Although animal fur is still sometimes worn by the wealthy, it no longer performs the basic need of protection. Animal fur prints have become an aesthetic feature in fashion and interior design, being used in the design and manufacturing of apparel and upholstery textiles.

Arts and Crafts Movement

In the second half of the 19th century, designers across Europe were focusing upon natural patterns expressed in distinctive regional motifs. If we look to the Arts and Crafts movement in Great Britain, the Art Nouveau movement in France, Modernisme in Spain, and the Jugendstil movement in Germany, we see that nature was an inspiration for the artists and designers from the 1850s through the turn of the century. Designers used stylized organic patterns of botanicals, birds, and insects to create textiles and wallpapers for interiors. These graphic images also carried over to the architecture of the period. Hector Guimard used intricate ironwork and patterned details for the Paris Metro stations. Others, like Antoni Gaudí, created designs for furniture and architecture that reflected highly stylized forms found in nature.

The Grammar of Ornament, written in 1856 by British architect and designer Owen Jones, was one of the first important books for pattern designers. Using illustrated decorative motifs from numerous sources, Jones created a huge library of patterns for designers and artists (Jackson, p. 10).

Working at about the same time as Jones, Christopher Dresser, originally trained as a botanist, approached pattern design through a scientific eye. Using plant forms, he created textile and wallpaper designs that were shown at the International Exhibition of 1862 in London. Dresser was a critical figure in the early melding of technology and design. Figure 5.12 shows one of his later designs for wallpaper.

William Morris, probably one of the most prolific and well-known British designers of the Arts and Crafts movement, returned to the basics of design and production by reintroducing hand block-printing and hand weaving to his creative designs. Using age-old block-printing and hand-weaving methods, Morris redirected the field of home furnishing

5.12

5.13

design by utilizing intricate patterns in printed fabrics and wallpapers (Jackson). Mellow vegetable dyes and native English plants with their natural flowing organic shapes were the basis for Morris's designs (Figure 5.13). Morris had a huge influence in all areas of the decorative arts.

Modernism

Through the first three decades of the 20th century, the Wiener Werkstatte established by Josef Hoffmann in Austria became a dominant force in pattern and surface design. The Werkstatte attracted numerous talented pattern designers who explored many new directions in surface design and produced thousands of important patterns that were used for upholstery, wallpaper, and apparel. Continuing to use block-printing methods of production, many of the Werkstatte patterns had organic motifs that were reduced to their simplest elements, but their woven textiles began to take on new dimensions.

FIG. 5.12 Christopher Dresser wallpaper design called "Sweet Peas" (1903). [Reprinted with permission of V&A Images/Victoria and Albert Museum.] FIG. 5.13 William Morris pattern. [Reprinted with permission of V&A Images/Victoria and Albert Museum.] FIG. 5.14 An example of an organic motif. [Reprinted with permission of V&A Images/Victoria and Albert Museum/Alamy.]

Throughout Europe, the mechanical processes of weaving provided a more formal linear framework that began to create an interesting contrast between the organic and geometric forms (Figure 5.14). The linear quality of architectural design was beginning to influence surface design.

The Bauhaus was also a part of the Modern movement. Although the Bauhaus followed Adolph Loos's dictate, "Ornament is sin," and did not teach surface decoration and ornamentation, Bauhaus wallpaper became a very successful mass-produced item that was used in the many new housing developments being built at that time. These wallpapers did not have conventional patterns but used painted textural effects that were printed in three tones of the same color, thus making it possible for the wallpapers to complement many different types of interior decor (Figure 5.15) (Jackson).

The weaving department at the Bauhaus created wall hangings, upholstery fabrics, and carpets that

5.14

adhered to a simple design and color vocabulary using circles, squares, and triangles. Anni Albers, a student of the Bauhaus from 1922 to 1930, designed "Wall Hanging" using a limited four-color palette. Her designs were austere, linear, and geometric, occasionally adding a raised relief for dimension (Figure 5.16). Other designers, like Gunta Stolzl and Lilly Reich, did some experimentation with color and printed textiles. While the Bauhaus was productive and highly influential over the history of Modern design, the actual school had a brief life; the Nazis closed the Bauhaus in 1933. The "less is more" philosophy of the Bauhaus has continued to endure, however, and is still taught in architecture and design schools today.

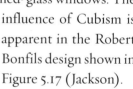

5.15

movement begun in 1907 with the paintings of Pablo Picasso and Georges Braque. This Cubist movement also had an impact on surface design and decoration that lasted through three decades. In the 1920s French pattern designers used Cubist designs purely for decorative purposes. Paul Rodier, a prominent textile manufacturer of fashion fabrics, also manufactured upholstery fabrics with Cubist designs by Picasso for use in home decor. Interest in Cubist designs spread to the United States, where, in 1926, Cheney Brothers of Connecticut produced dress fabrics inspired by stained-glass windows. The influence of Cubism is apparent in the Robert Bonfils design shown in Figure 5.17 (Jackson).

5.17

Cubism

Artists and designers, always exploring new means of communicating their individual philosophies, began to look toward the deconstructed geometric patterns of Cubism, an art

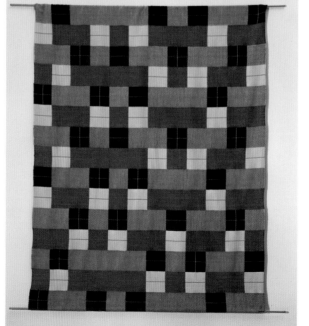

5.16

Op Art

The first part of the 20th century saw a shift in interpretations of

surface decoration from the natural designs of the Arts and Crafts movement through the deconstructed Cubist images. After World War II, Western culture expanded at an amazing pace. Manufacturing and mass communications grew at an unprecedented rate from 1958 to 1968. By 1960 over 85 million Americans owned televisions, and with that ownership, mass media advertising became a nightly occurrence. People desired the many new products being advertised on their favorite television shows. In addition, young people entering the workforce began to have a discretionary income of their own and began spending it in record amounts (Conran). Pop culture and art, with their images derived from science and architecture, were a result of the new and emerging mass media.

Designers began experimenting with skeletal plant forms; crystalline forms of minerals seen through the lens of a microscope; simple random organic images showing the contrast between line and mass; architecturally inspired patterns; abstract imagery of geological strata; leafless trees; and the larger, distorted and flattened images of the op art and pop art of the 1960s.

The 1960s were energetic times for the creative world of pattern design.

The design of textiles, wallpapers, graphics, and apparel was transformed by the "Carnaby Street" look. The Finnish company Marimekko, headed by Armi Ratia, revolutionized design in the 1960s with huge, bold, flat patterns that were hand screen-printed in vibrant colors or in graphic black and white. These large-scale patterns, usually printed on heavy cotton cloth, were used for dress fabrics, wall or window hangings, and upholstery for interior design (Figure 5.18a and b).

These bold, flat flower-power patterns led the way for op art-inspired psychedelic textiles. The textiles still used vibrant, flat, floral patterns, but they featured overlapping shapes with heightened colors adjacent on the color spectrum. These textile patterns were the inspiration for the design of the rock posters of the 1960s. Outlandish curvilinear

5.18a+b

FIG. 5.15 Bauhaus wallpaper with colored inks on tan woven paper by Josef Albers (c. 1929). [Reprinted with permission of the Busch-Reisinger Museum, Harvard University.] FIG. 5.16 "Wall Hanging" by Anni Albers (1927). [Copyright © 2006 The Josef and Anni Albers Foundation/The Museum of Modern Art/Licensed by Scala/Art Resource, NY.] FIG. 5.17 "Variations" by Robert Bonfils, Lyon, France (c. 1931). [Reprinted with permission of V&A Images/Victoria and Albert Museum/Alamy.] FIG. 5.18 Marimekko patterns in (a) bold colors and (b) black-and-white graphic patterns designed by Maija Isola (1964). [Photos by Judith Griffin.]

forms, difficult-to-decipher graphics, and contiguous and fluorescent colors were central to the theme of these posters.

Fashion was op art-inspired as well, with Italian designer Emilio Pucci becoming a trendsetter in printed motifs. Pucci, referred to as the "prince of prints," created intense abstract patterns that were used for fashion as well as furnishings. His Vivara and Paggio collections incorporated vibrant organic and geometric patterns, printed either in hot yellows, pinks, and oranges or deep blues, purples, and greens. Forty years later, Pucci's distinctive style is still evident in the line that has been carried on by his family (Figure 5.19).

5.19

5.20

Revivalism, Postmodernism, and Digital Design

The 1970s were not as energetic and hopeful as the post–World War II years. An economic recession, social unrest, and environmental concerns created anxiety among consumers. Everyone wanted to be safe and comfortable and looked toward "home" to make that happen. Designers did not experiment in new directions, but instead they used archived textiles and wallpapers as a source of inspiration (Jackson).

Downsizing seemed to be the theme of the 1980s, with smaller companies being acquired by large multinational firms. Pattern design was not moving forward, but still relied on the "document"

5.21

archives of past generations. However, an important part of the 1980s was postmodern design, which included ornamentation and references to historical styles, albeit sometimes taken to the point of absurdity. The Memphis group in Italy was an energetic force in the postmodern era, developing furniture and interior design using arbitrary, whimsical color and form (Figure 5.20).

The American architect Michael Graves, most noted for his postmodern designs, created textiles, interiors, and architecture with references to the past. In 1981, Graves designed printed textiles in collaboration with the Sunar Hauserman furniture company. In keeping with historical references, his patterns included scroll, fret, and tracery. Graves used color to relate to forces in nature. He used blue for the sky, yellow for sunlight, and green for plants. He also incorporated fantasy forms such as shells, dolphins, and swans as ornamental elements on his buildings. The 1990 Dolphin and Swan Hotels in Buena Vista, Florida, are a good example of his whimsical design (Figure 5.21).

The postmodern references to historical styles were not the only look at the past. The 1994 Henri Matisse retrospective at the Museum of Modern Art in New York had designers at fabric houses such as Osborne & Little, China Seas, and Kravet incorporating bright fabrics with Matisse-inspired free-form shapes into their 1995 collections.

This was not the first collaboration between art

FIG. 5.19 A printed motif by Pucci. [Courtesy, Fairchild Publications, Inc.] FIG. 5.20 This piece, "Casablanca," is a sideboard design by Ettore Sottsass and the Memphis group (1981). [Reprinted with permission of V&A Images/Victoria and Albert Museum.] FIG. 5.21 Swan hotel in Buena Vista, FL, by Michael Graves. [Copyright © Michael Graves/Taylor Photographics.]

5.22

and design. Prolific artist and sculptor Pablo Picasso created brightly hued graphic patterns for ceramic plates and bowls during the 1950s. Many of them were inspired by nature and had names such as "Bird in Flight," "Sun," "Still Life with Two Fish," and "Owl." Figure 5.22 shows a Spanish plate decorated with a bull.

Another collaboration between art and design was Judy Chicago's "The Dinner Party," an installation that traveled around the United States in the late 1970s (Figure 5.23a–d). It is a symbolic tribute to the achievements of women throughout history. Individual heroines are featured on 39 painted china plates and embroidered runners set on a triangular table. In addition to the plate settings, the "heritage floor" on which the table stood contained tiles inscribed to another 999 women. Some of the women represented by the plates were the Greek goddess Sophia (Figure 5.23a), the 16th-century Italian artist Artemisia Gentileschi (Figure 5.23b), the 19th-century American poet Emily Dickinson (Figure 5.23c), and the 20th-century American artist Georgia O'Keeffe (Figure 5.23d) (Chicago).

In 2001, *House Beautiful* magazine asked 14 international fashion designers to create one-of-a-kind dinner plates, applying their diverse talents to yet another area of home decor. Romeo Gigli's dinner plate theme was "Nature's Bounty." Tracy Feith said, "I tried to achieve an abstraction of the things that inspire me: the sun and water—the essential elements." Valentino's red rose pattern "symbolized romance, femininity, and elegance."

5.23a

5.23b

5.23c

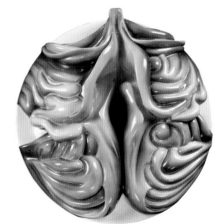

5.23d

96

5.24

"Place settings with personality" are Kate Spade's latest entrée into the home decor market. She has created dinnerware, flatware, and goblets, with names such as "Gramercy Park," which are reminiscent of the designs of Mondrian and Frank Lloyd Wright (Figure 5.24) (Macy's, p. A7).

Technology and Innovative Materials

The advancement of computer technology in the 1990s transformed pattern design into areas that once could only be imagined. Cables, computer circuit boards, techno-textiles (Moore, *Metropolis*, pp. 71–73), fabric environments, and microbiology affect design and reinforce the theory that we build what we see, as has happened throughout history. As technology continues to make rapid advances, we are able to see deeper and deeper into nature, and our design follows what we see—fresh new perspectives. Systematic structures, visible only through the microscope, reveal nature in a microcosm and allow us a deeper understanding of the structure of the universe. Just as Alice followed the rabbit down the hole in Lewis Carroll's *Alice in Wonderland,* we too are constantly looking to explore new horizons.

Many current designers are exploring these new horizons with materials that stretch our imagination and creativity. They are developing textiles and other materials with properties that repel and resist dirt and moisture and that are environmentally sound, innovative, and exciting.

Material ConneXion, created by George Beyler-

ian in 1997, has archives of over 1,400 unusual materials. It is referred to as a "petting zoo for new materials." The library, located in New York City, is an excellent resource for new and innovative substances. The materials are classified into eight categories: polymers, glass, ceramics, carbon-based materials, cement-based materials, metals, natural materials, and natural-material derivatives. The library also presents exhibitions showcasing some of its most innovative materials. In addition to the built environment, information is also available via the Internet, using Material ConneXion's database (Leland, pp. B1, B12).

Another source for new and unusual materials was Material-World held in Miami Beach, Florida, in fall 2003. It was the "largest fabric and sourcing event in the Americas" (*WWD*, August 5, 2003, p. 12). Vendors, designers, and manufacturers were all under one roof for sourcing, textiles, and technology.

Dorothy Cosonas, Unika Vaev's designer, has just introduced a line of Gore-Tex upholstery textiles reminiscent of both microscopic and nature-inspired imagery. With names like Terrain, Wavelength, Tetra, and Crossroads, these textiles are

5.25

FIG. 5.22 Spanish plate decorated with a bull by Pablo Picasso (1957). [Copyright © ARS, NY, and Réunion des Musées Nationaux/Art Resource, NY. Photo by Gérard Blot.] FIG. 5.23 From "The Dinner Party" by Judy Chicago includes the (a) Sophia plate, (b) Artemisia Gentileschi plate, (c) Emily Dickinson plate, and (d) Georgia O'Keeffe plate. [Photos by Judy Chicago © Through the Flower Archives (1979).] FIG. 5.24 Gramercy Park dinnerware by Kate Spade. FIG. 5.25 Unika Vaev pattern designs approved for Gore seating protection. [Reprinted with permission of Unika Vaev, Inc.]

5.26

resistant to soil, stains, abrasion, and flames, and they have antimicrobial properties (Figure 5.25).

Nanotechnology, developed by Nano-Tex, is producing highly advanced textiles that repel high levels of oil and water, have a hydrophilic fiber treatment, and also coat noncellulosic textiles with cellulose. Working with Unitika Fiber Ltd., a Tokyo fiber producer, Nano-Tex is designing textiles for the fashion and home furnishings market (*WWD*, August 5, 2003, p. 13).

Marcia Stuermer of Fossil Faux Studios in San Francisco has designed the Elemental Series, incorporating leaves, rocks, and grasses in custom resin panels. The panels, combining nature and technology in their manufacturing process, can be used for countertops, tables, screens, flooring, lighting panels, and wall partitions (Figure 5.26) ("Product Briefs," p. 201).

Ralph Lauren's daughter Dylan operates the two-story Candy Bar in the heart of New York City. At the center of the store is a $40,000 resin staircase that has red, yellow, and green candy featured in the stair treads. The stairs were designed by Joanne Newbold of Allen & Killcoyne and manufactured by Atta Inc. (Figure 5.27).

Architectural Materials

"You can't judge a book by its cover" is a well-known maxim. Well, can you judge a building's success by its skin? Innovative architectural materials are appearing all over the globe: a titanium-clad museum in Bilbao, Spain; a steel-clad concert hall in Los Angeles, California; and an aluminum-clad department store in Birmingham, England.

5.29a

The Guggenheim Museum Bilbao, designed by Frank O. Gehry, is noted for what have been referred to as "metallic flower" shapes. These were reportedly modeled by Gehry using a sophisticated aviation design computer program. The smooth undulating titanium rectangles (Figure 5.28) seem to float on the River Nervion. The museum has revitalized the industrial city of Bilbao.

The Disney Concert Hall (see Figure 3.1a on page 46), also designed by Gehry, features a dramatically curved steel exterior designed to look like a ship with its sail at full mast. "Gehry wanted to create the feeling of traveling along a ceremonial

5.27

5.28

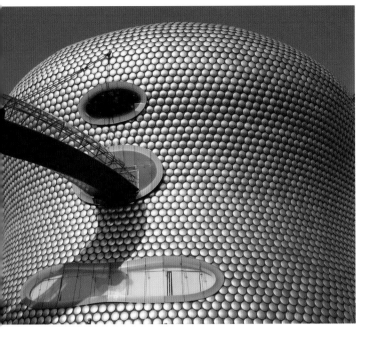

5.29b

barge to music" (*Los Angeles Times*). The Concert Hall is clad in 22 million pounds of primary steel joined out of 12,500 individual pieces that range from 13 inches to 110 feet long. No two pieces are identical, and some weigh as much as 165,000 pounds.

Jan Kaplicky and Amanda Levete of Future Systems in London designed the new Selfridges department store in Birmingham, England (Figure 5.29a). The mostly windowless building, clad in 15,000 aluminum disks, was inspired by a Paco Rabanne hammered-aluminum dress (Figure 5.29b). Architectural critics have compared the design to Guggenheim Bilbao, scales of a fish, a toadstool, or a soap bubble. "The store proves that adventurous, intelligent design can transform a city" (Rowan Moore, p. 82).

As we move further into the 21st century, technology will enable designers to transform the materials we use and the ways in which we use them. Designers will be inspired by these materials to create innovative new approaches to surface design and pattern. Experimentation with materials not yet invented will energize our professions and our creativity. If through the use of surface materials like titanium and aluminum designers can help revitalize city centers, imagine what the next decade might bring.

FIG. 5.26 Fossil Faux freestanding screen. [Reprinted with permission of Fossil Faux Studios.] FIG. 5.27 The stairway, designed by Joanne Newbold of Allen & Killcoyne, in Dylan's Candy Bar in New York. [Photo by Judith Griffin.] FIG. 5.28 Detail of the Guggenheim Museum in Bilbao, Spain. [Copyright © Colin Walton/Alamy.] FIG. 5.29 (a) Selfridges Department Store in Birmingham, England. (b) "Atomium Bruxelles" dress by Paco Rabanne (1969). [(a) Copyright © Richard Klune/Corbis. (b) Courtesy, Fairchild Publications, Inc.]

99

CHAPTER SIX

Furniture and Fashion

How to Wear Your Chair

When newspapers, periodicals, and museums are using titles like "She's Wearing My Chair," "The Library That Puts on Fishnets and Hits the Disco," and "Dangerous Liaisons: Fashion and Furniture in the 18th Century," it's clear that designers can no longer be pigeonholed into the specific and discreet disciplines of fashion, interiors, architecture, and graphics. Today's designers are multifaceted, well-educated individuals who bring to design an inter-disciplinary understanding of the elements of form, shape, color, and texture. With this understanding solidly implanted in our psyches, we look at design in a totally different way. Instead of upholstery fabrics being used solely for furniture, why not use them to manufacture garments? Architects mimic fashion designers as they create exterior spaces that look as if they should be dressed. When designing a building, architects can use steel fishnet, fabric-like membranes, or titanium cladding to alter the facade of the structure, making it more dynamic than a rectilinear box. Furniture, interior, and fashion designers can borrow form, shape, and texture from one another, thereby stretching the boundaries of their individual practice areas.

While trained in specific disciplines, designers are consistently creating new lines in other specialties. Frank Gehry designs buildings using innovative technologies and materials—like titanium for the Guggenheim Bilbao—and he also designs jewelry for Tiffany's and bentwood furniture for Knoll (Fig-

6.1

ure 6.1). Todd Oldham, originally a fashion designer (Figure 6.2a), now designs a line of accessories for Target and a line of contemporary furniture for La-Z-Boy (Figure 6.2b). Fashion designers Calvin Klein, Donna Karan, and Ralph Lauren have successfully developed elegant lines for home decor. Virtually every fashion design icon has commissioned an icon of architecture to design his or her

flagship store. The acknowledgment of the global interdependence of fashion, interior, and architectural design is no more evident than in the epicenters of the design world, from Rodeo Drive in Los Angeles to Rue St. Honore Fauberg in Paris.

The interdisciplinary approach to design is hardly new; designers have been "crossing over" into allied fields throughout history. Leonardo da Vinci (1452–1519), the archetypal "Renaissance Man," was a painter, sculptor, architect, engineer, and scientist, and in each area he was a huge influence on the world. William Morris (1834–1896), a prolific figure in modern design, created interiors, furniture, stained glass, tiles, wallpaper, and textiles (Figure 6.3). Charles Rennie Mackintosh (1868–1928), best known for his furniture and interior design (Figure 6.4), was trained as an architect. Haute-couture designer Paul Poiret (1819–1944) also designed furniture and interiors (see Figure 10.7).

6.3

What inspired these famous architects and designers to explore other avenues of design? Could it be that the crossover in the design disciplines seems natural to us, since all design students are taught the basic elements and principles of design? Could it be that this interdisciplinary creativity stems from our desire to discover new ways to utilize shape, form, texture, and new materials?

Form Follows Function

If we've learned only one thing from our study of

6.2a

6.2b

6.4

design in fashion, furniture, and interior design, it's that our basic instinct for form springs from necessity. In short, we design and redesign because we need things to work. We are continually redesigning the tools, appliances, furniture, and clothing that we need to survive and thrive. Our basic wiring seems to compel us to make these things perform better and appear more beautiful. The introduction of new materials and the discovery of new uses and variations of familiar ones also continually challenge us. Designers are thus always experimenting with new materials and tweaking their concepts and products, attempting to determine what works best in different applications. Design boundaries that existed when we had only wood and wool profoundly changed after plastic and nylon were developed. Architects and designers have always adapted and combined new materials presented to them by the circumstances surrounding their environments. Many times, the new materials utilized in architecture were developed in other disciplines to fill specific needs that had nothing to do with erecting well-designed buildings.

Why are new materials created? Is their development simply an answer to the depletion of existing materials? Do they become developed merely as new ways to showcase manufactured goods? Are they created out of necessity or boredom? Or, are new materials developed because we have an instinctual need to create better forms for the functions we require in our lives? As usual, history is instructive. We can clearly understand new developments in design if we recall the epical events that preceded their introductions.

International Exhibitions

In an effort to maintain their leadership in art and design, the French were anxious to find new directions for the 20th century. As a new style or modern design began to develop, exhibitions in which to showcase these new designs were planned. These international exhibitions showcased the work of fashion, furniture, and interior designers, using room vignettes that were fashion-oriented and decorative.

The Panama Pacific International Exhibition of 1915 in San Francisco was a major event in the world of art and design. At the time, French couture designers were trying to expand their export markets. They were designing dresses with wide skirts that were several inches above the ground. Their work indicated a new direction in fashion. Could this use of less fabric have been an economic response to World War I? This new "leggier" direction in fashion is represented in the 1922 Georges

FIG. 6.1 Bentwood furniture for Knoll, Inc. by Frank O. Gehry. [Reprinted with permission of Knoll, Inc.] FIG. 6.2 (a) Todd Oldham dress design (1994). (b) La-Z-Boy Snap sofa by Todd Oldham. [(a) Copyright © Michel Arnaud/Corbis. (b) Courtesy, La-Z-Boy.] FIG. 6.3 "Tulip and Trellis" tile by William Morris (1870). [Reprinted with permission of V&A Images/Victoria and Albert Museum.] FIG. 6.4 "The Willow Tearooms" in Glasgow, Scotland, designed by Charles Rennie Mackintosh (1904). [Reprinted with permission of T. & R. Annan & Sons Ltd.]

6.5

Barbier illustration "Woman in a Yellow Dress" (Figure 6.5).

Other important exhibitions followed. In Paris, at the *Salon d'Automne* and the *Salon des Arts Decoratifs*, contemporary furniture was the focus. Modern fashion with its innovative style and color was responsible for the modern design movement, and without the most prominent fashion houses showcasing these designs, the modern shapes, colors, and materials would not have been used in furniture and interior design.

The *Exposition Internationale des Arts Decoratifs et*

Industriels Modernes (International Exposition of Modern Industrial and Decorative Arts) took place in Paris in 1925. The term *Art Deco* was derived from the title of this exposition, which occurred during a cultural and commercial renaissance in France. All modern French decorative art exhibits were focused on the future (Benton, p. 157). The Exposition allowed the visitors to wander Paris streets and shop in the department stores and boutiques. The boutiques were part of Paris's postwar urban renewal project. They specialized in luxurious products, particularly those relating to the fashion and interior design industries (Benton, p. 158). Haute couture fashion was a major focus of the 1925 Exposition, since Paris was considered a "woman's city," with export of women's clothing totaling almost 2.5 billion francs in 1924 (Benton, p. 159).

This exposition also focused on the modernization and commercialization of interior design. The Art Deco style drew its inspiration from classical motifs. Classical three-dimensional sculpture, the use of smooth surfaces, and sumptuous, exotic materials used in highly stylized presentations characterized the Art Deco period (Massey, p. 91). The ornamentation of the Art Nouveau era was deleted, creating furniture and interiors with smooth, clean lines as shown in Figure 6.6. In addition to the change in shape and form, designers were beginning to experiment with rare materials. Emile-Jacques Ruhlmann (1879–1933), a furniture designer, used

6.6

6.7

department store in Los Angeles in 1928 (Benton, p. 108). Delaunay's designs, popularized through L'Herbier and Le Somptier's films, modernized the way women looked, creating an independent and professional appearance.

Paul Poiret (1819–1944), originally an haute-couture fashion designer, began a successful interior decoration atelier in Paris in 1912. Poiret developed a comfortable connection between women's high fashion and interior design. This crossover was typical of the Art Deco movement, which made it easy for him to design textiles for fashion and interiors (Massey, p. 96). Poiret used exotic textiles, patterns from nature, and strong colors, all with an Asian influence.

The 1925 Exposition introduced the world to modern forms of design. Art Deco was represented everywhere, in film, fashion, furniture, art, and product design. Utilizing both handcrafting and machine manufacturing, these new products were made of new materials. Aluminum, plastics, tubular steel, laminated wood and plastics, and exotic animal skins were some of the new materials introduced during this period. With new technology and materials, the design world was in the process of being transformed. What was once traditional was now modern and what was once ornate was now sleek, streamlined, and futuristic.

lizardskin, shagreen (sharkskin or galuchet), ivory, tortoiseshell, and exotic hardwoods (Figure 6.7).

Russian-born artist and fashion designer Sonia Delaunay (1885–1979), well known for her bold geometric patterns used in illustrations, paintings, and textiles, acquired several new clients as a result of her 1925 *Exposition Boutique Simultanée*. In 1926 Delaunay designed costumes and sets for Marcel L'Herbier and René Le Somptier's films *Le Vertige* and *Le P'tit Parigot*—two of the earliest films to include Deco interiors and costumes. She also designed the Art Deco interiors for the Bullock's

Postwar Development

The design world was still in a transformation mode when World War II began. Production of luxury furniture and fashion ceased, but technology did not. The manufacturing of durable goods was necessary for the war effort, but new materials and production techniques were needed. The materials that made aircraft design possible—lightweight metals, plastics, laminated wood, and glass—also created new technologies for the design of furniture and architecture. The materials used for parachutes, uniforms, and helmets launched fashion designers in new directions. The computer technology that was developed during the war years paved the way for the 3-D modeling that allowed architecture to take on the curvilinear metal-clad, anthropomorphic exteriors expressed in Frank Gehry's designs for exhibition and performance spaces. The advent of these new materials, technologies, and production methods helped increase our capabilities and freed our imaginations.

The baby-boom generation, born after the war, created a large population of young people with more discretionary income than their parents had at their age (Boucher, p. 423). By the early 1960s, this increased income allowed these young adults to purchase products and fashion previously available only to a middle-aged population. To keep up with the demand for innovative design, architects and furniture and fashion designers were looking to new materials and techniques for their new products.

logical advances. During the war, Eames was commissioned by the United States Navy to develop plywood stretchers and leg splints. After the war, Eames and his wife and collaborator, Ray Kaiser Eames (1912–1988), adopted his new techniques for molding and gluing plywood and reinforcing plastics with fiberglass for furniture design. Eames and Saarinen then collaborated on the "Conversation" armchair (1940) (Figure 6.8), a molded plywood shell chair shaped into three-dimensional curves with a single unit for both the seat and back. This chair won first prize at the Museum of Modern Art's Organic Design in Home Furnishings competition. The Eames's innovative techniques and materials appeared in their designs for seating, storage units, tables, and folding screens. Their greatest legacy was their belief that design could improve people's lives and create social change. Saarinen studied architecture at Yale University and later taught at the Cranbrook Academy of Art, where he met Charles and Ray Eames. He is best known for his design of the TWA terminal at John F. Kennedy Airport in New York. "Saarinen's 'Womb' chair (1946) and Charles and Ray Eames's 'Chair and Ottoman' (1956) are among the classics of 20th-century chair design" (Massey, p. 155). The furniture designed by the Eameses and Saarinen continues to be mass-produced by two American furniture manufacturers, Herman Miller and the Knoll Furniture Company.

Herman Miller also manufactured the organic furniture forms of

Furniture Design

Charles Eames (1907–1978) and Eero Saarinen (1910–1961) were two preeminent designers who emerged after World War II and rode the wave of new techno-

6.8

Isamu Noguchi's glass-top coffee table (1944) (Figure 6.9) and George Nelson's "Basic Storage Components" (1949). Mies van der Rohe's "Barcelona Chair" (1948) and Harry Bertoia's wire-mesh "Diamond Chair" (1952) (Figure 6.10) were also manufactured by Knoll. American corporate executives who wanted their postwar offices to reflect their own forward-thinking, global attitudes quickly adopted these sleek modern designs. Fortunately, most of the great postwar furniture designs, while originally created to furnish the residential architecture created by these same designers, adapted equally well to work settings.

Both Knoll and Herman Miller were also responsible for bringing these now-classic designs from the home to the office environments. Knoll and Herman Miller marketed these new furniture designs to many American corporations, that used the furniture and storage units designed by Eames, Mies, and Nelson in their staff offices. Knoll and Herman Miller created the contract interiors mar-

ket, revolutionizing the appearance and functionality of the corporate office, which became an open, organized, and efficient environment, utilizing desks, storage components, and ergonomic seating.

This organic Modernism was evident not only in furniture but also in the curved organic architecture of Le Corbusier, as exemplified in his Notre-Dame-du-Haute chapel at Ronchamp (1955), and vividly expressed in Frank Lloyd Wright's Guggenheim Museum in New York (1959) (Figure 6.11), and in Saarinen's TWA terminal at JFK International Airport in New York (1962) (Figure 6.12). The curved organic designs of the 1950s preceded the same thematic design carried out by Gehry by the end of the century. Of course, none of these 20th-century designs would have been possible without technological developments such as lightweight concrete, stainless steel, titanium, and computer imaging.

FIG. 6.8 "Conversation" armchair by Eames and Saarinen (1940). [Reprinted with permission of the Los Angeles Modern Auctions.] FIG. 6.9 Isamu Noguchi's glass top coffee table for Herman Miller (1944). [Copyright © The Noguchi Museum/Artist's Rights Society.] FIG. 6.10 Harry Bertoia's wire-mesh "Diamond Chair" (1952). [Copyright © Richard Bryant/Arcaid.] FIG. 6.11 Frank Lloyd Wright's Guggenheim Museum in New York (1959). [Copyright © ARS, NY, and Timothy McCarthy/Art Resource, NY.] FIG. 6.12 Eero Saarinen's TWA terminal in JFK Airport, NY (1962). [Copyright © Ezra Stoller/Esto Photographics, Inc.]

Fashion Design

France, the prewar leader in haute couture, was isolated from the rest of the design world during World War II. Shortages of materials forced designers to use wood and cork for the soles of shoes. Hats were created out of scraps of newspaper and ribbon. When the war ended and France was again open to the world, haute couture flourished, as the same new materials and techniques utilized in furniture design were introduced to clothing. The postwar period also saw a change in the everyday life of women. Although elegance was still required for evening attire, the modern woman needed clothing for daytime activities. The women who first entered the workforce during the war were still employed, and their numbers were growing, and these working women needed appropriate, professional clothing for the business setting.

Coco Chanel (1883–1971), born in France, was one of the most influential designers of the 20th

6.13

century. As a fashion designer she did away with the corset and created comfortable fashion with a casual elegance. She built an entire brand image around her simply tailored suits. Although immersed in the world of fashion, Chanel's vision as a designer was interdisciplinary. She felt that fashion was limitless. She said, "Fashion is not something that exists in dresses only. Fashion is in the sky, in the street, fashion has to do with ideas, the way we live, what is happening" (Anyara Aphorisms).

Chanel felt strongly about other areas of design and in another of her famous quotes said, "An interior is the natural projection of one's soul, and Balzac was right in giving it the same importance as to dress." When Chanel arrived in Paris in the early 20th century, rural furniture and a spartan environment shaped her style. She felt that women's clothes were too showy and their homes too chaotic and cluttered. "Chanel exercised the same purification in interior decoration as in dress." The Chanel style has been reinterpreted by a series of designers since her death in 1971. The fashion illustrations shown in Figure 6.13 are an example of Karl Lagerfeld's designs for the House of Chanel.

Another important fashion designer of the 20th century was Pauline Trigère (1908–2002). Trigère was born in Paris in 1908 and emigrated to New York in 1937. Trigère brought her European style and couture skills to America. She studied how the movement of the fabric related to the curves of the body. She draped and cut fabric directly on the body and never used a pattern. She understood how clothing could enhance the female body. Some of Trigère's most important contributions to fashion design were mobile collars, the reversible coat, cape-collared coats (Figure 6.14), and the jumpsuit. Multifunctional fashion is certainly not a new phenomenon. Trigère designed custom-made dresses and had a ready-to-wear clothing line in the 1940s. Her designs are very popular in vintage shops today. Trigère remained creative up until her death, designing black-tie canes and wheelchair accessories for elderly clients.

6.14

FIG. 6.13 Fashion drawings of Coco Chanel's tailored suit by Karl Lagerfeld. [Copyright © Massimo Listri/Corbis.] FIG. 6.14 Pauline Trigère's long red-and-black plaid cape coat (1969). [Reprinted with permission of Kent State University Museum. Gift of Pauline Trigère. Photo by Anne Bissonnette.]

Developments of the Late 20th Century

As we moved further into the 20th century, many new design concepts, materials, and directions developed in the United States and abroad. Indeed, as the globe began to shrink with the development of the commercial jetliner, design became more global and less parochial. Designers crisscrossed the world, borrowing concepts across international boundaries, their creations influenced by the broadest array of cultures. Designers were looking for innovative ways of expression, and as Asia, Africa, India, and South America became more accessible to Europe and America, there was an explosion of innovative design. The concurrent scientific revolutions that produced computer animation and 3-D modeling spilled over to produce a compelling new vision and perspective in design.

Whether they were involved in the design of fashion, furniture, or interiors, designers in the late 20th century thought and worked in three dimensions just like sculptors. Designers have always known that the wearer of a garment or the user of a piece of furniture will give designs a dimension of their own. However, fashion designer Issey Miyake sees distinct and stark differences between the soft draped clothing and the hard edge of furniture and architecture. "The final form of clothing design is determined by the way the body moves," he says. "Unlike architecture and furniture, clothing design cannot be accomplished without the wearer's participation." Miyake experimented with a beanbag chair that had a dual function. While it took on its complete shape only when a body was sitting on it, the beanbag chair could also be worn as a cape (Figure 6.15). Miyake said: "The physically closer the usage of discipline to the human body is, the more need there is for making use of all five senses" (Codrington).

While Miyake may be correct in his assessment, it's difficult to deny the sensation that the best of Frank Gehry's buildings give off—that they're breathing and moving under their curved smooth

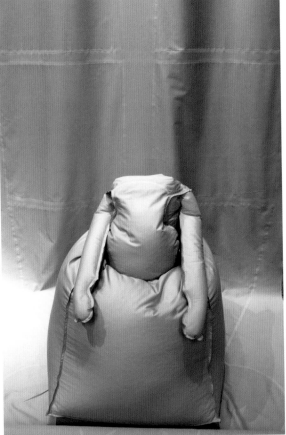

6.15

skins, much as a body breathes and stretches under a Miyake gown.

Furniture and fashion are intertwined and draw inspiration from similar sources. A parallel exists between dress, lifestyle, and furnishings. The inspiration for that parallel has become much more global in the past few decades. Everyone is traveling to far corners of the earth, and what was only once read and dreamed about is now a mere flight away. The Internet has made new designs and lifestyle trends universally accessible with the click of a button. However, questions remain: Is this globalism beneficial for designers, or does it create a generic look worldwide? Does our ever-shrinking world generate the creativity necessary for instilling new ideas and techniques for the design community? And do designers need this inspiration to maintain high levels of creativity?

In the innovative magazines *Metropolis*, *Surface*, and *Wallpaper*, up-and-coming designers are featured on a monthly basis; new technological advances and trends are described in vivid detail and illustrated through stimulating color photos. The latest in fashion, architecture, and design is evident on every page. One feature may describe how CAD or computer animation assist a designer in creating complex shapes and forms for dress or furniture design, while another describes a new "hands-on" plastic extrusion process that will create elegant forms in vibrant colors, but never duplicate objects.

Whether we are designing a chair or a dress, we are looking for similar attributes. We require a flexibility in furniture and fashion, something that can be used or worn anywhere, at any time, in a multi-

tude of combinations. Even though our wardrobes may consist of sportswear, formal wear, and business attire, we still have certain items that are flexible enough to make the transition from day to evening. Fashion in apparel has always changed with the season, but now it changes more rapidly than ever.

Furniture, unlike clothing, was once used year in and year out. Major suites of residential furniture were expected to last, unchanged for decades and even for generations, while fashion has always been more seasonal and, hence, mercurial. But this too is changing. In our more relaxed multifunctional environments we're looking for furniture that is as changeable as our clothing. The world of prêt-à-porter in fashion, with its ubiquitous in-stock items and seasonal adaptability, which we have taken for granted for decades, is now available in furniture. If we are bored with our living or working environments, all we need to do is shop at a local IKEA or Crate and Barrel and take a new look home with us. We wear different fabrics and looks for each season, and now our furniture can adapt to these seasonal changes as well. Slipcovers in dark, soft, cozy chenille can be used in winter, while lightweight linens and cottons are our furniture's summer outfits.

Even building interiors are more flexible. Significant interior spaces within Gehry's Bilbao museum can be quickly and effortlessly reconfigured from small, intimate areas to a large gallery that reminded the architect of the belly of a whale. Office environments, once constructed with rigid walled offices and conference rooms, are now planned with flexibility in mind. With the use of movable walls and open-plan furniture, interiors are now multifunctional.

FIG. 6.15 Issey Miyake's beanbag chair from "A-POC Making Exhibition" at the Vitra Design Museum (2001). [Copyright © Siemoneit Ronald/Corbis Sygma.]

The Beginning of the 21st Century

A few designers are difficult to place in the context of their time. Do they represent a continuation of postwar developments or are they emblematic of a complete break with the past? Although they worked in the late 20th century, does their work suggest that they actually need to be discussed with 21st-century designers? What about these designers might propel them into the next millennium? Is it that their designs evoke an emotional chord? Is it cutting edge or borrowed from our past? Are their production techniques and materials innovative? Will their designs be remembered as classics of the 21st century? As we observe their work, what is evident is their vision to explore new challenges in design. We can break these designers and observers into two groups: street fashion and high fashion.

Street Fashion

Street fashion of an earlier decade is epitomized by the work of British designer Mary Quant. More recently, many of the familiar names in street fashion are also familiar on the music charts. Their work and their inspiration are captured in the photography of Jamel Shabazz and Bill Cunningham.

Mary Quant

Mary Quant was one of the foremost fashion designers of the 1960s. She was influenced by the energy in the streets, by op art and pop art, and by the space age. Quant popularized the miniskirt and commercialized fun, hip fashion easily available to the average working girl (Figure 6.16). Quant's description of her own skillful antenna aptly describes the "tuned in" and "turned on" designers of the 1960s. Quant said that "good designers know that to have any influence they must keep in step with public needs and that intangible 'something in the air.' They must catch the spirit of the day and interpret it in clothes before other designers begin to twitch at the nerve ends." Quant's remarks indicate a reversal in the way designers began to think of themselves. Designers were abandoning the notion that they were society's self-appointed arbiters of taste and style. Instead designers were studiously copying what they were observing on the street, only tweaking what they saw by using new colors and materials. Everyone from the Beatles to Audrey Hepburn wore Quant's designs. Quant has also designed hosiery, home linens, and skin care products and is still working in London designing jewelry, umbrellas, and bags. In a recent CNN

6.16

interview, she said that "art and design schools offer a burst of energy and a network of ideas" and that "people who attend schools today are obsessed with design and it has become a way of life, they are very passionate about what they do" (*Design 360*).

Jamel Shabazz

Hip-hop, which was once just a small-scale, parochial musical style, has now become a major lifestyle and created a universal language. In the 1970s, fashion photographer Jamel Shabazz began photographing street fashion (Figure 6.17). It was clear that each person he photographed made his or her own fashion statement. It was also clear from Shabazz's photographs that a new fashion sensibility was emerging from the music of hip-hop and rap. What began with gold chains and baggy pants formed a multibillion-dollar industry featuring entire lines by well-known rappers and hip-hop artists. Sean John, the label of Sean Combs (also known at various times in his music career as Puff Daddy, Puffy, P. Diddy, and Diddy), and Phat Farm, the fashion enterprise founded by Russel Simmons, are major players in this urban lifestyle. Indeed, haute couture designers are now creating entire collections that evoke and sometimes mimic hip-hop clothing designers. As in the 1960s, designers are still copying and following that intangible "something in the air."

Bill Cunningham

With the street being a constant source of inspiration to designers, Bill Cunningham of the *New York Times* has been one of the greatest sources of trend-spotting in the world of fashion. Cunning-

ham has created ephemeral photo essays since the 1980s. His feature "On the Street" has been an excellent source of what New Yorkers are wearing and what is hot and what is not. His photo essays incorporate everything from crocheted shawls to bicycle messenger bags, Easter bonnets, animal prints, bold-color winter coats, short pleated skirts,

6.17

FIG. 6.16 Designs by Mary Quant. [Courtesy, Fairchild Publications, Inc.]
FIG. 6.17 Jamel Shabazz's street fashion. [Reprinted with the permission of Jamel Shabazz.]

113

or preppy Burberry plaids. Cunningham usually takes at least 20 pictures, which to him indicate a trend has been created (Trebay, 9A).

High Fashion

High fashion is well represented in the designs of Karl Lagerfeld and, in the realm of furniture and interior design, in the work of Patrick Norguet, Hoh Lik Phong, and the exhibitors at the annual Milan Furniture Fair.

Karl Lagerfeld

Fashion designer Karl Lagerfeld has been designing and creating fashion trends for the past 50 years. He has created collections and ready-to-wear lines for Fendi, Chloe, Chanel, and his own label, Lagerfeld Gallery. Lagerfeld, with his 18th-century powdered ponytail and skintight jeans, is a dynamic force in the world of fashion (Figure 6.18). He has produced everything from soft and fluid collections showing the body's silhouette to beautifully tailored box jackets rich in texture and color. Lagerfeld's collections are inspired by everything from the Hell's Angels to high-tech futurism. His designs are a fusion of old and new. He has combined the traditional Chanel jacket with denim skirts (Figure 6.19), and fishnet stockings and lace-up boots with flowing skirts and leather jackets. Lagerfeld, a man of many talents, has said, "I'm interested in a lot of things other than fashion. I hate nothing more than people who only look in one direction, which means

6.18   6.19

only in their direction. My fashion would be a bore if I did this. I get excited by everything I don't know, I don't do, I couldn't do, I would like to do, or that other people do better" (as quoted in Hastreiter). Fashion aside, Lagerfeld's interests are interdisciplinary and include photography, book design, architecture, and furniture. Lagerfeld's eclectic living environments include a blend of furniture styles, which incorporate a Louis XVI bed, Biedermeier designs, and Ingo Maurer hologram lights.

Just as Poiret represented a synthesis between fashion and interior design at the beginning of the 20th century, so do Karl Lagerfeld and Patrick Norguet, discussed next. Based in Paris, they have deep roots in couture design and have successfully bridged the worlds of fashion, furniture, and interiors. Paris thus continues to be a fertile ground for the development of interdisciplinary design.

Patrick Norguet

Paris product and furniture designer Patrick Norguet is noted for his blending of the old and the new, fashion and furniture, as well as plastics and wood. Norguet began his career in design by creating windows— for Louis Vuitton, Givenchy, and Christian Dior. Norguet is responsible for designing the "Rainbow" chair for the Milan-based furniture manufacturer Cappellini. This chair is made of multicolored plates of metaacrylate joined

by ultrasound waves. More recently, Norguet designed the soft, organic form of the "Apollo" chair (Figure 6.20). Cappellini also manufactures the Apollo. Norguet is also designing branded images and interiors for the French automobile manufacturer Renault and the Lancel luggage company.

Hoh Lik Phong

With chairs once again being the focus, Hoh Lik

6.21

Phong is the designer and owner of a hotel in Singapore, the Hotel 1929. The hotel is located in Chinatown in an historic building that has been given "Conservation" building status. This unique boutique hotel has a fun, quirky style, with each room having its own designer chair (Figure 6.21). The interiors of the hotel are not ordinary since they feature glass bathrooms and dozens of chairs from Phong's personal collection. These chairs range from the classics to the unusual and are displayed and used throughout the hotel.

Milan Furniture Fair

The Milan Furniture Fair is a huge exhibition of the latest innovations in the furniture market. The 2004 fair featured the furniture designs of new, up-and- coming designers as well as familiar names like

6.20

FIG. 6.18 Designer Karl Lagerfeld. [Courtesy, Fairchild Publications, Inc.] FIG. 6.19 Karl Lagerfeld design (1993). [Courtesy, Fairchild Publications, Inc.] FIG. 6.20 The "Apollo" chair by Patrick Norguet for Artifort, Netherlands. [Reprinted with permission of Artifort.] FIG. 6.21 Guest rooms at Hotel 1929. [Courtesy, Hotel 1929.]

115

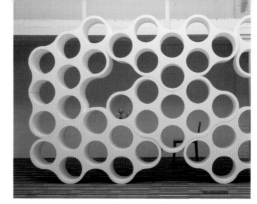

6.22a

Frank Gehry and Philippe Starck. What was most evident at the fair were the new materials and technologies used in the manufacturing processes. French designers Erwan and Ronan Bouroullec used a foamlike white plastic to create a modular, double-faced bookcase that when clipped together makes a room divider (Figure 6.22a). The clear, clean lines of Japanese designer Tokujin Yoshioka's "Kiss Me Goodbye" chair (Figure 6.22b), made of polycarbonate, and Dutch designer Peter Traag's "Sponge" chair (Figure 6.22c), utilizing polyurethane foam, were welcome additions to the fair. Reminiscent of the Eames fiberglass chair, the lightweight "Carbon" chair (Figure 6.22d) designed by Bertjan Pot and Marcel Wanders is made of a mixture of carbon fiber and epoxy. Architect Frank Gehry created "Superlight" (Figure 6.22e), an aluminum chair that is flexible and weighs only six and a half pounds, and Philippe Starck designed another lightweight carbon-fiber chair called the "Oscar Bon" chair (Figure 6.22f), which reminds us of the Eames/Saarinen "Conversation" armchair (see Figure 6.8). Using these inventive materials and methods to create curved and angular forms takes furniture to an exciting new level (Viladas, Farber, and Barbagelata).

6.22b

6.22c

6.22d

6.22e

6.22f

A Shared Aesthetic

Fashion, furniture, and architecture have developed a shared language of curves, color, shape, and texture that gives them an equally shared aesthetic. The use of a descriptive language overlaps the disciplines. We talk of ornamentation, fussy or clean lines, design being classic and timeless, and something having rich, warm elegance or being cold and stark. We discuss building a wardrobe or a structure and using the form or shape of a body or a building. Contemporary business suits can be boxy, and high-rise towers can be draped in fishnet. We combine antiques and modern in both buildings and fashion, using historical architectural or fashion details with modern shapes. When renovating an interior structure we might expose the bones of a building, thereby giving it a new, contemporary life. Or, we may deliberately build the "insides" of the structure on the exterior of the building, as architect's Renzo Piano and Richard Rogers did for the Pompidou Center in Paris (Figure 6.23).

Indeed, our most commonplace fashion accessories have been expressed in sculptural detail in central focal points in front of our most important new architectural statements. A *New York Times* photo essay by Bill Cunningham featured the "Extra Starch" that gives structure to the shape of collars, while "Collar and Bow," a sculpture created by pop artists Claes Oldenburg and Coosje van Bruggen, mimics the sweeping curves of Gehry's Disney Concert Hall in Los Angeles. "Collar and Bow" is intended to humanize the Concert Hall visitor's experience with some tongue-in-cheek everyday humor that exactly fits its setting. This sculpture will be constructed of fiberglass and steel and will be

6.23

installed in front of the hall in the near future. Whether or not the Concert Hall needs this extra sculpture is not at issue, but what is evident is that once again designers are drawing inspiration from the intimate but everyday elements of fashion and clothing and melding that aesthetic with the grandeur of a great and important structure.

As designers move forward in the new century, it appears that they will continue to attempt to create statements that resonate globally. They will continue to overlay techniques and methodology into designs and trends that are percolating up from every region of the world. Designers around the world now share a common language, thanks to the Internet and an integrated global economy that has the capacity to create fashion and furniture in copious amounts and in staggering styles, to store it and move it around the world with incredible speed, and to market it to an increasingly global consumer base.

FIG. 6.22 (a) Bookcase by Erwan and Ronan Bouroullec for Cappellini. (b) The "Kiss Me Goodbye" chair by Tokujin Yoshioka for Driade. (c) The "Sponge" chair by Peter Traag for Edra. (d) "Carbon" seating by Bertjan Pot and Marcel Wanders. (e) The "Superlight" chair by Frank Gehry for Emeco. (f) The "Oscar Bon" chair by Philippe Starck for Driade. [(a) Photo by Paul Tahon/Cappellini. (b, c, and d) Photos by Guido Barbagelata/Responsabile Realzioni Esterne EDRA spa. (e) Reprinted with permission of Emeco. (f) Reprinted with permission of Driade.] FIG. 6.23 The Pompidou Center in Paris, France, by Renzo Piano and Richard Rogers (1974–1976). [Copyright © Vanni/Art Resource, NY.]

CHAPTER SEVEN

Inspiration from Textiles

Everything Old Is New Again

Textiles have been part of culture and history ever since records have been kept. In written and oral accounts, in the form of pictorial representations, traditions having to do with fabric and its production have long been part of the development of civilizations. Because of the perishable nature of fabric, and hence the absence of actual materials, historians must often find evidence in images such as that in Figure 7.1, which shows a Greek vessel from 560 B.C.E. depicting weavers at a loom. Curiously, although numerous advances have been made in production and distribution, in many instances the fabrics that we use today for our clothing and environments are remarkably similar to those that were available hundreds of years ago. Technological progress has removed some of the drudgery of manufacturing, and synthetic materials have duplicated and improved upon some basic fibers, but counterbalancing the evolution of textiles for high-tech purposes is a revolution of sorts: Vintage clothing and textiles have never been more sought after. Whether a genuine 1960s Pucci print dress or a restoration fabric for drapery, old is good, authentic is admired, and vintage is most excellent.

The psychology of this phenomenon is a source for debate. Do we crave recognizable design successes from the past because we feel more comfortable with the known than the unknown? Is the ownership of an authentic textile part of our quest for status? Do we have nostalgia for a past that seems to have been a better time? Has the speed and ease of designing on the computer made it the equivalent of the industrial revolution, making us, like those involved in the Arts and Crafts movement of the late 19th century, long for products that were produced using techniques closer to "handmade"? Whatever the reasons for this phenomenon, the designers and manufacturers of textiles for use in apparel and interiors always have one eye on the past, and consumers are fascinated by vintage and collectible fabrics, associating quality and character with textiles from earlier times. To be able to assist their clients in capturing the qualities they desire and in order to understand the significance of contemporary developments in textiles, designers should have broad knowledge of textile history.

In Greek mythology, the idea of destiny is personified in the three fates, or goddesses, Clotho, Lachesis, and Atropos. According to that story, Clotho spins the thread of a person's life at birth, Lachesis

7.1

determines the length of the thread, and Atropos severs the thread at the moment of death (Trocmé, p. 13). This story illustrates how ancient and pervasive textile traditions have been, and how even our language demonstrates the lengthy international and multicultural saga of the development of fabric and fabric design. From the name of Clotho herself to the term for the patterned damask that reflects its connection with Damascus, Syria, to muslin, the plain-weave fabric from Mosul, now in Iraq, and to denim, which in the French *de Nîmes* reveals the city of its development as a woven textile, the study of textiles incorporates much of the history and geography of the world. Paisley is the name of a town in Scotland that was known for woven shawls patterned with the distinctive design that is known as paisley. Perhaps because of the production of cotton in India, and trade between Europe and India, many English textile terms originated in India—calico from the city of Calicut in Southern India and cashmere from goats from the Kashmir area of Asia. Kashmir referred also to floral and paisley pattern shawls used as wall hangings and as apparel.

There are many ways to describe textiles, but for the design professional it is important to be familiar with three major areas of description:

Substance, which answers the question, "What is the fabric made from?"

Structure, which answers the question, "How is the fabric made?"

Surface, which answers questions about the design on the face of the fabric.

The substance of a textile is its fiber content; the structure is the technique that is used to create it; and the surface is the application of design to the

7.2

fabric. While these three components will be considered separately, it is important to remember that it is the combination of these elements that gives a textile its characteristics. For example, a texture that is created in the structure of a fabric is also an element of its surface appearance. A substance such as silk can have a recognizable sheen that results from the fiber content but is also part of its surface appearance. As you gain knowledge of textiles, you will add to your design vocabulary so that a sample you describe for a client, such as that in Figure 7.2, is more than just a piece of fabric—it is a detail from a silk satin obi embroidered with silk and metallic thread.

Textile Substance: Fiber Content

As you study the overview of textile design presented here, it is important to remember that entire academic programs, industries, and careers are devoted to the investigation of this field. Perhaps this brief synopsis will arouse interest leading to further study.

In its broadest terms, the fiber content, or the substance from which a textile is made, is classified in one of two categories: It is either natural or manufactured.

Natural Fibers

A natural fiber is one that occurs in nature. The main categories are animal fibers, including silk from the cocoons of silkworms and wool from the hair of sheep, and vegetable fibers, including cotton from seedpods as well as linen from plant stems, or bast fibers. Other natural vegetable fibers are hemp, jute, and ramie. Natural mineral fibers include metallic threads such as gold, silver, and copper.

Silk

The first of the animal natural fibers that we will consider is silk. Because its origin is ancient and somewhat obscured by time, there has been abundant mythology about the development of silk. One of the most repeated legends is that as a Chinese princess sat in her garden, the cocoon of a silkworm fell from the mulberry tree's branches above her head into her cup of warm tea. As she picked it out of the cup, the cocoon unwound to produce a long filament of silk thread. Whatever the exact details of the "discovery" of silk, there is agreement that sericulture, the raising of silkworms and the processing of their cocoons for silk filament to be made into yarn and fabric, did originate more than four thousand years ago in China. By 1400 B.C.E., the cultivation and production of silk was highly sophisticated. The Silk Road refers to the path taken over land and sea to connect China to commercial trading centers in the Mediterranean, Red Sea, and Indian Ocean. The 13th-century travels of the Italian explorer Marco Polo and his father and uncle along these trading routes to visit the court of Kublai Khan, a journey that would be difficult even today, covering thousands of miles through deserts

FIG. 7.1 A terra cotta vessel with a loom and weaving scene (c. 500 B.C.E.) testifies to the long history of textile production. [Copyright © The Metropolitan Museum of Art. All rights reserved.] FIG. 7.2 Obi with carp, duckweed, and waves (detail) (late 18th century–early 19th century). Silk and metallic thread embroidery on green silk satin by Marubeni Corporation. [Copyright © 1992 Marubeni American Corporation. All rights reserved. Note card design © 1992 by Museum Associates, Los Angeles County Museum of Art.]

and over steep mountain passes, are a source of wonder (and some skepticism) even in our 21st century. Figure 7.3 shows the large landmass that stretches from China through the Middle East to Western Europe, and it is easy to trace the path of early traders, nomadic peoples, and travelers across this expanse.

According to Mary Schoeser, Middle Easterners brought the cultivation and weaving of silk to southern Italy in the 11th and 12th centuries (*World Textiles*, p. 76). From 1300 to 1600 the art and craft of silk

7.3

weaving developed to a great extent in Europe (Joyce, p. 12), and by the middle of the 17th century, Lyons, France, became the center of silk production (Lebeau). These beautiful silks produced at Lyons were in high demand as diplomatic gifts from one leader to another throughout the royal courts of Europe.

Silk has a luxurious feel and it drapes well. It takes dye well, although it fades when exposed to light. Several varieties of silk have an irregular surface appearance, such as doupioni, tussah, and raw silk. Silk is often used in apparel for special occasions and in upscale interiors.

Wool

Wool is an animal fiber produced from the coat, or fleece, of sheep. As with silk, there is an abundance of mythology about the origins of wool. At some point in our early education most of us are exposed to the legend of Jason and the Argonauts or to a similar heroic fable. A fleece of gold is stolen and Jason must retrieve it and safeguard it or risk losing everything. To do so, he builds a ship called the *Argo*, and he recruits sailors who become the Argonauts. After a long voyage fraught with perils comparable to that of Frodo in J.R.R. Tolkien's *Lord of the Rings*, Jason is successful. The ancient story of the protection of the golden fleece has been used to illustrate the importance of wool, which does have a long history. There is evidence that wool was used by Mesopotamian cultures along the banks of the Euphrates River in what is now Iraq, in the fourth century B.C.E. (Joyce, p. 12). Moreover, it was certainly made into felt before it was used in woven fabrics, because in order to have the strength to be made into yarn, the fibers have to be spun.

In *The Mummies of Urümchi*, Elizabeth Wayland Barber describes the clothing and textiles found at ancient gravesites in western China. Of the many fascinating points in this story—including the complexity of the weaves and the intensity of the colors of these woolen textiles—both woven and felted, that have been dated to the Bronze Age, about four thousand years ago, is the description of the mummies as having not Asian but Caucasian features, indicating that people were migrating through the East and West for many centuries.

It is thought that in Western Europe, sheep were raised in the British Isles before they were invaded by the Romans in the year 43 C.E., and that the Romans had wool factories in Britain to supply their armies with clothing and blankets (Trocmé, p. 13). England, Scotland, and Ireland became centers of wool production, and in market towns throughout

England, there are stories of competitions to produce a coat beginning from the fleece through the yarn production and weaving, cutting, and sewing, in the shortest amount of time. The process is diagrammed in Figure 7.4. There are several specialty animal fibers related to wool, such as mohair, camel hair, cashmere, and the fur of the camelid, which includes alpaca, llama, and vicuña.

Wool provides warmth and good insulation, and it does not hold static electricity, which makes it a good choice for carpets and other interior uses. It is warm and soft to the touch, has good elasticity, is lightweight in relation to the amount of warmth it provides, and does not absorb water. These qualities contribute to its popularity for cool-weather apparel.

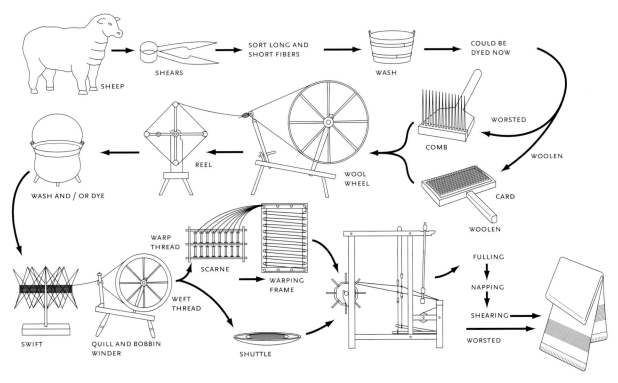

7.4

FIG. 7.3 Map of the Silk Road showing the path from China through the Middle East to Western Europe. FIG. 7.4 Processes in the transition of wool from fleece to fabric. [Based on *The Textile Tools of Colonial Homes* by M. Channing, Marion, MA: Channing Books & Whaleship Plans, 1971, p. iv.]

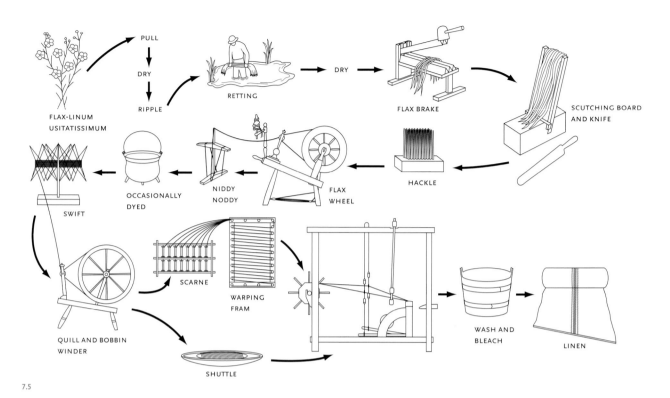

PULL

DRY

RIPPLE

FLAX-LINUM
USITATISSIMUM

RETTING

DRY

FLAX BRAKE

SCUTCHING BOARD
AND KNIFE

SWIFT

OCCASIONALLY
DYED

NIDDY
NODDY

FLAX
WHEEL

HACKLE

QUILL AND BOBBIN
WINDER

SCARNE

WARPING
FRAM

SHUTTLE

WASH AND
BLEACH

LINEN

7.5

Linen

Linen is probably the oldest fiber to be developed into fabric. Linen comes from the stem of the flax plant, and the whole group of linen and flax fibers are called *bast fibers*, referring to the inner part of the flax bark. These vegetable fibers are all processed in a similar way, which involves alternately dampening and drying the fibers so that they can be separated from the outer bark of the plant stems. This process is diagrammed in Figure 7.5. Cultivation of flax in what is now Iraq and Iran has been dated to 5000 B.C.E., and to 3000 B.C.E. in Syria and Egypt (Schoeser, *World Textiles*, p. 15). Flax has been cultivated for linen production in many areas of the world, and the process of making linen is very labor-intensive. Linens originating in Northern Europe,

including Belgium and Ireland, have been famous for their quality. Like wool, linen fiber has a wide range of sizes, and in general, long, thin fibers produce the best-quality fabrics.

It is misleading, and sometimes confusing, that the term *linens* is used to refer to the entire category of household items for bed, kitchen, and bath even if they are not made from linen fiber. This probably has to do with the fact that because of its characteristics, linen became synonymous with the kinds of soft, strong, absorbent, and easily washable fabrics that were needed for domestic use.

Linen is very strong; in fact, it is stronger when wet than when dry. It is very absorbent and dries quickly, and it is smooth and cool to the touch. These charac-

7.6

teristics make linen a popular fabric choice for table-cloths and napkins and for warm-climate apparel.

Cotton

Although Egyptian cotton has a revered place in textile history because of the fine quality of its fibers, evidence that cotton was cultivated and processed into textiles in ancient times has also been found in both India and in Peru. Cotton is the soft, fluffy fiber that lines the seed case of the cotton plant. To be used in textiles, cotton requires a lot of processing, first to be picked from the seed case and separated from the remaining seed, even before it

can be made into yarn. Separation from the seed is called *ginning* and the invention of the cotton gin in 1793 made it possible for a person to clean in one day as much cotton as had previously taken a year to clean (Weissman, p. 9). The scene in Figure 7.6 depicts the export of cotton across the Atlantic during the 19th century.

Cotton is strong, absorbent, and dries quickly, but it is prone to shrink. There are many different types of cotton, from the short fibers that are used in pillow stuffing to the very long and luxurious fibers of the "Sea Island cottons" (derived from the Egyptian species brought to the United States) that make

FIG. 7.5 The processing of linen from plant to fabric. [Based on *The Textile Tools of Colonial Homes* by M. Channing, Marion, MA: Channing Books & Whaleship Plans, 1971, p. v.] FIG. 7.6 The weighing of bales of cotton on the docks of Norfolk, VA, in preparation for export (1905). [Copyright © The Art Archive/Culver Pictures.]

high-quality textiles. These high-quality fabrics are used in upscale apparel and interior applications such as lightweight men's shirtings and luxury sheets and draperies, while the average and low-quality textiles are used in budget clothing and towels.

Manufactured Fibers

The manufactured fibers include those that are chemically produced, as opposed to being found in their natural state. The categories of manufactured fibers include those that are organic, such as the cellulose that is used to produce rayon, viscose, and acetate, and those that are synthetic, such as the chemical compounds that are the source of acrylic, nylon, polyamides, and polyesters. Included with these are the recycled fibers made from polythene beverage containers that are made into recycled fabrics such as the branded Polartec and Thinsulate.

Organic Manufactured Fibers

The first of the manufactured cellulose fibers, made from wood pulp, was viscose, which was developed toward the end of the 19th century in France. The first viscose yarn was exhibited in 1900 at the Paris International Exhibition. Rayon was the name adopted by the Americans in 1924. Rayon and acetate are cellulose fibers made from a process of converting cellulose into a liquid and then pushing it through tiny holes in a nozzle. Strands come out as a continuous filament and, like silk unraveled from a cocoon, do not require spinning, but can be further processed into spun yarns. Fabrics made from manufactured fibers are often the focus of advertising campaigns by the chemical companies that manufacture them. For example, Celanese featured champion skater Kristi Yamaguchi in its campaign to promote its acetate fiber, and her active, glamorous image supported the positive features of acetate (Figure 7.7).

These organic manufactured fibers take color extremely well; textiles made from them drape well and are durable for both apparel and interior uses. They are versatile in that filament rayon and acetate can have the appearance of silk, yet spun rayon can have the soft feel of cotton. Their durability makes them a good choice for interior spaces that are exposed to light and for elegant apparel at a mid-range price point.

Synthetic Manufactured Fibers

Synthetic fibers are made from compounds that do not exist naturally but are manufactured by a chemical process. The first synthetic fiber was

7.7

7.8

126

ducted in laboratories in New York and London, that led to the acronym NYLON (Trocmé, p. 72).

Polyester was introduced in 1946 under the trade name Dacron (Schoeser, *Fabrics and Wallpapers*, p. 22). Its early uses in textiles for apparel during the 1960s and 1970s brought some stunning failures as the first commercially produced polyester fabrics were low quality, uncomfortable, and difficult to clean. Most of these early problems have been solved, and the polyesters produced today are highly sought after for a multitude of uses. Acrylic is another synthetic that is often used in apparel and household items, where its similarity to wool has contributed to its popularity in sweaters and blankets.

Fabrics made from manufactured fibers are strong and durable, wrinkle-resistant, and quick-drying. Nylon has excellent elasticity. Acrylic is resistant to sunlight, so it has many interior and exterior uses. Polyester can be mixed with other fibers, such as cotton, before being made into yarn, so the resulting fabric is a *blend*. Manufactured fibers are finding many uses in the high-tech and activewear markets, where the positive aspects of their durability outweigh some of the negative connotations of having a petrochemical base and being nonbiodegradable. Patagonia, the California-based sport apparel company, has developed PCR fleece, a high-performance fabric made from used soda bottles.

nylon, which became available commercially in 1939 and replaced silk in women's stockings, which were required legwear during this era. Figure 7.8 shows a group of women from the post–World War II era, excitedly showing off the nylon stockings they were able to purchase after wartime shortages and restrictions had ended.

There are many theories for the source of the name "nylon." One is that as the term described a research project that was started in 1927 by E.I. Dupont de Nemours and Company and was con-

FIG. 7.7 Kristi Yamaguchi at the closing ceremony of the 2002 Winter Olympic Games in Salt Lake City, wearing a fabric of manufactured fibers especially suited for activewear. [Copyright © Getty Images.] FIG. 7.8 Women showing nylon stockings purchased at a hosiery shop in New York City in the 1940s, as wartime shortages began to ease. [Copyright © Bettmann/Corbis.]

The Structure of Textiles

In order for the fibers described in the previous section to be utilized, even after they are made into yarns, techniques must be applied to them to provide stability. These techniques form the structure of textiles, and they provide additional characteristics such as color, texture, and performance. To give color to a fabric, the fiber can be dyed before or after spinning into yarn; the fabric can be dyed before or after construction. If the fabric is dyed or painted after structure is made, it is called piece dye. If the yarn is dyed before the fabric is constructed, it is called yarn dye. The texture of a fabric is determined by the interaction of the size and quality of the fibers used with the construction methods. A textile's performance is dependent on the fiber's inherent qualities, the fabric construction techniques, and the appropriateness of the end use to which it is put.

Early Methods: Pressure and Linking

Before people employed tools to assist them in fabric construction, the techniques used to make textiles involved either pressure or some form of linking. Types of pressure include pounding or matting, and some early fabrics produced in this way include bark cloths, produced by soaking layers of tree bark and pounding it until the fibers break down and entangle. Felt is also produced by pressure and is a very early textile form, brought about by a combination of heat, moisture, and friction causing wool to become matted. The result is a warm and water-resistant cloth. If you have ever accidentally

7.9

put a wool sweater through the hot cycle on a washer and dryer, you have probably experienced the making of felt!

Thatching, plaiting, braiding, looping, knotting, and netting are early forms of textile construction that are based on linking. In these techniques, a fiber or yarn is interlaced either on itself or with another strand. Lace-making is related to these techniques;

even though its patterns are extremely complicated, it is still based on the twisting and looping of threads. Basketry is an example of plaiting, and it was probably the precursor of weaving. When flexible fibers such as linen and cotton were developed into yarns, a structure was needed to support them; that structure was the loom. The practice of spinning and weaving has been traced to ancient Egypt, along the Nile Valley, and pieces of linen fabrics have been dated to 5000 B.C.E. (Held). Figure 7.9 shows a copy of an Egyptian wall painting from the 19th century B.C.E., depicting women at work weaving and spinning.

Weaving

The process of weaving has changed little over the years, and although weaving equipment has become highly mechanized, it is still possible to experience the methods used in early weaving. Essentially, woven fabric is made on a loom using two sets of threads, the warp and the weft, or *filling* yarns. Generally, the warp threads are affixed to the frame of the loom from the top or back to the bottom or front, and held under some tension. The weft or filling yarn is interlaced across the warp. The edges of the fabric are called *selvages* and are often set up with extra threads for additional durability. The pattern of the weave is determined by the way the warp threads are arranged on the loom and the sequence in which they are crossed by the weft. Texture and color are important elements in the appeal of fabrics, and the many variations of these elements provide limitless inspiration to textile designers.

Textiles can be differentiated by their fiber content and weave structure. The weave structure gives texture to a fabric and affects the selection of the end use to which a fabric might be put. Smooth, strong fabrics constructed in basic weaves provide durable fabrics appropriate for apparel and interiors. They are used plain or as a background for designs added by printing. Patterned weaves show intricate detail that is structurally embedded in the fabric.

Basic Weaves

The basic weaves are plain weave, twill weave, and satin weave. Plain weave is the simplest and most basic weave, in which weft yarns pass alternately over and under the warp. Basket weave is a variation of plain weave, and is made when two or more filling yarns pass over and under two or more warp yarns. Twill weave is identified by the diagonal line on the face of the fabric. A familiar twill weave is seen in denim fabric in which the diagonal is visible because the warp is typically blue, while the filling yarn is white. Satin weave normally has a shiny and smooth surface, which is produced because only the warp or the weft is visible, not both. Patterned weaves include damask and brocade.

One of the least complex structures of weaving, yet one that has produced some of the most splendid examples of decorative art of textiles, is the tapestry weave. It is essentially a plain weave, but one in which the warp is completely concealed so that only the patterns created by the weft are visible. It is a "discontinuous" weft, one that can start and stop across the width of the textile, thus offering many

FIG. 7.9 "About Women (De Gynacaeo)" from the encyclopedia *De Universo* by Rabanus Maurus (c. 780–856). [Copyright © A.M. Rosati/Art Resource, NY.]

opportunities for pictorial design. The word *tapestry* was originally used to describe any type of wall hanging, whether woven or embroidered (Figure 7.10). As we understand it today, tapestry refers to a weaving technique but also describes a wall hanging in which the threads form a picture. Although it has a long history, tapestry weaving continues as a form of contemporary art.

During the Renaissance, between about 1300 and 1600, the art of tapestry weaving was important in both France and Belgium, and the French cities of Aubusson and Gobelin were principal tapestry weaving centers in the 17th century, so much so that tapestries are referred to by these names to indicate the weaving techniques used. After the French Revolution (1789) tapestry as an art form declined, but tapestries from this period can be seen in museums around the world. Many of the

tapestries of the Renaissance have religious themes. In addition, some of the most detailed and intricate examples of the art of tapestry weaving show historic events and serve as documentation of the ideas that were important to wealthy people of this era. For example, "The Astronomers," shown in Figure 7.11, is from a set of tapestries titled "The Story of the Emperor of China," which was woven between 1697 and 1705. It confirms not only the interest of Europeans in what they considered to be the exotic and mysterious Far East but also their interest in astronomy.

Far from Renaissance Europe, another form of tapestry weaving was that practiced by the Native American Navajo people. The technique was adapted from the Pueblo tribes, who were using this method to make blankets and rugs prior to the arrival of the Spanish. Navajo textiles are

7.10

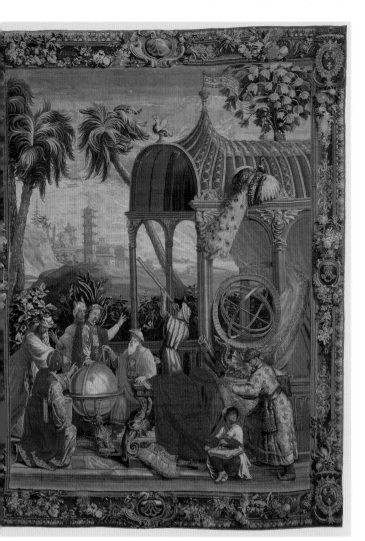

tern used for aprons, tablecloths, and napkins. Madras is a plaid fabric in plain weave that is named for the location of its origin in India. It is usually cotton and is typically woven using strong colors. Tartan is a plaid fabric in twill weave, of which there are many variations, some more authentic than others. It originated as an apparel fabric used in Scottish kilts, and each tartan was a very specific pattern that identified the wearer as belonging to a certain family or clan. Dobby describes a plain fabric with a simple geometric pattern such as a small diamond or fleur-de-lis woven into it that is repeated and closely spaced. Dobby also refers to the loom attachment that allows these small patterns to be woven.

highly prized today by owners and collectors. Figure 7.12 shows a Navajo blanket woven between 1860 and 1863, known as the "Chief White Antelope Blanket."

Other than its tapestry variation, plain weave has relatively little surface interest and is most often used as a background for printed designs. Stripe and plaid fabrics can be plain weave, with the surface interest created by color variation in the weft (horizontal stripes) or warp (vertical stripes) or changes in the warp in combination with changes in weft to form a plaid. Gingham is a plain-weave check with two colors of warp and filling yarn. It is a classic pat-

FIG. 7.10 Detail of the Bayeux Tapestry, "Horses Tumbling in a Swamp," which depicts the Battle of Hastings (Centre Guillaume le Conquerant, Bayeux, France). [Copyright © Erich Lessing/Art Resource, NY.] FIG. 7.11 The tapestry "The Astronomers" from the series "The Story of the Emperor of China" (1697–1705). [Copyright © The J. Paul Getty Museum.] FIG. 7.12 The "Chief White Antelope Blanket" (1860–1863). [Reprinted with permission of the Indian Arts Research Center at the School of American Research.]

Patterned Weaves

Although complex patterned weaves were hand-made prior to the mechanization of textile production, these textiles were relatively scarce and made only for royalty or the wealthy. Fabrics such as damasks and brocades were made more readily available after the introduction of the Jacquard loom in 1801. Damask, typically a two-color floral design, which was produced in Syria from the fourth century and in Europe from the 15th, is distinctive because its pattern is reversible. Brocade is similar to damask in that the design is produced entirely by the weave structure, but in brocade, additional filling yarns are added to supplement the pattern with areas of additional color. The Jacquard loom, shown in Figure 7.13, has been referred to as the first computer because the woven patterns were controlled by a series of cards with holes punched in them. Not really a loom but an elaborate addition, the Jacquard attachment was affixed to both weaving looms and knitting machines to increase productivity in the production of complex patterns.

Knitting

Besides weaving, knitting is the most common structure of textiles. Although it may be related to the ancient network systems used in Peru well before the arrival of Europeans in South America, knitting needles have not been found there. Most of the Peruvian networks are structured with consecutive loops or knots. Figure 7.14 shows the structure of the looped network compared with the knit stitch produced with needles.

Because of the looped structure of knit, it is a flexible textile. One of the first uses of the knit structure in apparel was for articles of clothing that

7.13

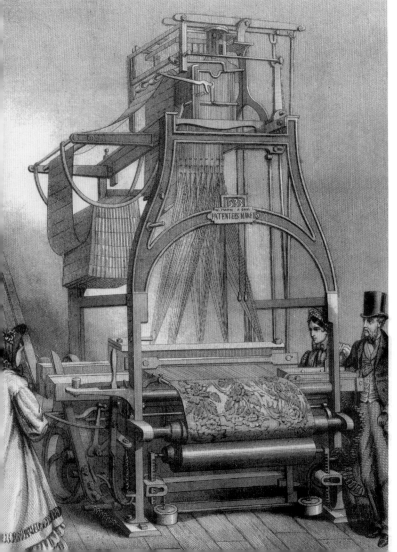

7.14

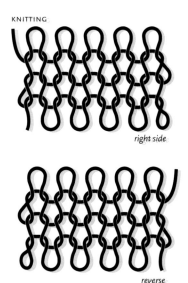

KNITTING

right side

reverse

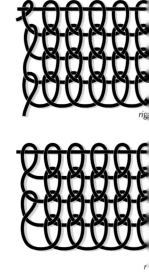

LOOPING

ri

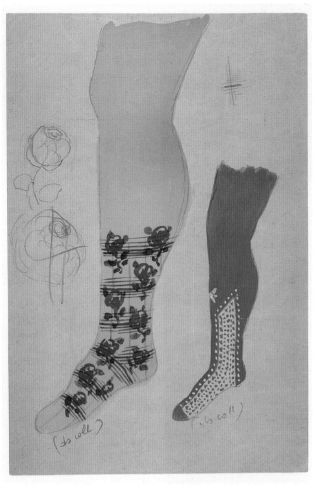

7.15

changed so that apparel, especially women's clothing, had to be less restrictive and allow more freedom of movement. The characteristics of knit fabric fit perfectly with this trend toward comfort, and developments in machinery to produce knit fabrics led to lower costs and increased popularity. There are basically two types of knit textile products, piece goods and full-fashioned products. Piece goods refers to yardage that is produced for apparel manufacturers who cut and sew garments from it. Because of the looped structure of knit textiles, it has not been used extensively in interiors; however, with the development of fine yarns and fine-gauge machinery, sheer curtains and other drapery fabrics are increasingly being produced using knit technology. Besides yardage, knits are manufactured as finished products, such as socks, hosiery, T-shirts, and sweaters that come off the knitting machines virtually completed. At the beginning of the 20th century, machine-knit fabrics were still primarily used for hosiery and lingerie. At the beginning of the 21st century, most of us live almost completely in knits for casual clothing, and knit textiles are gradually finding more popularity for interior uses. Fine, strong yarns have been developed that increase the durability of these fabrics for sheer draperies and backing fabrics for upholstery.

required flexibility for movement—socks and hosiery. The stocking frame was invented in England in 1589, when hand-knit silk stockings were very fashionable. Fancy silk stockings for men and women were produced in France in the 17th century (Figure 7.15). But it was not until the further mechanization of knitting and the development of suitable yarns that knit fabric became the important textile construction that it is today.

After World War I ended in 1918, lifestyles

The fundamental knit constructions are weft knit and warp knit, and each of these produces different types of fabrics. While either construction can produce a plain or jersey knit, weft knits can produce the rib knit, which includes double knit and interlock, as well as links and links, which creates a texture by creating a variety of stitches. Weft knit-

FIG. 7.13 The Smith Brothers patented Jacquard Power Loom (1862 engraving). [Copyright © The Art Archive/Culver Pictures.] FIG. 7.14 Comparison of knitting and looping. [Based on *Textiles of Ancient Peru and Their Techniques* by Raoul D'Harcourt, Seattle: University of Washington, 1962, p. 104.] FIG. 7.15 The "Album de modèles" (c. 1880) shows women's silk, jersey stockings. [Copyright © Laurent Sully Jaulmes Les Arts dècoratifs/Musèe de la Mode et du Textile, Paris. All rights reserved.]

ting uses one continuous horizontal strand of yarn; it includes circular knits, which are produced in a tube for T-shirts and socks, and flat knits, which are produced in flat shapes that are sewn together to make a garment. Warp knits, by contrast, have at least one strand of yarn per needle and are produced on vertical beams, similar to the warp on a loom. The major types of warp knits are tricot, which is usually a plain knit, and raschel, which produces a variety of surface textures including lacy effects.

Other Structural Effects

Velvet, corduroy, chenille, velour, and terry cloth belong to a category of fabrics that are looped pile or cut pile. Fabrics with these surface characteristics can be produced by either weaving or knitting, and they are used extensively for apparel and interior applications.

Lace is another category of specialized fabrics. Although lace is sometimes included with gauze weaves, in structure it has more in common with knitting than weaving, based on patterns of looped and crossed threads. Antique lace, or lace with a vintage appearance, is very popular in apparel and interior uses, and handmade or early machine lace or antique linens with lace trim are highly prized.

Textile Surface Design

Textile surface is created either by application of an embellishment such as embroidery, by the manipulation of threads during the process of construction, or by painting or printing. The art of ornamenting textile fabrics was one of the earliest of human inventions, and probably had to do with those ever-present human characteristics, vanity and the pursuit of status. There are many historical references to the embroidery of textiles for important members of society and to the ornamentation of religious vestments. The Babylonian cultures were known to value embroidery, and the technique of surface decoration with stitching spread throughout the Mediterranean. With the rise of the Persian empire in the sixth century B.C.E. until its decline in the sixth century C.E., decorative textile arts were practiced in ancient Persia, and woven tapestries were produced and exported to other parts of the ancient world, including the Roman empire, which adopted of many of the textile techniques practiced by the people it conquered.

Occasionally, structure and surface are so interconnected that they cannot be described separately. For example, the pleated and crinkled structures created by Mariano Fortuny, Mary McFadden, and Issey Miyake all beg the question of surface versus structure. Fortuny's pleating process for his silk evening gowns remains a mystery to this day, even though they were made in the 1920s and 1930s, and the permanent pleating of this natural fiber has not been replicated since. Two of the Fortuny gowns are pictured in Figure 7.16. Mary McFadden also works with a pleating technique, although her designs are executed in a synthetic fabric, and while the gowns are exquisite, the thermal effects used to produce these fabrics are better understood. Figure 7.17 shows an evening gown designed by Mary McFadden in the late 1970s–early 1980s.

7.16

7.17

Quilts, Needlework, and Coverlets

The textile arts that are recognized to be traditionally American cover a wide range of styles and techniques and are sources of inspiration for designers. These techniques include combinations of appliqué and embroidery known as *broderie perse*, pictured in Figure 7.18, in which motifs are cut from chintz and sewn to a backing fabric; traditional patchwork quilting, in which patterns are made from pieces of fabrics in different colors and patterns; and embroidered samplers, which feature a variety of stitches, usually spelling out the alphabet, numbers, various decorative motifs, and the name of the maker.

The textile skills of earlier generations of American women also included knitting, spinning and weaving, lace making, and rug hooking. From the colonial era until the present, masterpieces of creative expression have been created through needle-work, quilts, and coverlets. Although these skills are no longer the necessity that they once were, art quilts and quilt guilds are a feature of contemporary life.

Printed Textiles

Many of the most recognizable textiles are those with printed surface designs. In describing a textile design, the motif is the basic image, the layout is the arrangement of the motif, and the colorway is the selection of colors. Fabric prints are sometimes classified into groups of patterns identifiable by motif, such as floral, geometric, pictorial, ethnic, abstract, or novelty. This is not an exact science, but it is a convention to enable designers to have a vocabulary of design themes.

Most of us are familiar with the printed textiles that we use, live with, and wear every day, but these

FIG. 7.16 Mariano Fortuny's "Delphos" gowns. Fortuny's pleating process remains a mystery. [Reprinted with permission of Kent State University. Gift of Mrs. Susan G. Rossbach (left) and gift of Mrs. Miriam Whitney Coletti (right). Photo by Anne Bissonnette.] FIG. 7.17 Pleated evening gown with belt by Mary McFadden (1970s–1980s). [Reprinted with permission of Kent State University. Gift of Joanne Toor Cummings. Photo by Anne Bissonnette.]

7.18   7.19   7.20

were preceded by very sophisticated forms of printed textile surface design, such as those seen in Japan during the Edo period (1600–1868). The practice of traditional *shibori* methods of tie-and-dye produced stunning examples of fabrics that functioned as works of art. In the technique of shibori, a design is created by tying, sometimes individually wrapping, small pebbles in tiny bundles, dyeing the fabric, and then untying to reveal a pattern in the areas that dye has not penetrated. One of these is shown in Figure 7.19, a vibrant design created on silk.

Other sophisticated methods of fabric surface design include batik, in which wax is used to allow areas of fabric to resist dyes, *devoré* or burnout velvet effects, in which a design is created by the removal of surface areas on the fabric, and many other techniques that fall into the category of textile art because they are produced as one of a kind or in very limited production.

Dyed and block-printed cottons from India were popular in France and England in the 17th and 18th centuries. The term *indiennage* refers to hand-printed cottons from the south of France that took their inspiration from textiles produced in India. This style of fabric is still available in the south of France, and is a sought-after souvenir for travelers to that region. Originally, wood blocks were used as stamps to create patterns, but these were replaced by copper plates that had been used for printing books on paper. Using these copper plates, the pattern repeat size could be larger and include finer detail. *Toiles de Jouy* were cotton fabrics with a single color design printed by this method, and were named for Jouy-en-Josas, near

7.21

7.22

Versailles, France, where many were produced. Toiles were also produced in Ireland, where a larger repeat size enabled vignettes of life to be represented on fabric. Romantic scenes or those depicting country life are popular motifs, and toile maintains its popularity now in both apparel and interior fabrics. Box 7.1 describes the crossover between apparel and interior uses of these traditional printed fabrics. Figure 7.20 shows an example of toile.

Another popular style of printed cotton is chintz. Chintz originated with printed cotton imported into Europe from India, and the name derives from the Indian *chitta*. It is thought that the painting of designs may have originated to disguise imperfections in the fabrics or to simulate the appearance of decorative embroidery. Figure 7.21 shows a floral design imitating embroidery from the 1750s or 1760s. Whatever the reason for their popularity, these printed cotton fabrics with mostly floral designs became very fashionable and were produced throughout France, England, and America. Chintz is recognizable not only for its signature multicolor floral designs but also for the polished or glazed surface of the fabric. For nearly four centuries, the popularity of chintz has come and gone, and it remains a classic printed fabric.

Many of the toile and chintz designs available today are reproductions or variations of historic designs, such as the cabbage rose and floral motifs designed by William Kilburn in 1792 (Figure 7.22).

There are many levels of interest in fabric designs from the past, ranging from authentic

FIG. 7.18 This example of the combination of embroidery and appliqué is known as *broderie perse* (c. 1855). [Reprinted with permission of the Charleston Museum. Photo by Carlton Palmer.] FIG. 7.19 This butterfly design pattern was created using traditional Japanese shibori, which is a tie-and-dye technique. FIG. 7.20 A bed hanging made of toile. [Copyright © Philadelphia Museum of Art/Corbis.] FIG. 7.21 A chintz design that imitates embroidery from the middle of the 18th century. [Reprinted with permission of V&A Images/Victoria and Albert Museum.] FIG. 7.22 A chintz pattern designed by William Kilburn (1792). [Reprinted with permission of the Victoria & Albert Museum.]

BOX 7.1

What's Good Enough for the Couch Is Good Enough for the Closet: Toile de Jouy prints cross over from home decor to trendy duds.

By Valli Herman-Cohen

Sometimes, blending in with the wallpaper is a great way to stand out in fashion. This spring, apparel and home furnishings merged with such speed that the gap that once separated the two became nearly imperceptible. Suddenly, trendy scenesters and hip interior designers were of the same mind. Toile de Jouy, an almost fussy print of 18th century scenes, got hot.

"The environment of the body and the environment of the home have totally converged," said Fran Sude, creative director of Design Options, a Los Angeles-based color and trend forecasting company. About three years ago, Sude noticed that "not only are the colors crossing over, but the prints and the trends are." Sofas and skirts of late have shared everything from chambray and chenille to chalk stripes and tapestry.

New York designer Miguel Adrover illustrated the high-fashion potential of castoff upholstery in his fall 2000 debut collection, which included a coat made from neighbor Quentin Crisp's mattress ticking. Though high-fashion designers have marched on to new prints for fall, namely 1960s Marimekko, mainstream fashion collections and many more home furnishings makers are fixated on the toile prints of the 1760s.

This fall, many more affordable versions of toile will be showing up on skirts and handbags, as well as home furnishings from such companies as Anthropologie and clothier J. Jill. Though some of the finest examples of the print can cost more than $200 for a yard of upholstery material, a range of makers offers it for less than $30 a yard, not a bad price for a piece of history.

Toile de Jouy was named for the town near Versailles,

France, where Christopher Philip Oberkampf created single-color prints with finely engraved copper plates. He introduced scenes that represented the time period, such as groups of aristocrats or peasants in activities associated with their 18th-century lives. The storytelling quality of the scenes derived from the printing process, said Brunschwig and Fils company archivist Judy Straeten. "This was technique that was coming out of books," she said. "The first use of copper plates on fabrics was on toile."

Today, those scenes of hunters, historic moments, or simple pastoral pleasures have become both quaint and hip. Then and now, the fabric was used mostly for interior decoration, and some for apparel. Its latest resurgence began last October when designers Suzanne Clements and Ignacio Ribiero put toile in their first collection for the French sportswear firm Cacharel.

They not only launched a 21st-century revival of the print, but also of the fashion house, which will likely make toile part of the new corporate image. The British designers updated the antique print by cutting it into slim hiphugger slacks, zippered skirts and cheery accessories that mixed with ginghams, Oriental prints and even western shirts. Now the look is coming to your local mall.

A longtime staple, it was easy for the home decor market to seize upon toile almost immediately. Shelter magazines from the homey *Country Living* to the hip *Elle Décor* and *House & Garden* promoted it in ads and editorials, often mixed with ginghams, checks and plaids. Nationwide, interior designers have witnessed a renewed interest in patterns once reserved for the most traditional homes. "Just the last couple of months, several people have asked for it," said Torrance interior designer Ellen Cantor.

Though the prints are most often on plain cream or white backgrounds, they are nevertheless fairly complex and intense, making some of them unsuitable for small spaces. No problem. Pillow makers sometimes feature a single scene or offer them as powerful accents. With subjects that can range from floral bouquets to Napoleon's conquest of Egypt, the patterns of all sizes also have long been popular for papering walls, covering windows or adding an arty, European feel to home decor.

"Many new homes are very large, mega-mansions," said Cantor. "With lots of architectural details, a lot of them look like they are French or Italian villas. In order to decorate them properly, they are looking to period patterns."

Cantor client Susan Tyssee of Huntington Beach chose several toile patterns for her new Redondo Beach home. "It's very crisp and fresh looking," she said, "but it also has a kind of vintage feeling to it at the same time." Her husband has vetoed any all-toile rooms, so Tyssee and Cantor are using the patterns mostly as accents. "It becomes too heavy when the whole room is done in it," Tyssee said. But she likes the look: "I wouldn't mind having a skirt in it."

Consumers this spring were of the same mind. "It was one of the few things that sold well this season, in terms of apparel, accessories or home," said David Wolfe, creative director of New York-based trend forecasting firm Doneger Design Direction. Toile prints are continuing for fall, he said, though often with nontraditional, darker backgrounds. Toile's sudden acceptance illustrates how easily trend information is shared between different users of textiles.

"I think home furnishings are moving at the same speed as apparel," Wolfe said. The proliferation of fashion designers with their own lines of home fashions has aided the crossover. "In the past, Bill Blass apparel had nothing to do with Bill Blass home furnishings," Wolfe said. "Now they make sure that the home furnishings relate very closely to the image the apparel projects."

Having designer labels outside the closet appeals to many consumers. "People are having more fun with their homes, and home fashions always fit," said Wolfe. "You don't have to worry that your couch is going to gain weight."

What's more, a designer suit can cost as much as a leather couch, causing people to refocus.

"The clothing industry is downsizing," said Sude. "Clothing is becoming secondary as more people invest in homes, kids, cars. What is interesting is that the same culture[s] that used to go out of the home to entertain now are entertaining in their homes. They want the home to be like what the outside environment used to be."

Once inside, the line between clothing and sheets often blurs, a trend that mail-order firm Garnet Hill has explored as its designers swap print patterns for sheets, pajamas, dresses and more. Their cooperation isn't so much "a strategic calculation of matching this sheet with that sweater but a cross-pollination of the same sensibility and design approach," said Sarah Santa Maria, Garnet Hill's fashion designer.

"If a piece of artwork is gorgeous and we feel it is special, then the design can look beautiful on a sheet and sophisticated on the right piece of fashion." The company's best-selling linen dress this spring featured a passion rose pattern that's slated for flannel sheets this winter.

Tying trends into the fickle fashion market poses some risks for home furnishings makers, who still have a slower turnaround and often more conservative customers. Garnet Hill skipped toile this season and next because they already offered toile flannel sheets four years ago. They weren't a hit with consumers, who had yet to benefit from fashion's latest endorsement. Their python-print sheets got a cool reception, too. Seems no one really liked the idea of crawling under the covers with a snake.

reproduction to sources of inspiration for contemporary versions. If a fabric is being used in a restoration, for example for reupholstery of an antique, it is important that the modern textile replicates the original as accurately as possible. In authentic reproductions, the fibers and the fabric width and every feature of the design are duplicated. In the use of historic designs as inspiration for contemporary fabrics, research forms the basis for designs that can then vary greatly from the originals, suggesting the past without documenting it in every detail. Textile designers for both apparel and interior fabrics utilize the past in their contemporary collections.

Another example of the keen interest in preserving and replicating the designs of the past was the exhibi-

7.23

7.24a

tion of mid-century textile designs "Marimekko: Fabrics, Fashion, Architecture," at the Bard Graduate Center in New York in 2003. Marimekko is a design company based in Helsinki, Finland, and its aesthetic captured the optimism of the 1950s with brightly colored large-scale prints for fashion and interiors. Figure 7.23 shows a bedroom done in Marimekko fabric with the signature colorful, oversize patterns for which the company has become known.

The Past Is Present

Whether it is because the future is ever uncertain or because mass media has made design inspiration from the past more accessible, textile designs from

7.24b

past eras are increasingly popular, and it is important for all designers to have a grasp of the major trends and vocabulary of textiles over the centuries.

The concept of looking back for inspiration in textile design is not new. One of the most renowned designers of the Arts and Crafts movement, William Morris, was inspired by medieval textiles, and many of his textile pattern designs were adapted from designs he saw in the collections of the Victoria and Albert Museum in London. Like some of the designers who are practicing today, he was dedicated to making historically accurate textiles, using authentic discharge printing methods in which the whole piece of fabric was dyed, with bleach applied to areas that would get additional color. In addition to printed fabrics, Morris and his workshops produced embroideries, wallpaper, woven textiles, carpets, tapestries, and furniture. Figure 7.24a shows "The Orchard" tapestry designed by William Morris and woven in 1890. Compare it with Figure 7.24b, "Concert at the Fountain," a tapestry woven in Belgium in about 1570–1580. Medieval influence, espe-

7.25

cially in the treatment of flowers and trees, is very apparent in the Morris tapestry, woven almost four hundred years after the Belgian example.

If use of patterns for textile design recurring over time is nothing new, neither is the exploitation that has been connected with textile production. From sweatshops to child labor, to the connection of cotton production to the institution of slavery in the southern United States, abuses have occurred that should not be overlooked when considering the beauty and value of textiles. Figure 7.25 shows workers at a loom at William Morris and Company in the early 20th century. The youth of the workers and the cramped quarters in which they appear to be working would be cause for concern today. The advent of high-tech machinery and computer-controlled production has in much of the industrialized world eliminated the menial jobs that led to exploitation in the past, but because of economic pressures brought on by competition in the global economy, fiber and textile producers must be vigilant to ensure that workers throughout the world have good working conditions and livable wages.

Another skeleton in the closet of textile production has been environmental contamination from chemicals in processing and dyeing. With the use of the Internet, it is increasingly possible for consumers to monitor the environmental performance of fabric manufacturers and make purchasing decisions based on this information. Additionally, new developments in textile design, in which laser and ultrasound technologies are used to create surface patterns without dyes and chemicals, hold great promise for environmentally responsible textile production.

Textiles often symbolize the importance of the wearer or owner. Both apparel and interior textiles are a reflection of affluence and position in society. Historically, textile color was significant because the cost of dyes was also a reflection of wealth. Fiber content has carried value, as have the techniques utilized in creating the structure and surface design of textiles. In our contemporary society this idea carries through in the significance of designer labels. With more frequency, textile designers are involved in the creation of designer apparel and home products. Textiles hold a unique position in our lives because they can be useful and decorative at the same time. As this chapter has shown, for as long as fabrics have been made, they have been a source of aesthetic pleasure.

FIG. 7.23 A Marimekko bedspread with colorful, oversized patterns. [Copyright © Arcaid/Alamy.] FIG. 7.24 (a) "The Orchard" tapestry by William Morris (woven in 1890). (b) "Concert at the Fountain," an early 16th century Belgian tapestry. [(a) Reprinted with permission of V&A Images/Victoria and Albert Museum. (b) Copyright © Giraudon/Art Resource.] FIG. 7.25 Young Workers at William Morris and Company in the early 20th century. [Copyright © The London Archives.]

CHAPTER EIGHT

Trend Forecasting

Seeing What's Not There... Yet

The ability to spot trends is an important skill for anyone interested in making a career in the design professions. Whether we like it or not, the majority of us, regardless of our inspiration and creativity, will eventually confront the big question: How do we turn our design interests into a career? When Dustin Hoffman's character Ben in *The Graduate* was faced with an uncertain future and a family friend, Mr. McGuire, advised him with that one famous word, *plastics*, he was predicting a trend. Ben had other things on his mind, as many recent graduates do, and as shallow as the recommendation seemed in the context of the character's larger concerns and feelings of alienation, it was nonetheless an accurate glimpse of the growing industrial and commercial uses of synthetic materials. What is the early-21st-century equivalent of "plastics"?

Information Gathering

Designers are concerned with forecasting trends because most of their work is done well ahead of the time that their product or concept is released to the public. It is critical to be able to recognize trends and to extrapolate from them. Each day is an opportunity to create a time capsule—a snapshot of culture at a particular point in history. A journal or scrapbook record of ideas and notes about potential trends can be an important resource for a designer. What is in the news? What geographic areas of the world are in focus? What current national or international events will have a force in shaping the future? What is happening in music, art, and cinema?

This sort of information gathering includes being aware of events in the media: broadcast news, weekly news magazines, as well as international, national, and local newspapers. Editorial opinions and advertisements should also be studied. Keeping track of potential trends means following business news, cultural news, and politics and staying attuned to changes in the way people live. Walk into a branch of one of the large chain booksellers. Look at the placement of books and new merchandise in the entry area. New books, best sellers, and books that reflect current cultural phenomena are often displayed in this area, so this is a snapshot of trends on any given day. How many books are about celebrities? How many are about food, fitness, and dieting? Are there books about politics and world affairs? Money and business? Look at the best-seller lists for fiction and nonfiction. What do the titles and subjects tell you about the interests of the reading public and about the popular culture?

Advertising and marketing professionals keep close watch on trends. Before developing products, designers should be aware of the kinds of activities that will be increasing in popularity. What geographic areas are gaining population? What lifestyle changes are occurring? Is technology causing changes in how people live? Are cultural changes occurring? How are geographic and demographic changes affecting population density and distribution? How are economic and cultural changes affecting lifestyle? What effect will these changes have in the future?

The Trend Toward Interdisciplinary Approaches to Design

In the mid-1990s when the authors of this book forecasted a trend toward an interdisciplinary approach, the worlds of fashion, interior design, architecture, and graphic design were very distinct from one another. Yet there were indications that designers were reaching across boundaries that had separated not only the products but the process of design. Ralph Lauren had begun presenting his clothing in a setting that suggested an entire lifestyle and to offer home products as well as apparel. Since then, it has become commonplace for clothing designers to expand into home products; brands such as Gucci, Claiborne, Armani, and Burberry have added furniture, wallpaper, linens, and carpets to their offerings. Responding to that trend, interior designers and producers of textiles for interiors have begun to cross over into the design of apparel and accessories (Kaiser; Mechling). Figure 8.1 shows a recent advertisement that reflects this crossover, in which Kate Spade handbags serve as architectural detail and bed linens are worn as clothing.

Designer as Researcher

As forecasters, designers should cultivate not only the capacity to recognize trends but the intellectual ability to see what implications a trend has for related industries, the economy as a whole, and the various manufacturing, service, or technology sectors. Like market researchers, trend forecasters look at demographics: the birth rate, the growth or decline of different age groups, and life expectancy. They study lifestyle, family or household size, and

144

8.1

income statistics for different groups and ethnic mixes. One activity shared by all trend forecasters is the insatiable gathering of information. Trend forecasters read, watch, and listen to everything they can about everything that is happening in the world—in politics, culture, and the arts—not just news about design.

Professional Forecasters

Trend forecasters and market researchers look at values and lifestyles and how people are spending their time and money. In employment, what skills are in demand? How much leisure time is there, and what kinds of activities occupy that time? Are events formal or casual? What is the level of interest in health, fitness, and nutrition? Thanks to the Internet, much of this kind of information is readily available. Current statistics on many subjects can be found at the Bureau of Labor Statistics (www.bls.gov). The Bureau of Labor Statistics is a government agency that compiles information on opportunities in career areas. By becoming aware of the information available through the Bureau of Labor Statistics, trend forecasters can analyze potential areas of growth in the economy. Another source of economic information is the National Retail Federation. This organization publishes a weekday online summary of articles with links to the sources of the articles on its Web site at NRF Smart Brief. Another source of retail trend information is *Plunkett's Retail Industry Almanac* from Plunkett Research. The almanac offers analysis of major retail business trends and markets. These business sites provide important access to historical information and statistics and to current profiles of different types of retailers. Articles on subjects such as emerging technologies, shopping center development, and online retailing help product developers analyze potential markets and marketing trends.

Forecasters translate emerging trends into specific recommendations for clients, predicting not only product styling but also material and color. As we have seen in Chapter 4, people make psychological and cultural associations with specific colors, and these associations influence color trends and color cycles. Whether the color of large, durable items such as cars or refrigerators influences interior and fashion colors or vice versa, it is certain that color selection, and awareness of color trends, is an important aspect of design (Brannon pgs. 182–185).

FIG. 8.1 This Kate Spade advertisement details the creative mixture of apparel and home products. [Reprinted with permission of Kate Spade, NY.]

Trade organizations such as the Color Association of the United States (See Box 4.1) and the Color Marketing Group monitor developments in color; they sponsor annual meetings at which members discuss and evaluate changes and produce predictive reports.

Additionally, forecasters have a large role in predicting textile trends in fabrics for interiors and fashion, since many decisions are made prior to the conversion of fiber into yarn and fabric. Fiber producers are among the first industries to require information about trends in color, texture, and quality, since their production cycle can take a year and a half. Textile trade shows such as Première Vision, Moda-In, and the International Fashion Fabric Exhibition are gathering points for designers in search of the latest predictions for color and trends. Trade groups such as Cotton Incorporated and the Wool Bureau have departments devoted to trend research. They provide fabric libraries and color and style forecasting to the producers of these fibers and to the manufacturers of products using these fibers. Fashion forecasting services like Promostyl and Here & There include color ranges in their seasonal projections. Some forecasting services provide a unique focus: Design Options, for example, reports on the latest trends from the West Coast. Market weeks such as Magic International in Las Vegas and West Week at the Pacific Design Center in Los Angeles, although too close to the selling cycle to provide forecasting for some segments of the fashion and interiors industries, certainly serve as barometers of the retail climate. Box 8.1 presents an interview with a professional fashion forecaster.

BOX 8.1

Interview with Fashion Forecaster Wendy Bendoni

WEAR YOUR CHAIR: *What led you to become interested in the field of trend forecasting?*

WENDY BENDONI: Well, I think it started in college when I took a field experience trip to London. My instructor set up a meeting with Cotton Inc., and we learned about trend forecasting. "Trend forecasting?" I was amazed that someone's job was to research fashion trends by looking at what was being worn on the street, runway, and current events. I also liked the idea that this job involved being creative but still had a business angle. The business side of it pertained to determining what was a marketable product. Since my major was fashion marketing, this job was a perfect match to everything I was studying. I knew then that I had to become a fashion forecaster.

WYC: *How did you get started in your career, and how has it developed over time?*

WB: I learned about my job through the college's career center, which I was very friendly with. I had this phobia about not having a job when I graduated from college, so I made it my business to take charge of my future. I was a junior in college when I first heard of an opening at a fashion forecasting-retail reporting office. I accepted an internship at Bill Glazer & Associates (BGA), but I also accepted an internship at a special events department at I.Magnin (high-end retailer). I told you I had a fear of not getting a job, so I overextended myself to see which career would best fit my lifestyle. I worked all the time, but I was also learning about two amazing careers.

After four months at both jobs, I discovered that I was much more cut out for fashion forecasting at BGA. BGA offered me more of a chance to execute all that I had learned at college as well as a chance to learn more of what interested me, fashion. I started as a shopper, whose job was to shop for the "hot sellers" each month, then worked my way up to the photographer. To become a photographer, I went back to school and studied journalism. This helped me with my reporting and photography skills. This was over 15 years ago, and I am now the European correspondent and travel to Europe on a regular basis.

I also have added on to my job title and have become the Director of Educational Services for SnapFashun (BGA's sister company). Once again using my college work, since my minor was in computer science, I often created programs that had a fashion angle. Yes, at the time I was one of two girls in the whole computer program. This was "old school" programming! I was the only girl who was interested in anything having to do with fashion. SnapFashun (www.snapfashun.com) is the perfect match for me because it offered fashion and computers in one. I then decided that I would introduce all schools to this idea and in 1990 this was a new idea to everyone.

Traveling is a key part of my job, but I think it is important to say that I still have time to raise a family and to keep in touch with all the other interests in my life. Whether it is traveling to Europe for BGA or traveling to New York for Snap-Fashun, it is still important to keep a balance between family and your career. I also have a chance to work at two different companies and always challenge myself with new ideas and new concepts. I think it is important when you choose your career to consider what works best for you in your interests. Since you spend most of your days working, you'd better love what you do. I have therefore chosen my career and not just a job, and to me there is a difference. I love what I do!

WYC : *Describe the variety of services that a trend forecaster provides. How do you keep up with emerging trends?*
WB: We offer many services, but they are all made to tell our subscribers (retailers and designers) what is happening in fashion on the street, runway, and retail. Lifestyle is also an important factor when determining trends, and part of our job is just to be aware of our surroundings and how it can affect fashion. BGA/SnapFashun's specialty is being practical when determining fashion trends (salable items) as well as being computerized. When I say computerized, I mean offering our clients SnapWest, which e-mails them every week with new details, trends, and silhouettes. Fashion trends seem to end as fast as they get started, so we have to

make sure our clients receive the information as fast as it develops. Some of our services such as Report West and Xtract (www.snapfashun.com) offer a CD-ROM, with the same detailed sketches found in the reports saved as Adobe Illustrator files (CorelDraw). In fashion, as in technology, it is all about keeping up with what is available and executing it as fast as possible.

WYC: *Our book is geared toward a multi-disciplinary audience. Do you have insights to share about the similarities and differences in the use of color in, for example, fashion versus interior design?*
WB: Fashion and interior design are one and the same, thanks to what is being called the "lifestyle" trend. Lifestyle has to do with the consumer shopping habits and creating a new market in one convenient area. For example, if a customer is buying into the global market trend and purchased an India-inspired skirt, retailers would use the same motivation to get her to buy India-inspired pillows for her apartment. This is genius; you now can captivate your customers to dress themselves and their surroundings. Stores such as Anthropologie and Urban Outfitters are doing just that. Pottery Barn Teen is also working on this idea of pulling from fashion and applying that to their interior trends. There are services that focus on just this called *lifestyle.* They pull from what is being seen on the runway and what is being sold at better-end home stores to determine trends in "the market."

WYC: *What advice would you give to those just entering the field?*
WB: I would say that if you are interested in fashion forecasting, you need to start by being aware of all of your surroundings and start by working at retail. Yes, I said retail; you need to learn how the consumer shops, and what merchandise sells, and why some merchandise doesn't sell. I worked at Nordstrom for six years, and this taught me all I needed to know to start to help determine what to look for when shopping and tracking trends. Yes, there are other factors but this is a key contributor. I would also recommend getting very friendly with your career center and start working on what internships are available. Good luck!

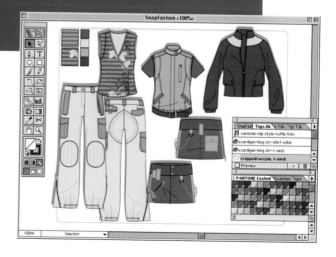

Where Do Trends Start?

It may seem easy to identify a trend once it has developed, but designers should be able to predict trends before they have completely evolved. Some of us may think of trends as vast and encompassing, but essentially, it takes only one person to start a trend. Look at yourself. You are a unique individual with interests and attitudes that are entirely your own, yet your tastes and pastimes may be part of a trend. From a broad perspective, trends are made either by insiders or outsiders. Insiders are people who follow the status quo and fit with the mainstream of society. Outsiders are those beyond the mainstream. Trends can begin at any point on this spectrum, as a continuation of a current tendency or as a reaction to it.

In *Fashion, Culture and Identity*, Fred Davis describes the prevailing theories of how fashion is made and identifies the concept of "key persons" as arbiters of style (p. 146). In *The Tipping Point*, Malcolm Gladwell compares the development of a fashion trend with that of an epidemic; he explains how something that begins accidentally with a very few people can spread quickly into a trend. He takes the example of the reemergence during the 1990s of the almost-forgotten brand of shoes Hush Puppies. The people who started this trend were outsiders who were wearing Hush Puppies precisely because they were so out of fashion as to be unique and available in thrift shops for bargain prices. When a stylist used this brand of shoe in a fashion shoot, a trend was launched. Within a couple of years the production of the shoes had quadrupled (Gladwell, p. 4).

Case Studies: Trend Research

In the section that follows, information is presented on a range of topics that might serve as a basis for the development of trends. This kind of informal evidence shouldn't be confused with scholarly research. These case studies are provided as discussion points and as a model for the gathering of information from a wide variety of readily available sources, including popular magazines and newspapers. The categories are consumer behavior, demographics (age, gender, and ethnicity), art and culture, and lifestyle.

Trendspot 1: Consumer Behavior

One of the first indicators of a trend is consumer behavior, as the buying habits of the public give clues about changes that are occurring in economics, culture, and lifestyle. Consumer behavior is seen not only in the spending or saving of money but in the purchasing choices that people make. These choices can suggest underlying shifts in the ethos of an era. For example, contemporary consumers appear to follow contradictory impulses in their attempt to decide whether more is better or less is better.

More Is Better

In *I Want That! How We All Became Shoppers*, Thomas Hine makes the observation that "being a good consumer is an important part of being a grown-up in contemporary society, especially for women" (p. xiv), and he draws a parallel between shopping and nurturing (p. 40). Shopping has not always been the all-encompassing and even patriotic activity that it is today. Mass production and the development of the consumer credit industry have changed our

BOX 8.2

Ideas and Trends: Not for You, Mr. Trump

By David Carr

The National Magazine Awards took place last week, honoring a coven of magazines built on long thoughts, gorgeous designs and an aspiration for the finer things in life, however unattainable.

Editors for publications like *The New Yorker*, *W* and *Gourmet* all marched up to the winner's podium. But also taking the victory mile was a far-less-known magazine, one that meets consumers where they actually live: *Budget Living*. The glossy homage to cheap chic was cited for general excellence in the category of magazines with circulations from 250,000 to 500,000. It beat the likes of *Teen Vogue* and *Details*.

While many magazines these days push $100 pens, $10,000 stoves and $100,000 cars, *Budget Living* has focused on a simple thought: You are indeed what you consume, and you are a moron if you pay too much for it.

That may not be much of a news bulletin at a time when Wal-Mart, Costco and Target have conquered the retail industry with low pricing. But the large media companies still seem stuck on William Blake's maxim that the road to excess leads to the palace of wisdom, and they miss a more common point: Everyone, including, and perhaps espe-

cially, the wealthy, loves a good deal. Why else would the parking lot of Costco be clogged with Mercedeses and its aisles dotted with shoppers in furs?

Budget Living's message, "Spend Smart, Live Rich," counterintuits the conventional wisdom that people buy magazines to see how the other half lives. The six-times-a-year magazine is more concerned with sofas that start at $250 than with fueling unattainable consumptive dreams.

When Donald E. Welch started *Budget Living*, he was told by many big publishers that a magazine with the word "budget" in the title would never succeed in a country hooked on glamour and luxury. He disagreed. "Part of being tasteful is not being a sucker in what you buy," he said.

His magazine, of course, was started on a shoestring and runs frugally. *Budget Living* suggests that to a new generation of adult consumers, the only thing embarrassing in searching for a good deal is not finding one.

Most of the magazine racks will continue to be reserved for lifestyle voyeurism, with fanciful goods arrayed over impossibly beautiful people. But the success of *Budget Living* suggests that readers will want to read those magazines while sitting in a recliner that looks like a million bucks and costs a fraction of retail.

Reprinted with permission of the New York Times, May 9, 2004.

ideas about our needs and wants. Lizabeth Cohen, in her social history of consumerism, *A Consumers' Republic: The Politics of Mass Consumption in Postwar America*, traces the development of our assumptions about the acquisition of material wealth to what she calls the "golden era of postwar prosperity that lasted approximately from 1945 to 1975" (p. 125). Much of trend forecasting in the area of consumer behavior is based on the presumption that markets will continue to grow and that people will maintain their desire to possess new and better products and that bargain shopping will continue to develop as a

trend. There are certainly indications that the quest for a good deal is seen by many as one of the essential drives. Box 8.2 provides a look at an award-winning magazine devoted to bargain shopping.

Less Is Better

In seeming opposition to the outright acquisitive instinct of bargain hunting are products and services that counteract the chaos of modern life, such as spa treatments, wellness concepts, or noise-canceling headphones. While still evidence of consumerism, products of this type demonstrate a rise in the trend

8.2

accumulate less, live more

jantzen

dive into life
www.jantzen.com

8.3

toward reflection of the inner spirit. Similarly, and especially since September 11, 2001, there has been an upsurge of interest in ethics, values, dignity, and spiritual faith as an antidote to materialism (Foster). An example of this value system is the magazine *Real Simple*, in which the underlying theme is that in the pursuit of a genuine life, small pleasures lead to personal fulfillment. We now talk about clothing with a conscience and ethical consumerism. American Apparel, the company that began with an antisweatshop mission, has opened a community boutique in the fashionable Robertson Boulevard district of Los Angeles (Figure 8.2). There are many indications that people are rediscovering idealism and supporting companies that have humane working conditions (Ito). Even mainstream companies are tapping into this concept in their advertising campaigns. In an interesting twist,

the swimsuit ad in Figure 8.3 is selling a product by encouraging customers to accumulate less!

Trendspot 2: Demographics

In the mid-20th century, during the period following World War II, the demographic standard in the United States was the white, suburban nuclear family. We only have to look at popular media from the 1950s and 1960s for models of this family structure in which roles were tightly constructed. Television programs such as *Father Knows Best*, *Leave It to Beaver*, *Ozzie and Harriett*, and even the cartoon *Jetsons* showed what was then the norm: a man, the husband, whose primary role was to be the provider; a woman, the wife, whose primary role was to take care of the household; and a couple of children who basically did as they were told. If we continue to use media as a mirror, we see the development of a variety of family and household structures, which reflected cultural and demographic changes occurring in society, with classics such as *The Bill Cosby Show*, *The Golden Girls*, and *A Different World* leading up to more recent programs like *Queer Eye for the Straight Guy* and *The Sopranos*. Trends in society and culture are also seen in Spanish-language *telenovelas* and other culturally specific programming wherever an audience exists. With the development of cable television stations devoted to the airing of decades-old programs, it is possible to survey and document the cultural changes that have taken generations to occur.

Youth and Age: Multigenerational Shoppers

Consumer research itself has been the subject of much investigation into its own effectiveness; Figure 8.4 takes a satiric look at reliance on demographic information. Whether a link can be made between salmon eating and interest in retirement planning is open for debate. However, what marketing researchers who analyze buying habits have identified is a group of 45- to 64-year-olds whom they've named *multigenerational shoppers*. In their surveys these researchers have found that in a growing number of households, several generations are represented—grandparents, their child, and the grandchildren. In some cases the grandparents' parents are still living, making four generations under one roof (Kauf; Nova Marketing). Marketers look at this trend as an opportunity to develop retail settings in which the individual who does the purchasing for these multigenerational households can conveniently locate a wide variety of products rang-

ing from diapers for the grandchild to denture cream for the grandparent.

Youth and Age: Is Youth Wasted on the Young?

In *Branded: The Buying and Selling of Teenagers*, Alissa Quart writes, "It is common for mothers and daughters in upper-class areas to wear the same expensive brand-name clothes. While the mother strives to look twelve years younger, the daughter strives to look twelve years older. They meet in between" (p. 16). Although there has been some

FIG. 8.2 American Apparel community store, a Los Angeles–based manufacturer of knitwear, sportswear, and comfortwear. [Photo by Penny Collins.] FIG. 8.3 A Jantzen ad that encourages customers to accumulate *less*. [Courtesy, Jantzen Apparel, LLC.] FIG. 8.4 A "Boox" cartoon about consumer research. [Artwork © Mark Alan Stamaty.]

backlash to the promotion of sophisticated products for children, advertisements in teen magazines still provide evidence of the marketing of a wide range of choices of consumer items for this age group. Teen films often promote ideas of beauty and success based on being rich, thin, and popular. The concept of the teen years as prime years for consuming products to achieve this goal is further reinforced by the availability of credit and cash cards for teenagers. Companies seek to capitalize on the spending power of teens and young adults with products directed at this market, such as soft drinks in changing fashion flavors that appeal to teens' enjoyment of the new and unique, and flavored tobacco products with names such as Mocha Taboo and Midnight Berry (Walker, "Sprite Remix"; Grimes, "Mocha Puffs and Berry Notes").

Another newsworthy development in our contemporary society, in which children dress to look older and adults dress to look younger, is the concept of a "reemerging adult style of dressing" (Bellafante, "The Power of Adult Clothes"). Casual trousers, T-shirts, and sneakers are making way for tailored suits, dresses worn with jackets, and serious shoes in many workplaces and social environments. People are living longer, and older people are doing more and are challenging accepted notions about aging. For example, Marvin Traub, the former president and chairman of Bloomingdale's, was heading a business consulting firm, a new venture at the age of 77 (Rozhon). Past age 70, Joan Rivers, whose career has spanned more than 40 years, is performing comedy for audiences half her age (La Ferla). And at 94, famed architectural photographer Julius Shulman was busier than ever with photo sessions and three books in the works (Nakano). Statistical information shows an increase in the number of people living to the age of 100 or more (Dominus).

Youth and Age: If You Can't Be Young, at Least You Can Look Young

Perhaps as a corollary to improved longevity, there has been increasing acceptance of cosmetic surgical procedures and apparent acknowledgment of the high importance of physical appearance. Popular media, with television shows such as *Extreme Makeover*, illustrate the value that our culture places on a certain type of looks. Teeth whitening, nose straightening, and wrinkle removal have all become progressively more popular procedures (Kuczynski). In its June 2004 issue, *Vogue* magazine featured a story about plastic surgery under the headline "Shopping for Surgery," calling it the "new cultural obsession" (Levy).

Gender: Changing Roles and Expectations

In that limited world of the mid-20th-century sitcom, no self-respecting male breadwinner head of household would have taken much interest in his own clothing or grooming. All that has changed and continues to develop so that increasingly there are many options for fashion and grooming products and services for men, including magazines, spas, and upscale specialty stores (Quintanilla; Rendon). While traditionally male sports have dominated some television networks, women have their own television network, Lifetime, and men now have Spike TV. GQ magazine has increased its fashion coverage. For their part, women's roles have expanded too, with the stereotypical "helpless female" image receding and do-it-yourself courses at home centers being directed toward women's interests in home repair and construction. The popularity of television programs like *Trading Spaces* and other home renovation shows is evidence of the growing interest among women in home repair. Increasingly, home centers such as Lowe's and Home Depot offer demonstrations and classes (Warner). Figure 8.5 shows a stylish young woman using a cordless drill for do-it-yourself home improvement.

8.5

Same-Sex Marriage as a Social Movement

In 2004, the 50th anniversary of *Brown vs. Board of Education*, the Supreme Court decision that found racially segregated schools to violate the educational rights of minorities, weddings of same-sex couples were performed in San Francisco and Boston. These occasions gave promise to the potential that the inequities gay people have encountered in health insurance, family issues, and other social matters would begin to be addressed. While some decried the marriages, many Americans were supportive, and any lingering doubts about gay rights may one day seem as distant as the lunch counter sit-ins of the civil rights era (Rich).

Ethnicity: Awareness and Blending

The National Museum of the American Indian, part of the Smithsonian Institution in Washington, DC, which opened in the fall of 2004, is focusing interest on the ethnicity and culture of Native Americans. This museum, which is a monument to the customs and history of the indigenous tribes that were displaced by European settlers, has a prominent location on the National Mall. In a coun-

try in which the vast majority of people are from immigrant backgrounds, balance has not always been achieved in recognizing the importance of respect for ethnic and cultural heterogeneity. The 2000 national census, which allowed people to identify themselves as belonging to more than one racial group, and the popularity of biracial celebrities like golf pro Tiger Woods and singer Mariah Carey have helped to focus attention on the gradual change of racial definitions, as have politicians and public figures who are partners in interracial marriages, such as Senator Mitch McConnell and Secretary of Labor Elaine Chao.

Ethnic blending, racial ambiguity, and the fusion of racial characteristics have emerged as themes in several recent art exhibitions. The interest by Japanese teenagers in the vibrant hip-hop culture and their adopting of style details such as braided Rastafarian hairdos is seen on many college campuses. This Afro-Asian aesthetic is captured in the work of artist Iona Rozeal Brown shown in Figure 8.6. The racial mix of white Spaniards with

FIG. 8.5 Do-it-yourself home improvement projects are appealing to an increasing number of women. [Copyright © JLP/Sylvia Torres/Corbis.]

native Indians and with Africans who had been brought to Mexico as slaves was the exhibition theme of "Inventing Race: Casta Painting and Eighteenth-Century Mexico" at the Los Angeles County Museum of Art in 2004. Figure 8.7 portrays racial mixing among different family groups. During the 18th century, paintings such as this served as promotion for Spaniards to settle the areas of Mexico that were being colonized at that time.

8.6

154

Trendspot 3: Art and Culture

Museum exhibits, art and architecture, musical and dance performances, films, and other aspects of culture such as dress and grooming shed light on trends. For example, taken on its own, a new building in a city center may not seem striking. But taken in the context of several renowned architects being commissioned to design important civic structures in several urban centers, that is probably a trend.

Visual and Performing Arts

In recent years the architecture of public gathering spaces devoted to cultural activities has received as much or in some cases even more attention than the work on display. (See also Chapter 9.) Frank Gehry's Walt Disney Concert Hall in Los Angeles (See Figure 3.1a) has received critical acclaim that has made it almost as much a destination as attendance at the performances it was designed to show-

8.7

8.8

case. Such is also the case with the new concert hall at the world headquarters of AOL Time-Warner at Columbus Circle in New York, designed specifically for Jazz at Lincoln Center (Figure 8.8). Similarly, the Milwaukee Art Museum, originally designed by Eero Saarinen, and updated in 2001 with the addition of the Quadracci Pavilion by Santiago Calatrava, draws visitors not only to the art collection but to the buildings that house it. The environments created by, and programs presented by, galleries, muse-

ums, and concert facilities serve as a reflection of the cultural interests of the public.

Trends can also be analyzed in relation to the work that is done by contemporary artists and designers as well as by the choices made by curators to present work from past eras. Recent exhibitions of black-and-white photography including the work of Diane Arbus (Figure 8.9) have focused interest on this art form that exposes detail so effectively. The recent death of Henri Cartier-

FIG. 8.6 "Untitled I (Female)" by Iona Rozeal Brown explores racial categories by blending dress and hairstyles normally associated with specific ethnicities. [Copyright © Iona Rozeal Brown.] FIG. 8.7 "Human Races (Las Castas)" painting by an unknown artist (18th century). [Copyright © Schalkwijk/Art Resource.] FIG. 8.8 Jazz at the Lincoln Center opening gala in the Frederick P. Rose Hall. [Copyright © Ramin Talaie/Corbis.]

8.9+8.10

YOU KNOW BLACK AND WHITE ISN'T OLD, IT'S ART.

The HP Photosmart 790 not only produces glorious color, but something even harder:
glorious, gallery quality black and white. Sometimes, black and white says the thing best.

Bresson, one of the pioneers of photo-journalism, has occasioned a retrospective of his black-and-white images, notably his photos of the liberation of Paris at the end of World War II. At a time when computerized color printing makes possible the use of several million colors, it seems that a reaction is occurring in the interest in, and appreciation for, the classic black-and-white. Printers, such as the one shown in Figure 8.10 that produce high-quality black-and-white output, are in demand. In cinema, the current popularity of large, epic adventures that portray clearly defined heroes and villains seems to fill our need for answers to basic questions in an increasingly complex era.

Fashion

Perhaps it is the concerns of our unsettled era that take us back in fashion to a previous time of unrest—to the hippie and psychedelic looks of the 1960s—such as those presented by Jalian in 2004 (Figure 8.11a). Grim realities of life are also kept at a distance with a return to femininity in fashion in both interiors and clothing. This is seen in the fall 2004 collections of Ungaro (Figure 8.11b), which reflect the opulence of 18th-century France shown in the 2004 "Dangerous Liaisons" costume and furniture exhibition at the

8.11a+b

Metropolitan Museum of Art. The Museum of Modern Art's 2004 exhibition "Fashioning Fiction" is an example of how fashion photography has blurred the line between advertising and art, with photographers such as Robert Avedon and Steven Meisel (Bellafante, "Art That Wears $780 Shoes").

Trendspot 4: Lifestyle

A close examination of life-style, including emerging trends in the location and size of living spaces; preferred leisure activities; health, diet, and fitness concerns; and technological advances will serve as a useful barometer of our contemporary culture. In "Our Sprawling, Supersize Utopia," David Brooks analyzes the growing interest in and demand for exurban housing, residential developments beyond the standard suburban plan. According to Brooks's statistics, not only living space, but working space has moved to the

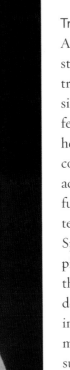

suburbs and beyond, as "ninety percent of the office space built in America by the end of the 1990s was built in suburbia, much of it in far-flung office parks stretched along the Interstates" (p. 48).

Along with this love of wide-open spaces has come the increased popularity of golf, which combines business, social, and athletic endeavors in a unique way (Smith and Kiger). An emerging sport activity is parkour, which has also been known as traceur and freerunning, in which practitioners utilize any environmental architecture as a springboard for leaps, jumps, and slides, without the assistance of any board or blades (Bahney). For the armchair athlete, video games, video lounges, and elaborate home entertainment centers continue to gain participants. "Cocooning," the increased desire to stay at home, was identified by Faith Popcorn almost a generation ago, but as it continues, conveniences such as home beverage dispensers (Figure 8.12a) and cosmetics coolers (Figure 8.12b) bring commercial appliances into the domestic arena.

Along with the focus on domestic life, family celebrations and parties have gained in importance, with milestones such as *quinceañera*, bar and bat mitzvah celebrations, and weddings becoming increasingly lavish affairs with increasingly large budgets (Quart). Family reunions and family vacations are fea-

8.12a

8.12b

FIG. 8.9 "A Young Brooklyn Family Going Out for a Sunday Outing" by Diane Arbus. [Reprinted with permission of the Estate of Diane Arbus/The Museum of Modern Art/Licensed by Scala/Art Resource.] FIG. 8.10 Ad for an HP printer. FIG. 8.11 (a) The hippie era revisited in "Jon in Ocean Pacific Polo Shirt and Jalian Shorts" by Jalian (2004) and (b) Ungaro collection by Giambattista Valli (fall 2004). [(a) Courtesy, Lisa Eisner. (b) Reprinted with permission of Emanuel Ungaro.] FIG. 8.12 (a) Free Delivery sky box by Maytag. (b) Biszet B11 cosmetics cooler. [(a) Reprinted with permission of Maytag Co. (b) Photo by Jonathan Kantor.]

tured as travel destinations, with resorts and hotels offering increasingly family-friendly options.

And would a house be a home without a dog? Increasingly, "man's best friend" has come to be interpreted more and more literally, as options for canine clothing, gourmet treats, and pet health care increase. Dogs appear prominently in advertising campaigns, films, and television, and dogs have been known to write books, presumably with the help of their owners (Iovine). One of these, *Sweetie, from the Gutter to the Runway: Tantalizing Tips from a Furry Fashionista*, includes illustrations by well-known fashion illustrator Ruben Toledo. The Coach advertisement shown in Figure 8.13 captures in one image ideas about "home sweet home," symbolized in the increasingly pricey care, comfort, and clothing lavished upon pets. Seated together on what appears to be a sofa is an entire family of well-dressed pooches, sporting their quilted dog jackets and legacy dog collars.

When people do leave home, there are an increasing number of budget airlines available, such as Ted (the last three letters of United) and Song (a subsidiary of Delta). These airlines offer not only discounted fares on popular routes but friendly, casual service, and in the case of Song, flight attendant uniforms designed by Kate Spade (Estabrook). Security concerns have influenced the travel habits of many Americans, and domestic travel has outpaced international in recent years. Urban areas have spruced up to make visitors more welcome, and public art projects, such as the work shown in Figure 8.14 by Takashi Murakami in Manhattan, provide a source of entertainment for tourists.

Health and fitness trends reflect a culture that is

8.13   8.14

increasingly concerned about physical condition and well-being yet is surprisingly complacent. The popularity of health regimens, such as centers where weight loss is monitored, low-carbohydrate diets, and personal fitness trainers is in striking contrast to the growing epidemic of obesity. Similarly, the environment has suffered as clean air standards and pollution standards are being pushed by the demands of big business and big power and oil companies even though the short- and long-term health impact of these changes has raised concern among scientists and physicians (Barcott). Although alternative fuel sources are being developed on a small scale, and hybrid technologies are already in use, the United

analysis of the growing health concerns related to fast foods, he calls diabetes "the growth industry for an ever-expanding nation" (p. 126). Perhaps in response to demand for healthier alternatives, fast-food chains have begun to add fresh fruit and salads to their menus and are offering alternatives to fried foods. Box 8.3 presents a humorous image of the demise of "super-size" with commentary on its cultural impact.

One of the areas of highest impact when analyzing lifestyle is technology. The digital revolution has only begun, as access to the Internet has exploded with search engines such as Google. David Hochman describes Google as "many things to many people, and to some, perhaps too much: a dictionary, a detective service, a matchmaker, a recipe generator, an ego massager, a spiffy new add-on for the brain" (p. 1). This unlimited availability of information brings with it many questions about how to evaluate the content of Internet sites and how to apply critical thinking skills to the vast stores of information hovering in cyberspace. The Internet provides quick connections to international media, making possible the nearly instantaneous transfer of news from almost every corner of the globe. Online shopping, online dating, and online research have gained popularity, influencing the ways that people socialize and form communities.

Telephones, which were once a communications revolution in themselves, have changed from wire to wireless, and cellular telephones have become so

States has maintained its dependence on petroleum products with environmental health, economic, and political repercussions.

Diet and fitness statistics show that even very young Americans are increasingly overweight as a sedentary lifestyle, cuts in physical education budgets, and the quality of lunch programs take their toll. In *Fat Land: How Americans Became the Fattest People in the World*, Greg Critser documents how the American idea that bigness equates to power has influenced food industries, so that a serving of McDonald's French fries, which had 200 calories in 1960, now provides over 600 calories (p. 28). In his

FIG. 8.13 A Coach advertisement with clothing for pets. FIG. 8.14 "Reversed Double Helix" in New York by Takashi Muramaki. [Copyright © Thomas Loof.]

BOX 8.3

Supersize, We Knew Thee Too Well
By William Grimes

Dealing a crippling blow to the American lifestyle, McDonald's announced last week that it would phase out its "supersize" French fries and soft drinks. The downsizing, part of a broader plan to simplify the menu at the company's 13,000 restaurants in the United States, would slim the 7-ounce fries down to 6.2 ounces and bring the 42-ounce drink down a full 10 ounces. The move was announced just a few days after Size USA, a national survey of the American body, revealed that the median weight for Americans had increased by four pounds since 1994, and that the average American woman now wears a size 14, up six sizes since World War II.

Yes, the supersize fries and drinks were excessive. The soft drinks, in particular, were so large they should have come with a lifeguard. But why should the company be responsible for monitoring its customers' calories? The House of Representatives is scheduled to take up this very question on Tuesday, when it debates the so-called cheeseburger bill, designed to protect companies like McDonald's from lawsuits by overweight customers.

Consumers, especially American ones, were born to consume. Banish supersizing, and where does that leave Texas toast, foot-long hot dogs and Starbucks grande lattes? Wave farewell to the all-you-can-eat buffet. Prepare for sweeping changes at the multiplex, where the size charts for popcorn, candy and sodas make McDonald's look like a spa. The government might want to reassess jumbo eggs, which are, blatantly, eggs that have been supersized.

If consumers need protection from their constitutional right to pursue plus-size happiness then perhaps it is also time to slice a couple of feet off the king-size bed and about 500 pounds from the Cadillac Escalade. (I will leave unmentioned some of the very personal supersizing opportunities I receive via e-mail.)

The McDonald's decision could be good news or bad news for Morgan Spurlock, whose documentary film "Super Size Me" records his ballooning figure and soaring cholesterol count as he eats an all-McDonald's diet, morning, noon and night, for a month. The film is scheduled for release in May, but by that time "supersize" may no longer resonate. "Can I supersize that for you?" will be nothing more than a colorful bit of Americana, like "twenty-three skidoo," "oh, you kid" and "you bet your sweet bippy."

Americans will be healthier, perhaps, but make no mistake, something precious has been lost.

Reprinted with permission of the *New York Times*, March 7, 2004.

---

ubiquitous that they have their own fashion accessories, such as the cell phone necklace shown in Figure 8.15. Increasing numbers of customers are giving up their land lines and using wireless service only (Tahmincioglu).

The sort of comfort that we expect from products that we use and wear reflects the influence of technology as materials become more sophisticated. For example, the shoe designs of Yves Béhar for Birkenstock shown in Figure 8.16

8.15

combine streamlined style with aesthetics and environmental considerations made possible with high-tech materials and methods. Computerized body scanning has made possible custom-fitted clothing at increasingly affordable prices, and has also allowed the collection of data to be used for body size trend analysis (Sciolino). Apparel manufacturer Levi Strauss and Philips Electronics have prototypes in the works of products that combine

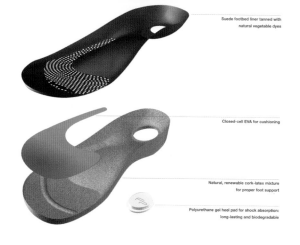

Suede footbed liner tanned with
natural vegetable dyes

Closed-cell EVA for cushioning

Natural, renewable cork-latex mixture
for proper foot support

Polyurethane gel heel pad for shock absorption:
long-lasting and biodegradable

8.16

utility clothing with wearable computing through, for example, wiring in the lining of a coat that can connect built-in electronic devices (Pescovitz). In furniture, high-tech materials and computer modeling have influenced design, presenting increased opportunities for ergonomic choices.

In the four trend categories identified in the preceding section—consumer behavior, demographics, art and culture, and lifestyle—a pattern emerges as the trends identified in each area converge, and the picture is one of a dynamic society. Family and social structures are less rigid than they once were. We expect and demand a good deal when we shop, we like our homes and conveniences, and we like to pamper ourselves, our families, and our pets. Our society both influences and is influenced by art and culture. We're aging and gaining weight, but maybe we're getting more interesting.

Responsive and Responsible Design

We have shown in this chapter that in addition to being creative and technically skilled, a designer is a trend forecaster. In this capacity, a designer functions as a decision maker—first making note of important events and developments that will influence society and then making design choices that accommodate this knowledge. Forecasting is perhaps the most important function of the designer. It is certainly the area in which the designer can bring about change. The designer can do much more than choose the newest shade of blue or the softest textile for a new upholstery fabric. A forward-looking designer is responsive to social and environmental trends: sustainable production, affordable housing, accessible public and private spaces, and emerging technologies that allow for manufacturing processes that have a less harmful impact on the environment.

The categories that we have examined provide a broad overview of possibilities for analyzing trend development. It is important for designers to remain aware of changes. We have identified some consumer, demographic, cultural, and lifestyle trends in the preceding sections, and we have suggested how these demographic and lifestyle changes will influence the types of products and materials that will be useful in the future. One of the more intriguing aspects of the design function is to be able to sort carefully through layers of information from this wide range of sources, looking at what's there, making connections from one layer to another, seeing, and then inventing, what's not there . . . yet.

FIG. 8.15 Cell phone necklace. [Copyright © Don Hogan Charles/The *New York Times*.] FIG. 8.16 Shoe designs for Birkenstock by Yves Béhar. [Photo by Hunter Freeman. Courtesy, Birkenstock and Fuseproject Inc.]

CHAPTER NINE

Design and the Shopping Experience

Whether you think of shopping as a chore or as a source of entertainment, there is no denying that it plays a large part in contemporary culture. At a design level, retail is a showcase for new ideas and retailers provide a public space in which new products and concepts about their presentation are tried. To some extent, we are all consumers, but as designers, we should be able to step outside the role of customer and think critically about what we observe in shopping centers and malls, whether they are "real" or "virtual." More and more, what we observe includes the incorporation of design to form a larger picture of how people live, what products and services they want, and the trends and ideas that influence those desires.

This chapter will assist you in thinking about and analyzing different types of physical retail spaces and their designs and uses (Figure 9.1a–d). We will discuss the visual merchandising of products (Figure 9.2) and the development of consumer tastes in the evolution of shopping from the early trading post to the virtual trading post of e-tailing. Retail space used to refer to the physical setting in which products were presented to customers. Because of changes in technology, retail transactions moved beyond brick-and-mortar locations, first to print catalogs and then to shopping networks and the Internet. The environment that you see and experience in a retail setting and how that environment affects you take on a new meaning when approached from an interdisciplinary perspective

9.1a

9.1b

9.1c+d

The Rise of Multicategory Design

Toward the last decades of the 20th century, designers and architects whose careers had been established in one specific area of product design began, both individually and collaboratively, to broaden their perspectives and develop merchandise in new categories. Although there are some very early examples of designers who explored a variety of media and presented a wide range of well-designed products, such as Sonia Delaunay, Charles Rennie Mackintosh, and others described in Chapter 2, this trend escalated during the late 1980s, and it has continued unabated since then. Designers, especially those with well-established brand identities, looked to new merchandise categories to extend their product range by providing an array of choices for customers already familiar with the style and quality of their products. An example is the line of jewelry designed for Tiffany and Company by architect Frank Gehry (Figure 9.3).

What are the reasons for this trend? What accounts for the tendency of consumers to follow designers and retailers who look outside of a narrow product category and create a look that suggests an entire way of living? In advertising, the trend is demonstrated in promotions that project a whole concept rather than individual items.

9.2

9.3

9.4

For example, the image in Figure 9.4 entices the imagination of the viewer as it blurs the lines between fashion and furniture. Is this an advertisement for apparel, home furnishings, or just a suggestion of a luxury lifestyle in which shopping is a primary activity?

The interplay of the disciplines of fashion, textile design, interior design, and architecture is well represented in Ralph Lauren's flagship store in New York. The setting, the exquisite 19th-century Rhinelander Mansion (Figure 9.5), is located at Madison Avenue and 72nd Street in Manhattan. The interior, with its welcoming oak staircase inviting all visitors to feel part of this luxurious atmosphere, presents merchandise in ornately carved oak showcases, which contribute to the elegant ambiance. As design boundaries are blurred, so are distinctions between merchandise categories.

In display vignettes, apparel and interior fur-

nishings are seamlessly melded to portray the Ralph Lauren lifestyle, "old money," which includes many forms of luxury leisure activities such as yachting and polo. One can escape urban life in the comfort of the atmosphere of the store's old-world-style "gentlemen's club."

Oprah Winfrey, in an interview with Ralph Lauren for her magazine, articulates the essence of the appeal of his products when she says, "Ralph Lauren sells much more than fashion: He sells the life you'd like to lead. To own a creation of Ralph Lauren's, whether it's his red patent leather boots, his signature Polo shirt, or an ottoman from his furniture

9.5

FIG. 9.1 (a) Sephora is an example of a high-end specialty retailer, carrying a specific selection of products for a target customer. (b) Mass-market retailer Wal-Mart caters to a budget-conscious consumer. (c) Costco is an example of a warehouse retail setting. (d) The IKEA store is an example of a home center retail setting. [(a) Courtesy, Fairchild Publications, Inc. (b) Copyright © Ralf-Finn Hestoft/Corbis. (c) Copyright © Jeff Zelevansky/Reuters/Corbis. (d) Copyright © Lou Linwei/Alamy.] FIG. 9.2 The Weathervane boutique features designer clothing in a gallery-like setting. [Photo by Judith Griffin.] FIG. 9.3 Architect Frank Gehry showing his jewelry collection. [Copyright © Marsaili McGrath/Getty Images.] FIG. 9.4 A fashion and lifestyle statement in a single image. [Copyright © Roy Botterell/Corbis.] FIG. 9.5 The architecture of the Rhinelander Mansion, the flagship store of Ralph Lauren. [Courtesy, Fairchild Publications, Inc.]

collection, is to savor a taste of the American dream" (Winfrey, p. 220).

In comparison to the Ralph Lauren store, Donna Karan's flagship location, located in the same Madison Avenue neighborhood of New York City, is a reflection of a lifestyle aimed at a stylish, contemporary consumer (Figure 9.6). Shiny, hard-edged architectural elements constructed of plastic laminate, natural stone, and stainless steel display clothing, accessories, and home furnishings that suggest a hip, urban life. The bustle of the city is at the same time subdued by areas of uncluttered spaciousness and the inclusion of a water garden. A sleek, polished concrete beverage bar presents a calming atmosphere, where the consumer can escape from the pressures of the city. Both stores are excellent examples of design in the retail setting.

Both Ralph Lauren and Donna Karan started their careers in the apparel industry, but as their businesses expanded, they both began to explore the addition of textiles, home furnishings, and accessories to their already popular lines of fashion merchandise. Both apparel brands were already recognized by consumers, so the addition of a wider range of products was a natural business develop-

ment. These designers are representative of the interdisciplinary trend, and their retail stores are excellent examples of current approaches to store design, in which the presentation of merchandise suggests a lifestyle experience. The Lauren family continues to diversify its product range, as Dylan Lauren, the daughter of Ralph Lauren, has expanded the famous lifestyle to include designer sweets. She is co-owner of Dylan's Candy Bar (see Figure 5.27), an upscale candy and ice cream shop on Manhattan's Upper East Side (Moore).

The Evolution of Store Design

Contemporary retail spaces such as Donna Karan's and Ralph Lauren's flagship stores in New York City reflect the public images of their founders. However, the "lifestyle" concept, in which a wide variety of types of product are presented together rather than in separate stores or distinct departments, is relatively recent in the history of store design. In the United States, the development of retailing parallels the settlement of the nation, first in the cities of the East Coast, and then across the frontier. In the mid-19th century, stores in Eastern cities mimicked the design of those in European capitals. In the sparsely populated and less urban towns across the growing nation, general stores developed from trading posts that had served the early settlers.

Over time, the brick-and-mortar Main Street has been transformed in many ways—from the general store to the mall, with its assortment of department stores, boutiques, and specialty stores, to warehouse, off-price, and discount stores. Popular taste then

9.6

9.7

went back full circle to the simulated Main Street, as seen in the growing popularity of human-scale pedestrian malls in the large urban areas that tend to be in the forefront of such trends. In Los Angeles, for example, The Grove at Farmer's Market recaptures the atmosphere of the commercial center of a small town, complete with cobblestone walks, streetcars, kiosks, and landscaped gathering places (Figure 9.7).

Designers, developers, and city planners have recognized the need for public areas offering resting and recreational opportunities that humanize urban spaces; in many upscale shopping areas the focus has shifted from obvious selling to providing an atmosphere that encourages consumers to linger comfortably and perhaps eventually make a purchase. Leslee Komaiko captures this spirit in her survey of malls saying, "Going to the mall has become an all-take, no-give, fun-for-the-entire-family free activity, like an afternoon at the beach or the park. Show me what you've got and I'll maybe show you the money at some future date" (p. 6).

FIG. 9.6 The interior of the Donna Karan store communicates a contemporary, urban feeling. [Courtesy, Fairchild Publications, Inc.] FIG. 9.7 The Grove at the Farmer's Market in Los Angeles. [Copyright © RMA Photography Inc.]

167

9.8

Borders, Barnes & Noble, and other book and music merchants have incorporated comfortable lounge seating areas, cafés, and listening booths into the design of their retail spaces (Figure 9.8). Similarly, household product retailers Pottery Barn and Restoration Hardware offer their clientele an opportunity to literally make themselves "at home" in the midst of store merchandise and to relax in living-room vignettes prevalent throughout the stores. At IKEA, customers lounge in model living areas while making selections of merchandise already coordinated by store design staff.

The Retail Environment

The traditional architecture and space planning of retail stores included segregated departments and

merchandise. Except at the high-end designer shops, there were few opportunities for rest and relaxation during the shopping experience. Store spaces were divided predominantly by merchandise categories. In today's retail settings, merchandise is often shown in lifestyle vignettes, combining items that represent different categories of design so that everything a particular shopper might desire is found in close proximity. With access to comfortable seating areas, the consumer has plenty of time to make purchasing decisions. In Urban Outfitters' Anthropologie stores, for example, items supporting the visual displays are part of the merchandise for sale. This combination of fashion, furniture, and home and garden accessories is an excellent example of the interdisciplinary approach to store layout and visual merchandising (Figure 9.9).

Directing Traffic in the Retail Store

In studying different approaches to the design of retail environments, we begin to understand some of the changes that have taken place in the design of retail store customer circulation patterns, the placement of architectural barriers, and the use of wayfinding techniques and environmental graphics. Circulation patterns in the retail environment are crucial in moving the consumer from one area to another; the control of customer traffic patterns and the accessibility of merchandise can be important sales tools (Figure 9.10). Similarly, placement of aisles and displays can influence the mood of the consumer. Wide aisles and elegant displays suggest an upscale ambiance, while clustered racks of merchandise, notices of price reductions, and product demonstrations create a "bargain basement" atmosphere.

9.9

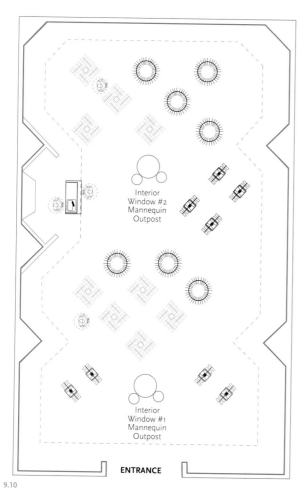

Interior
Window #2
Mannequin
Outpost

Interior
Window #1
Mannequin
Outpost

ENTRANCE

9.10

following the yellow brick road. From the customer's perspective, this use of color is a key "wayfinding" device.

Navigating the Retail Environment

The term *wayfinding* was coined in 1960 when architect Kevin Lynch used it to refer to maps, street numbers, directional signs, and other elements as wayfinding devices in "The Image of the City" (Muhlhausen). Applied to interiors, wayfinding includes color changes, signage, lighting, floor plans, and other systems that help people understand how an unfamiliar environment is organized. In the retail environment, wayfinding is essential and takes different approaches for different categories of retailing.

Although wayfinding can include details such as the organization of traffic flow, it is much more than that, since, ideally, it is taken into consideration in the project design and planning stages. Some of the elements to be resolved in wayfinding are clearly marked entry and exit points, graphic devices to provide direction and spatial orientation, audio devices such as self-help telephones, and tactile devices such as changes in surface treatments to communicate direction to different destinations (Muhlhausen).

Signage graphics are an important aspect of wayfinding. They are used in different ways in the various types of retail environments. For example, warehouse stores and home centers usually have large and clearly defined aisle signage, with text in readable font styles, some more effective than others. On the other hand, consumers rarely expect bold aisle signage in department or specialty stores. Signage in department stores becomes an integral

One traditional approach to the control of retail traffic flow has been the construction of architectural barriers that force consumers to take certain paths through as much merchandise as possible to encourage impulse buying. An example of this is the placement of elevators and escalators so that consumers are compelled to walk through the sales area before being able to move to the next level.

Another important aspect of circulation and flow of traffic is color. Changes in floor color, floor surface, and pattern direct the consumer to take a certain path, similar to Dorothy in *The Wizard of Oz*

FIG. 9.8 Bookshop on Bertelsmann Boulevard in Düsseldorf, Germany. [Copyright © Aleksander Perkovic/Laif/Aurora.] FIG. 9.9 The interior of the Anthropologie store shows a mix of fashion and accessories. FIG. 9.10 This diagram of a store interior floor plan shows the arrangement of merchandise, display, and cashier areas. [Illustration © Craig Gustafson/Presentations Plus.]

9.11

Marketing and Customer Service

Service has long been an important factor in the success of retail establishments. Delivery of service refers to the entire experience of shopping from the moment the consumer enters the retail environment until merchandise is selected, purchased, and packaged. Different retailers have different philosophies and strategies about delivery of service. Store employees range from the neighborly, friendly Wal-Mart greeter to the helpful Nordstrom sales associate to the nearly invisible sales staff at various chains. Some fashion retailers seem to encourage sales staff to take a snobbish attitude toward customers, portraying the shop as a bastion of design only available to a small "in" crowd.

Marketing refers to the analysis of who the customer is and how the customer can be satisfied. This is an increasingly important consideration, as retailers compete for a share of the spending of a very well-informed consumer. The field of "retail anthropology," recognized by Malcolm Gladwell and described in his 1996 *New Yorker* article "The Science of Shopping," explains the growth of market research and the increasingly sophisticated methods of analyzing consumer tastes and trends. Marketing professionals collect data and pore over customer profiles to guide retailers in the building of a customer base and brand loyalty (McNamara, 2001).

In some ways, the development of retail practices over time can be seen as a transition from full service to self-service, with customers doing the work or performing functions that clerks previously were paid to do. The traditional approach to service in a retail setting is humorously presented in the British

part of the merchandise display, sometimes indicating the designer or brand and notifying the consumer about discounts or promotions (Figure 9.11).

Location of displays is a key feature of store design and visual merchandising. Endcaps, or end-of-aisle displays, are used for products that are being promoted by the retailer, such as seasonal merchandise. The end-of-aisle is a prime location for quick turnover or for showcasing a combination of products that feed the consumer's imagination and whims, resulting in increased sales. Point-of-purchase displays, which are strategically located just adjacent to cashier areas, offer impulse merchandise that becomes more tempting the longer the customer waits in line (Figure 9.12).

9.12

sitcom *Are You Being Served?* The program is still widely shown on public broadcasting stations throughout the United States, even though the last episodes were made 20 years ago. Set in a fictional London store, it recounts the antics of the staff of the clothing department. Although exaggerated, the show portrays an era in which the service staff, with its rigid hierarchies, frequently outnumbered the customers.

In current retail practice, one trend is toward self-checkout, Internet connection, automated price-scan stations, and minimal staff. Whereas each department or section of a store used to have its own checkout area, which often included a wrapping desk, at many retailers there are now cashier locations in only a few places, with a centralized area for gift wrapping and other customer services. The supermarket concept of putting a variety of items into a shopping cart has expanded outside the grocery store into home and fashion centers and chain stores such as Target. With merchandise tagged with bar-code price labels and the swipe of a debit or credit card, customers can navigate the retail environment efficiently and independently.

Types of Retail Stores

Because of the way the retail industry has developed, and because it is constantly changing, there is a great deal of overlap in the way that the various types of retail stores are defined. A store can fall into more than one category. For example, a retailer can be defined not only by its size and the mix of merchandise but also by its pricing strategies and the level of customer service offered. In response to the 2005

announcement of a planned merger between Federated Department Stores and May Department Stores Company, experts began to reevaluate traditional store definitions, looking more at the function of stores than the square footage or price points. The definitions offered here should provide a vocabulary of working terms, but they are not intended to be absolute descriptions.

Department Stores

Originally descendants of the general stores that helped to clothe and furnish a growing country, department stores have changed a great deal over their nearly 150-year history in the United States. As the name suggests, a department store carries a variety of categories of products in one location. In the growing economy of the post–World War II United States, department stores proliferated along with the development of malls and became anchor tenants as these shopping centers multiplied through the 1960s and 1970s. But since the 1980s, many department stores have consolidated or downsized, and have eliminated their appliance and furniture departments.

The design of the traditional department store depends, of course, on its size and location. For example, the flagship Macy's store in New York occupies a city block and has eight floors of selling space, while many other urban and suburban Macy's stores have a much smaller footprint and fewer floors. In general, however, department stores carry a wide range of categories of merchandise and, at least to begin with, offer it at full price. Customers may be attracted more by selection than low price,

FIG. 9.11 Store interior signage used to announce discounts, sales, or brand promotions. FIG. 9.12 Point-of-purchase displays—areas near the checkout counter, often cluttered with items to encourage impulse purchases.

171

and these stores inspire customer loyalty in other ways, such as by providing personal shoppers to assist busy clients with personal wardrobe choices or with gift selection.

Department stores also gain status and customer loyalty by presenting community events, such as the annual Macy's Thanksgiving Day Parade in New York City, imaginative seasonal window displays, or support for local charities (Figure 9.13). Kohl's department store encourages community involvement by sponsoring Kohl's Kids Who Care in order to recognize and reward youth participation in philanthropic activities. Another way in which the department stores earn customer loyalty and compete with lower-price retailers is by controlling the manufacture of private label products. By developing their own brands, department stores control the design and manufacturing of goods under their own labels, offering only slightly altered versions of popular items to compete with designer-name products.

specialty store selling only cosmetics, and Crate & Barrel, which carries only household items and furniture. Specialty stores can be large or small, high-end or low-end, and can be discounters, such as Payless Shoe Source. Stores such as Abercrombie & Fitch, Old Navy, and Kenneth Cole are private-label specialty stores carrying just their own brands of merchandise. Pottery Barn, which as its name suggests began by specializing in dishes and glassware, added a Pottery Barn Kids division featuring children's furniture, linens, and even party supplies. These expanded lines of merchandise categories are offered in some traditional Pottery Barn locations as well as in freestanding Pottery Barn Kids stores.

Because of the wide range of retailers that can be classified as specialty stores—from auto parts stores to bridal shops—there is no particular formula for store layout and design. A department store or specialty store can also be referred to as a chain store when it is managed from a corporate headquarters.

Specialty Stores

In contrast to the department store, which carries many different types of merchandise, specialty stores limit their stock to a particular category, such as shoes, hats, or women's clothing, or to a group of related categories, such as women's apparel and accessories (Figure 9.14a). Some examples are Sephora, a

Discounters or Mass Merchandisers

Larger than department or specialty stores, and normally carrying a much wider range of different categories of merchandise, the discount store or mass merchandiser is a retail operation that sells goods at less than full retail price (Figure 9.14b and c). Examples of the discount store are Wal-Mart and Target, which use such volumes of merchan-

9.13

BOX 9.1

Luxury, low price mix as some malls blend merchants

By Lorrie Grant

Mall developer Westfield Group will announce Wednesday that it plans to include "cheap chic" discounter Target (TGT) alongside Neiman Marcus (NMGA) and Nordstrom (JWN) as one of five anchors at a high-end mall it is redeveloping in Los Angeles' San Fernando Valley.

The $300 million redevelopment of the Westfield Shoppingtown Topanga mall is to be complete next year.

The move reflects a growing trend in retailing to experiment with bringing what have been mostly freestanding "big-box merchants"—from discounters such as Target to specialty retailers such as Best Buy (BBY) or Bed Bath & Beyond (BBBY)—into malls as anchors.

The idea of mixing a luxury experience with low-price convenience under the same roof reflects widespread acceptance of discount shopping. "The owners of department stores and luxury stores had an attitude many years ago about this, but today they are saying these are the same customers," says Richard Green, vice chairman of Westfield's U.S. operations.

The move also is a realistic response to consolidation within the department store sector that has pushed developers such as Westfield to try something different. This will be Westfield's eighth Target store as a mall anchor.

The Australia-based mall developer also has put discount giant Wal-Mart in its Westfield Shoppingtown Parkway mall outside San Diego. It has seven Best Buy stores as anchors for some of its 67 U.S. malls across the country.

Meanwhile, the Irvine Co.'s Irvine Spectrum in Orange County, Calif., will have Nordstrom and Target as co-anchors when it's completed next year. Warehouse club Costco was a replacement tenant for Spotsylvania Mall in Fredericksburg, Va.

In general, malls depend on anchors to draw customers to their line-up of shops. Adding "big boxes," which are growing even as department stores are struggling, can do that, as well as add categories of merchandise not generally available now in malls. That helps them compete with one-stop megastores, such as Wal-Mart Supercenters.

"Years ago, malls were fashion-driven. You couldn't get a bike," Green says. "But today, you can get a bike in Target, along with housewares, sporting goods, etc."

The big stores are adding to the pressure on malls with continuing rapid expansion and with more locations in close-in suburbs and city centers.

"Regional malls were once the principle option for a shopper wanting to purchase discretionary merchandise; now, they are one of many," according to a report by the International Council of Shopping Centers. Most malls are in high-traffic suburban areas and draw customers up to 25 miles, the report shows. Only four regional malls were built in the USA last year. Five are underway this year. To fill those, developers still are likely to seek complementary—or alternative—retailers to department stores.

Consumer surveys continue to register department store complaints about too much sameness in merchandise, cluttered stores and poor customer service. Sales at department stores open at least a year nudged up just 1.6% last year, and that was the first gain since 2001, according to Redbook Research.

Department stores are trying to help themselves by doing more to differentiate themselves—and by acquiring competitors. Sears and Kmart expect to close their merger next month. Mat Department Stores bought Marshall Field's last summer. Federated Department Stores is in talks about a possible merger with May. Store closings because of overlap are seen as the inevitable result of such consolidation.

"There are fewer and fewer department stores to go after to anchor the malls," says John Melaniphy III, executive vice president at retail real estate consultant Melaniphy & Associates.

Reprinted with permission of USA Today.

dise that they can negotiate very competitive wholesale costs with suppliers in order to maintain low prices at retail. The acceptance of discount shopping and the trend toward the mixing of different types of retailers in one location is illustrated in the article in Box 9.1, which describes how the consumer's interest in value has influence the selection of the mix of stores in shopping centers.

FIG. 9.13 The Macy's Thanksgiving Day Parade. [Copyright © Shannon Stapleton/Reuters/Corbis.]

Off-Price or Outlet Stores

Another type of retail store that traditionally caters to the price-conscious consumer is the off-price or outlet store. These stores carry manufacturer overruns, closeouts of seasonal merchandise, or surplus inventories from other retailers. Examples of off-price apparel stores are TJ Maxx, Loehmann's, and Marshall's. Designer manufacturers that operate their own retail stores, such as Ralph Lauren, also operate outlet stores to close out excess inventory and items from past seasons. Often, these outlet stores are grouped together in outlet malls, typically located away from urban centers but on well-traveled routes near theme parks and other tourist destinations.

9.14a

Boutiques

Sometimes similar to the specialty store in its merchandise offerings, but not in size, the boutique is a small shop that usually carries the latest merchandise in a well-designed setting. Normally only a few pieces of each item are stocked, with custom tailoring available. Clients are individually assisted by trained sales associates who keep records of their preferences and contact them when new merchandise arrives. Box 9.2 presents a profile of a sales associate in an upscale clothing retailer where the emphasis is on personal service.

9.14b

Big Box or Warehouse Stores

An innovation in retailing that has gathered momentum since the last decade of the 20th century is the big box or warehouse club, which usually has a no-frills atmosphere that features a concrete floor, industrial shelving, and piles of shipping palates used as tables.

9.14c

174

Interview with a Designer Sales Associate: Deborah Stone

Located on Montana Avenue in Santa Monica, California, Weathervane has for more than 30 years been a magnet for those interested in cutting edge and unique pieces from the fashion world's most creative designers. The selection of merchandise and the interior environment of the store reflect the aesthetic sensibilities of the store's owner, Jan Brilliot, who keeps the inventory current with regular buying trips to the fashion centers of Europe to provide answers for her clients to that age-old question, "How should a woman dress?"

Jan Brilliot's specialty store caters to busy women with full lives, and she approaches relationships with her clients on a long-term basis. Deborah Stone, the focus of our interview, worked as a designer sales associate for six years at Weathervane, and her reflections on that experience provide insight into the differences among the many different types of shopping experiences available to the consumer.

WEAR YOUR CHAIR: *What led you to become interested in working at Weathervane?*
DEBORAH STONE: I had shopped there and liked the clothes. It was always a nice experience in a pleasant environment where I felt comfortable. I connected with the whole atmosphere on an aesthetic level. I had previously lived in New York, where there was greater access to designer clothing than there was in Los Angeles when I first settled here. I had several years of familiarity with Weathervane, but as a student at that time, I didn't have a large clothing budget. After finishing my degree in fashion marketing, I saw a small notice in the window of Weathervane and was hired.

WYC: *Have your experiences working with such unique clothing influenced your ideas about your own wardrobe?*
DS: Yes, when you're in an environment with like-minded people, it's easier to try something new, to put pieces together in an imaginative way. I look at clothing as art, so it was wonderful to have this in common with my colleagues. I don't dress from top to toe in a single designer, and this was a great opportunity to experiment with clothing, and it broadened my scope of possibilitles.

WYC: *How would you characterize the differences in service between a specialty store such as Weathervane and, for example, a department store?*

DS: Weathervane offers very personalized service. In many high-end department stores, it seems difficult to have the kind of personal attention that we were able to provide. All of the designer sales associates have established relationships with clients and are very responsive to their needs.

WYC: *Describe, if possible, a "typical" client and the shopping experience at Weathervane.*
DS: Most clients are busy women, some professionals and others not in the work force or young moms, and most have a strong interest in fashion and like a nice, uncrowded, responsive environment. The shopping experience is a collaborative effort, but it is always all about the client. I developed close relationships with some of my clients, but it was never about me and never went beyond the store. I gave psychological support when it was called for, without an invasion of their privacy. You have to be a very good listener. It's personal yet a little removed. I think people respond to honesty and respect.

WYC: *How does the interior design of the store affect the shopping experience?*
DS: The physical setting is very clean, modern and uncluttered. The hanging clothes are on racks that are set into wall alcoves, and shelves are built into the wall. Most of the clothing is around the perimeter of the store, with select pieces on two large tables. It is very functional, open plan, very minimalist. The circulation is good; the clothes are very accessible. The interior design makes the shopping experience pleasant and comfortable, intimate but not intimidating.

WYC: *If your clients had a change in fortune, and had to shop at the lower end, could you still find good products for them?*
DS: Yes, of course. I'm in private wardrobing now, which is probably a field that is viable only in large urban areas, but basically I assist clients in coordinating their clothing options, editing and building wardrobes. I'm happy in thrift shops, flea markets, the bargain basement, low-end or high-end—I'm an equal opportunity shopper!

WYC: *Do you have any advice for those just entering the field?*
DS: Aim high. That's where you get exposure to the best situations. Go with your strongest interest, what you love and feel passionate about. Be open.

FIG. 9.14 (a) Specialty store, Urban Outfitters. (b) Discount store, Burlington Coat Factory. (c) Mass merchandiser, K-Mart. [(a-c) Courtesy, Fairchild Publications, Inc.]

These stores feature oversize shopping carts or large rolling flatbeds and a very broad merchandise mix, with many categories of merchandise but few individual selections within each category and with multiples packaged in quantity. The check-out counters rely on do-it-yourself packing, offering no assistance with bagging, boxing, or carry out.

The warehouse store shouldn't be considered low-end though. For example, at Costco, with a club membership, in addition to such necessities as multipacks of paper towels, the customer can purchase collector's items of Limoges enamelware from France. *USA Today* recently reported that an original Picasso drawing with a listed price of $40,000 was sold on the Costco Web site. The popularity of these warehouse stores is evidence of the fact that shopping, specifically bargain-hunting, has become a common form of recreation. In an article about the quest for good deals, a shopper is quoted, "Getting name brands at a discount price is a duty" (Earnest).

Home centers such as Expo, Lowe's, and IKEA are a variation of the warehouse store in the way in which merchandise is presented. They carry a vast assortment of products. Customers of these retailers are expected to have a certain amount of knowledge of products, their function, and their location within the store as well as no fear of the phrase "Some assembly required." Design and remodeling consultation services are available along with educational workshops in which customers can develop home-repair skills. The IKEA motto, "We shall offer a wide range of well-designed, functional products at prices so low that as many people as possible will be able to afford them," is the reverse of the snob appeal of expensive designer-brand household items.

Thrift Shops

Thrift shops have long been part of the retail landscape, but in recent years they have lost the aura of shame that was once associated with secondhand merchandise. Vintage clothing and furniture are very much in demand, especially among students or young professionals, who tend to have limited financial resources, by costume and set designers for the entertainment industry, and by those seeking an interesting alternative to mass production done offshore. Thrift shops are usually run as nonprofit entities for fundraising, and they include stores such as Goodwill, Discovery Shops, and Salvation Army Thrift. Flexible layout is a key design element since the stock is usually donated merchandise that is constantly changing. In some ways these stores resemble garage sales with assorted clothing, furniture, and appliances all sharing the sales floor.

A variation of the thrift shop is the consignment shop, which is stocked with items that the owner, a private individual, has agreed to sell at a certain price, of which the shop proprietor takes a percentage. Consignment shops that carry vintage clothing and furniture often have devoted customers who scour these shops for collectibles. The popularity of vintage clothing with celebrities who choose to appear in these classic pieces for award shows has increased interest in these rare and one-of-a-kind fashions.

Airport Shops

Airport shops make up a growing retail niche. As airline economies and unforeseen events increase the amount of time needed to allow for travel delays and security and check-in procedures, the captive audience for airport retailers increases, as does the quantity,

9.15

quality, and variety of shops. Retail opportunities in airports, especially those serving as hubs for transfer, are increasingly being developed. "The airport retail market, already at $20 billion, is expected to grow to $40 billion by 2010, and the average sales per square foot can be 30 times that of shopping centers" (Schaffer, p. 5). Figure 9.15 shows a planned airport retail area.

Virtual Retailing: Shopping Through Media

There are several types of retailing that do not rely on brick-and-mortar locations, but instead on a form of media. Catalog retailers are associated with the print medium, shopping networks with the medium of television, and electronic retailing, or e-tailing, with computers and the selling of goods on the Internet. Catalog shopping, which was once the only way that people in remote situations could make purchases, originated as a way for retailers to reach customers in regions far from store locations. Although catalog shopping still serves customers in remote areas, it has also become popular with people whose hectic schedules prevent shopping during regular business hours and those who prefer the convenience of mail order to the store experience.

Although many retailers with brick-and-mortar

sites such as Eddie Bauer, J. Crew, and Williams-Sonoma produce merchandise catalogs to augment the business conducted at store locations, there are also catalog retailers without any physical store locations. An example is Levinger, a specialty catalog aimed at readers and book lovers, which features selected merchandise targeted to this very specific interest group.

The catalog concept has evolved further with the development of interactive shopping media, such as cable shopping channels and Internet shopping. The Internet site eBay combines features of auction and consignment in its huge array of new and used merchandise and collectibles. It also provides chat opportunities to users of the site. In the past catalog retailers had to contact the customer, but with these virtual retail sites, it is the customer who contacts a Web site or cable channel. The Internet offers bountiful shopping opportunities as well as services that parallel those in traditional retail venues. The online shopping services characterized in Figure 9.16 are an example.

Another retail opportunity that relies on interactive media is the product tie-in with television broad-

9.16

FIG. 9.15 An airport shopping area. [Copyright © Hashi/ Getty Images.]
FIG. 9.16 Online shopping allows many to enjoy the convenience of 24/7 access to merchandise. [Copyright © Images.com/Corbis.]

casts, in which consumers can place an order online for merchandise that is featured in televised events, soap operas, or other programs (Rosenbaum).

What's Next?

Not too long ago, income was almost the sole determiner of access to well-designed products. Now good design is featured in mass media and is available at almost every price range. At one time, fashion, interior design, art and design students, and professionals seemed to have a monopoly on design knowledge. Through their education and professional training they were familiar with such names as Michael

9.17

Graves, Le Corbusier, or Nicole Miller and might covet items designed by these stars. Now the 21st-century consumer is, for the most part, equally well informed about these persons and products. The media, including television networks and specialized cable programming, the Internet, and fashion and lifestyle periodicals, are contributing to the consumer's awareness of well-designed clothing, furniture, and small appliances. As new products become more visible through these many forms of media, and the ease of distribution of products is increased by efficient methods of transportation, the sophistication level of the consumer grows. The apparent conclusion drawn by marketing and advertising professionals is that this

leads to increased demand for well-designed and well-priced products.

Consumers can now choose to shop in a luxury setting with personalized service, in a warehouse setting where they know they can get what they want for a lower price, or in the privacy and comfort of their homes through catalog shopping or interactive media.

Marketing professionals seem fairly confident of the level of design awareness among consumers and of the consumers' sophistication and knowledge about products and their value. For example, the Michael Graves kettle with bird whistle designed for Alessi, pictured in Figure 9.17, is available through a variety of sources at different prices. Pure devotees of Michael Graves will want to visit the Graves Design Studio Store in Princeton, New Jersey, to acquire this iconic piece of kitchen equipment, or at least order from the store's catalog. But the same kettle can be purchased through other catalogs or, perhaps slightly used, on eBay. Another choice might be a facsimile of the kettle with the bird whistle replaced by a twirling bauble and a slightly altered handle design, available at Target stores.

Again, perhaps responding to the media and to the accessibility of products, consumers seem ready for a new type of brick-and-mortar shopping experience when they venture out—the "concept store,"

9.18a

9.18b

where the emphasis is on the education of the consumer. These stores are appearing in urban areas throughout the United States. In the concept store, which has the feel of a showroom, the customer is welcomed and encouraged to examine and try whatever product lines are being offered. Maytag, the maker of household appliances, has introduced concept stores in which customers can test its products by bringing their own dirty laundry and dishes (Eastman, 2002).

Similarly, for Mac computer aficionados, the new Apple Stores devote half their retail area to "after-the-sale" services that include instruction in how to use computers and demonstrations of Mac products by professionals. In these stores there is a club atmosphere as regulars eagerly trade secrets of the Mac operating system (Eastman, 2002).

As we move forward, contemporary store design is providing notable examples of a trend toward the retail store becoming a public space that has more in common with a museum or art gallery than with a merchandise emporium. The Italian company Prada recently invested a reported $40 million in its New York boutique designed by the Dutch architect Rem Koolhaas (Figure 9.18a). When it first opened, the project received both raves and ridicule, but the idea that a fashion house would devote such resources to

making a design statement that features an interior space that the architect calls "the Wave" is revolutionary.

In a retail climate in which merchants analyze the productivity of each square foot of sales area, Prada has made history by going against the grain of traditional store design. This suggests how the future of some shopping experiences might evolve. The store has the feeling of a gallery, featuring both new and vintage Prada items, and legions of Prada fans, like pilgrims reaching a sacred destination, troop through the store, paying homage to these items and to the interior space that houses them.

The building of Prada flagships known as *epicenter* stores has continued, with the collaboration of significant figures from architecture and fashion: The locations in Beverly Hills and Manhattan were designed by Rem Koolhaas, and the store in the Aoyama district of Tokyo was designed by Swiss architects Jacques Herzog and Pierre de Meuron (Figure 9.18b). These stores are examples of retail space design that has made shopping a recreational activity with the evolution of commercial spaces into cultural spaces. Designers can lead the way by working to create interesting and inviting shopping environments that present intelligent and aesthetically pleasing products.

FIG. 9.17 The Michael Graves bird whistle kettle is now available at several different market levels. FIG. 9.18 (a) The Prada Store store in Manhattan, designed by Rem Koolhaas, and (b) The Prada store in Tokyo, designed by Jacques Herzog and Pierre de Meuron. [(a) Reprinted by permission of the *New York Times.* (b) Courtesy Fairchild Publications, Inc.]

CHAPTER TEN

When Life Became Style

This chapter discusses advertising, branding, and lifestyle and the relationship of each to fashion design, interior design, and graphic design. Graphic design for the creation of identifiable marks or logos serves as a connection to branding, layout, and advertising. What do these terms mean, what do they have in common, how do they interact, what common elements of design do they share, how do they differ, and why are they important to designers? To understand their importance we must first define these terms.

To advertise is "to make a public announcement of a product or business so as to increase sales" (*American Heritage Dictionary*). These paid announcements appear in newspapers and magazines, on signs and posters, on television, and as banners on the Internet. Brand or branding, which was originally a mark burned on the skin of animals to denote ownership, has evolved to also mean "a trademark or distinctive name identifying a product, aesthetic, or manufacturer" (*American Heritage Dictionary*). We can define *lifestyle* as an individual's whole way of living, which seems to be a perfectly straightforward response, but the answer is not that simple, for our 21st-century lifestyles are constantly changing. When we open our daily newspapers, monthly magazines, drive on our highways, littered with billboard advertising, we are deluged with new products, brands, and philosophies that we are told we cannot live without. *Lifestyle*, as a contemporary term, encompasses our mode or characteristic of existence, combining demographics, psychosocial needs, and life

10.1

stages. A humorous lifestyle example appears in "Cathy" (Figure 10.1), where Irving's expensive sunglasses make a lifestyle statement for him, creating a fantasy persona.

The Purpose of Brand Advertising

Brand advertisements, whether they are trying to sell cars, clothing, furniture, or personal hygiene products, certainly influence our lives. Which SUV can climb a mountain (adventurous), which dress will actually "get the guy" (happily married), which sofa portrays the right image (successful), and which deodorant will actually keep you dry (cool)? If you desire any of these lifestyle attributes you will buy these products. Advertisers try to answer these questions to facilitate your decision-making process. In the cartoon *Fashion Fatigue* created by Roz Chast (Figure 10.2), the featured charac-

fashion fatigue
BY ROZ CHAST

10.2

ter is questioning what kind of utilitarian objects her life represents. Advertisers focus on whether or not we would actually change our teakettles or soap dishes to suit our lifestyles.

Just by observing students and faculty on your college campus, you will see clothing, backpacks, computers, shoes, jewelry, and cars that can be identified by brand. Whether it is the apple on our classmates' laptops, the swoosh on their running shoes, or the golden arches on the wrappers on their lunches, brand identification is part of our daily lifestyle (Figure 10.3a–c).

The most effective brands or logos transcend languages—they are evocative and instantly recognizable. Some are pictograms or marks like the "apple," and some are words like "Coke." When consumers are given a choice, they usually purchase the branded product they know best (Keiser p. 78). How are these brands or logos conceived, and most of all, what do they have to do with designers?

The Evolution of Brand Advertising

If we think about how the design process evolves or how different areas of design are interrelated, we can visualize the design process as a never-ending cycle or chain of events, with each area overlapping the next (Figure 10.4) (Hanks, p. 58; Koberg, p. 20).

We can illustrate the relationship between advertising, branding, and lifestyle with another graphic (Figure 10.5). Companies need a strong brand image to identify their products, for without this image, the advertising agencies on Madison Avenue cannot successfully promote the products. The public wants a product that will make their lives better,

10.3a

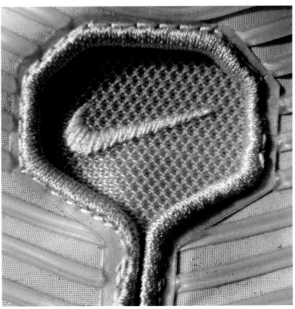

10.3b+c

FIG. 10.1 A *Cathy* cartoon about lifestyle. [Cathy © 2002, Cathy Guisewite. Reprinted with permission of Universal Press Syndicate. All rights reserved.] FIG. 10.2 A *Fashion Fatigue* cartoon that relates to lifestyle choices. [Reprinted with permission of Roz Chast.] FIG. 10.3 (a) Apple computer with logo. (b) Nike swoosh logo. (c) McDonald's sign with logo. [(a) Copyright © Hugh Threlfall/Alamy. (b) Copyright © David Crausby/Alamy.]

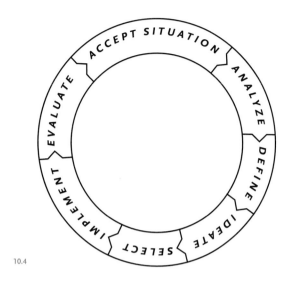

10.4

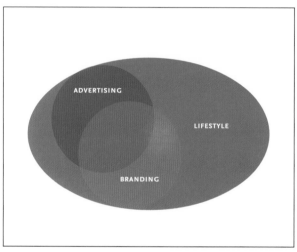

10.5

papers," says James Twitchell, "we listened to the same radio programs. Of all the radio formats that originated in the 1930s, the soap opera was the best suited to play a central role in encouraging mass consumption" (*Lead Us into Temptation*, p. 106). Everyone needed to buy products and radio, through its daytime soap operas, which provided the sales format. Advertising agencies actually began to make references to the products within the shows' dialogues and then followed with commercials selling the same product. The concept of "product placement," if not the term, has a long history in advertising. The Detroit auto manufacturers followed this advertising strategy by allowing television producers free access to automobiles for promotion in movies and TV shows. Television actually popularized the automobile. Whatever car your favorite actor was driving helped you to visualize the star's lifestyle, and you wanted to emulate it. Today Internet advertising and instant messaging are bombarding you with offers of products, vacations, and dating services to assist you in achieving and maintaining your desired lifestyle image.

Designers are part of this ever-changing advertising, branding, and lifestyle trend. They design the logo or brand to make the product identifiable and desirable. Even as design students, they participate in creating the products or services to be sold. Fashion design students may interest manufacturers in their senior runway collections; interior design students may sell a custom-designed piece of furniture to a leading furniture company for inclusion in its product lines. As interns, they sell their design services to the clients of their employers. Industrial design students are frequently being hired by major

easier, or "more complete," thereby enhancing their self-image. Thus begins the lifestyle segment of this chain of interrelationships.

Mass advertising and consumption had its start in your great-grandmother's living room with the radio. "While we did not all read the same news-

automobile manufacturers to design cars. Designers and design students are also among the trendsetting consumers who purchase, use, and help to popularize these products as part of their individual lifestyles.

Creating a Brand Image

"Buildings age and become dilapidated, machines wear out, people die, but what live on are the brands," says Sir Hector Laing (as quoted in Temporal, p. 1). In this section, we examine how brand images are born and what efforts go into ensuring their survival.

The Beginnings

How are brand images created, why are they created, and why are they so important? They are created to identify and sell ideas and products, but this is far from a new phenomenon. Trademarks have been around for centuries (Figure 10.6). Stamps or markings were used on pottery and bricks by the ancient Romans, Greeks, and Egyptians to identify the maker (Johnson). Coats of arms indicated which kingdom or family warriors came from. In the Middle Ages bell makers, jewelers, and silversmiths used stamps, while paper makers used watermarks to indicate the maker. In 1266, England passed the Bakers Marking Law, requiring bakers to stamp or pinprick their loaves of bread. In Paris, furniture makers as early as the 1750s signed their work with marks. Collectors of antique artifacts look to these ancient stamps and marks to determine the identification, quality, and value of an object. Dating back to

10.6

the beginning of the 20th century, we see fashion and interior designers and architects in the United States and Europe adopting logos and brands for their furniture and fashion.

20th-Century Lifestyle Pioneers in France

The formation of the *Société National des Artistes Décorateurs* in Paris in 1901 was a significant event in the history of design. This group of dynamic and talented designer-decorators included Hector Guimard, the architect of the Métro entrances in Paris, and Eugène Gaillard and Eugène Grasset, whose design work was displayed and sold in department stores. Their aim was to increase the public awareness of

FIG. 10.4 The design process—circular format. [Based on *The Universal Traveler: A Soft-System Guide to Creativity, Problem-Solving, and the Process of Reaching Goals*, by Don Koberg and Jim Bagnall, Los Altos, CA: William Kaufmann, Inc., 1976, p. 20.] FIG. 10.5 The interrelationships of design. FIG. 10.6 Silver horse trapping with heraldic symbol of Samaritan people from the necropolis of Nejzac Belogorsk, Crimea. [Reprinted with permission of The Art Archive/Historical Museum of Republic of Crimea Simferopol/Dagli Orti.]

design and decoration through publications and exhibitions.

By 1923, after many years of presenting annual exhibitions at the Pavillion Marsan in Paris, the Société began to show whole room settings created by individual designers. Everyone interested in all facets of design attended these events, and the images of these designers began to be publicized, creating identifiable furniture and brands. People who wanted to emulate the lifestyles embodied in the displays purchased the complete room settings, furniture, or products created by these fashionable designers for their own use.

Just before the start of World War I, Paul Poiret (see Chapter 2) and his wife, Denise, became famous for their lavish *fêtes de Bacchus.* At these parties, fashion and interior designers and artists came together, all looking for new directions. Perhaps, never before had the three worlds so comfortably and profitably overlapped with one another (Adam, p. 71). After sales from his first couture collection reached a million francs, Poiret began exploring areas of design other than fashion. Not only did he design furniture, textiles, and scents that were available to the public in his Paris boutique *Ateliers Martine* but Poiret also began to decorate patrons' homes, creating his branded image with brightly colored trees and flowers painted on the walls and low furniture upholstered in shimmering or boldly patterned fabrics (Massey, p. 96). Poiret's bold colors and imagery were adopted from the Fauves, a group of painters active at the turn of the 20th century that included Raoul Dufy and Henri Matisse (Massey, p. 95). Poiret's crossover between fashion and interior

design was typical of designers during the Art Deco movement (Figure 10.7).

During this time the art, furniture, and couture clothing markets in Paris began to boom. Paris became a mecca for artists and designers. As Parisians became more affluent, they changed their lifestyles and renovated their homes (Adam p. 95). In order to assist with this huge undertaking, people began to hire designers and decorators like Eileen Gray, who was known in Paris for designing homes and apartments in some of the wealthiest arrondissements (subdivisions of the city). Decorating became an important aspect in the lives of the Paris elite; they changed their decor almost as often as they changed their dress (Adam p. 243).

Eileen Gray, Sonia Delaunay (see Chapter 2), Le Corbusier, Robert Mallet-Stevens, and others helped form the *Union des Artistes Modern* (UAM). This group was created to remove unnecessary ornamentation from design and integrate furniture and architecture (Adam). This new era in design continued to merge the design disciplines of fashion, interiors, furniture, architecture, and graphics, thus creating more identifiable branding and lifestyle images.

Although not part of the UAM, Gabrielle "Coco" Chanel was part of the emerging modernist trend. Her use of jersey made it possible for women to participate in activities that they could not do before. She made sports clothes a part of women's wardrobes and made significant contributions to lifestyle imaging. Coco Chanel's influence reverberated throughout the 20th century (Figure 10.8). Her Chanel No. 5 Perfume, in its Art Deco bottle, launched in 1923, was the first perfume to be branded with a designer's name (Sischy).

10.7

Mass Marketing of Branded Design in Europe

In 1921, Gray, who was best known for designing furniture, lacquer work, screens, and rugs, opened Jean Désert, a shop that would allow the French public easier access to her designs. Anyone desiring to emulate her lifestyle approach could commission her to design furniture or rooms for their homes. Although her work was well known in Paris, she never signed or dated her furniture or accessories, and they were not mass-produced. In the late 1920s she was greatly influenced by the Modern movement and her designs began to be devoid of ornamentation, with tubular steel, glass, and wood reflecting her new image (Adam, p. 131) (Figure 10.9).

Other designers who gained popularity during the 1920s had individual galleries, ateliers, or

10.8

10.9

FIG. 10.7 Interior of a room on Poiret's barge, designed by Martine and exhibited at the Exposition of 1925. [Copyright © Bibliotheque des Arts Decoratifs, Paris, France/Archives Charmet/The Bridgeman Art Library.] FIG. 10.8 A design from House of Chanel. [Courtesy, Fairchild Publications, Inc.] FIG. 10.9 Furniture by Eileen Gray (1929). [Reprinted with permission of the National Museum of Ireland.]

187

creations in Paris. Among them were furniture designer Emile-Jacques Ruhlmann, who designed furniture, light fixtures, fabric, and household accessories exhibiting amazing attention to detail, and Jean Dunand, whose furniture and lacquer pieces were exhibited at the Galerie George Petit. Maurice Dufrêne, whose design studio La Maîtrise was opened in the Galeries Lafayette department store, and Paul Follot, whose Grand Salon was in Bon Marché, were among the first interior designers to be featured in stores that had formerly sold only clothing.

The XX Salon des Artistes Décorateurs' 1930 exhibition gave the public a first look at the innovative steel furniture designs of Marcel Breuer, Herbert Bayer, and Walter Gropius. These Bauhaus designers, along with Le Corbusier and Mies van der Rohe, were part of the Modern movement in design, whose philosophy was to remove unnecessary ornament from architecture, interiors, and furniture (Figure 10.10a–c). Many of their tubular steel furniture designs began to be mass-produced, and they established international reputations as designers and architects. The Museum of Modern Art in New York supported the development of this trend by exhibiting plans and photographs of their work in a 1932 exhibition, bringing the Modern move-

10.10a

10.10b

10.10c

ment to America. Their classic furniture is still licensed and manufactured by Knoll and Herman Miller with many other manufacturers creating inexpensive knockoffs for mass consumption. Thus, we can all be part of the Modern movement lifestyle.

America Follows European Trends

Similar approaches in design were also taking place in the United States. In the design of interiors, household accessories, appliances, and fashion, an American lifestyle aesthetic evolved in the 20th century.

Residential Interior Design and Household Accessories

Elsie de Wolfe, a former actress, was considered the first interior decorator. She was a chic, successful businesswoman who, in 1905, distributed business cards using a trademark of a small wolf with a flower in his paw (Figure 10.11).

Ms. de Wolfe, or Lady Mendl, as she was later called, was a trendsetter in the field of interior design. Photographs of many of the rooms she designed were published in magazines, and they were copied by a public anxious to follow these new trends. She objected to the darkness and clutter of Victorian design and invented a new clean English country look (Figure 10.12). Ms. de Wolfe wrote *The House in Good Taste,* which treated home decoration as a branch of fashion (Smith). Ms. de Wolfe was very talented and capable of designing everything from a table setting to an entire house, creating a complete lifestyle image. She wrote articles for popular

ideals of every country and every time.

Consequently, she is able to re-create for every patron of hers a significant reflection of a distinct individuality. A visit to her rich studio is a revelation to every beauty lover—a revelation both of her personality and of unsuspected possibilities in plaster and metal and cloth and wood.

ELSIE DE WOLFE

INTERIOR DECORATIONS
ANTIQUE FURNITURE   OBJÊTS D'ART

677 FIFTH AVENUE   NEW YORK CITY

10.11

10.12

FIG. 10.10 (a) "Wassily" chair by Marcel Breuer (1925). (b) "Barcelona" chair by Mies van der Rohe (1929). (c) Chaise lounge by Le Corbusier and Charlotte Perriand (1927). [(a) Copyright © The Museum of Modern Art/Licensed by Scala/Art Resource, NY. Gift of Herbert Bayer. (b) Copyright © The Museum of Modern Art/Licensed by Scala/Art Resource, NY. (c) Courtesy, Cassina, Inc.] FIG. 10.11 Elsie DeWolfe trademark. [Photo by Judith Griffin.] FIG. 10.12 Corner of Main Salon in Elsie De Wolfe's studio. [Photo by Judith Griffin.]

10.13

The Kitchen Buffet is really cafeteria procedure. A stack of trays and tableware is laid out on the counter, and food is taken directly from the stove by the guests.

10.14a

Cleanup can even be a part of the evening's pleasure, if managed properly.

10.14b

lifestyle magazines, and the women of the day used her ideas to freshen up their homes and add a bit of individuality to their lives.

Russel Wright, another influential midcentury modernist, and his wife, Mary Wright, can be said to be the inventors of lifestyle marketing. Without the Wrights, Martha Stewart and Ralph Lauren would not have been as successful (Albrecht, p. 11). Wright designed inexpensive, mass-produced dinnerware, furniture, appliances, and textiles that he and his wife felt created "easier living" for the American lifestyle. Wright used many new materials for his products, among them spun aluminum and melamine (Figure 10.13).

The Wrights' designs were featured in exhibitions, books, advertisements, and demonstration rooms in department stores. In 1950, the Wrights co-authored the *Guide for Easier Living*, which described in great detail how to create the perfect home. The book included information on planning, designing, and maintaining an efficient home for modern living. The book is filled with charming illustrations depicting many types of situational activities for a middle-class lifestyle (Figure 10.14a and b).

The American Modern dinnerware line, marketed in 1939, made Russel Wright a household name. The magazine *Living for Young Homemakers* con-

10.15

ducted a poll in 1951, and consumers indicated that they used Wright dinnerware over all other manufacturers' names featured on the list. Wright was the only individual designer on the list (Albrecht, p. 163). For the first time, American dinnerware, perhaps the most commonplace of all household products, became identified with the name of one designer (Figure 10.15).

Russel Wright was a pioneer in design and lifestyle for the modern, suburban, post–World War II family. He knew that the men and women returning from the war would begin a new lifestyle, and he helped pave the way. In the economic boom that followed the war, families in the United States began to make substantial purchases. The GI Bill made it possible for returning soldiers to borrow money, obtain an education, start businesses, and purchase new labor-saving products. Everyone in

the 1950s had high expectations and looked forward to a new upwardly mobile lifestyle.

A predominant part of this upwardly mobile lifestyle included some of the most exciting new electronic inventions, the television being the most significant. With the advent of the TV (as it quickly came to be known), people were not only able to hear about products and lifestyle but they actually became voyeuristic observers. Evening TV began to be watched by thousands of households, and people wanted to purchase what they saw advertised on their favorite TV shows.

One of those shows, the *General Electric Theater,* was viewed weekly by thousands of households. It featured situational dramas and comedies with advertising for the most current GE products. Long before becoming president of the United States, Ronald Reagan was the program's host, and GE

FIG. 10.13 Spun aluminum tableware by Russel Wright. [Photo by Anita Calero. Copyright © Cooper-Hewitt National Design Museum.] FIG. 10.14 (a) "Kitchen Buffet" and (b) "Cleanup with Guests" cartoons depict middle-class lifestyle. [Source: *Guide to Easier Living*, by Russel and Mary Wright. Reprinted with permission of Gibbs Smith, Publisher.] FIG. 10.15 Dinnerware by Russel Wright. [Photo by Anita Calero. Copyright © Cooper-Hewitt National Design Museum.]

used his voiceover to sell its appliances. By 1954 the *General Electric Theater,* according to the Nielsen ratings, had won top-ten status. One of the most remembered segments was the "Kitchen of the Future," in which Ronald and Nancy Reagan advertised the most innovative, time-saving features and appliances available to the consumer of the day. Standing in the "totally electric home," they told viewers, "When you live better electrically, you lead a richer, fuller, more satisfying life. And it's something all of us in this modern age can have." Their motto, expressed by Reagan weekly, was "progress in products goes hand in hand with providing progress in the human values that enrich the lives of us all." The *General Electric Theater* became "the leading institutional campaign on television for selling ideas to the public" (*General Electric Theater*). We can easily envision the advertising, branding, and lifestyle paradigm in this GE example, and we can see how important it was in creating this new, "satisfying" lifestyle (Figure 10.16).

10.16

Fashions for a Casual Lifestyle

Clothing design was also a part of this new suburban lifestyle, and Claire McCardell took a significant lead in the design and creation of women's sportswear in America. She created practical, beltless dresses with loose armholes and usable pockets. She used comfortable materials like corduroy and cotton. Women could move in her clothing, and her designs were fashionable and beautiful. McCardell was a revolutionary force in midcentury design (Figure 10.17).

Bonnie Cashin, whose designs were a significant part of the 1950s and 1960s, shared McCardell's interest in comfortable, casual clothing. Cashin designed clothing using "real hardware" closures, clean lines, and uncomplicated styles. A trip to Japan inspired Cashin to pioneer the "layered look," allowing women to change their outfits according to changes in the temperature (Swank Vintage). Her later clothing designs included the use of canvas, jersey, leather, and tweed (Figure 10.18), which she incorporated into her popular "dog leash" skirt and loose-fitting turtlenecks.

Shelter and Lifestyle Magazines

During the burgeoning 1950s, monthly lifestyle magazines were beginning to gain a strong foothold in American

10.17

10.18

homes. These magazines were designed to teach the wives of military veterans how to create comfortable domestic environments and included recipes and articles on home decorating, entertaining, and child rearing. *Good Housekeeping, Ladies Home Journal,* and *McCalls* were among the most popular. *Good Housekeeping,* which was started in 1885, was the original shelter magazine, and it continued to provide stimulating information about running a home. It was also known for testing consumer products and advertising them when they met with the *Good Housekeeping* "Seal of Approval" (www.TodayinHistory.com).

Current Lifestyle Magazines

New shelter and lifestyle magazines continue to be published monthly, but women are no longer the sole audience. With titles like *Martha Stewart Living, Country Woman, Dwell, Metropolis, Wallpaper, Architectural Digest, Men's Health, Real Simple, Self, Town and Country, Prevention, Lifestyle, Vegan,* and *Gaylife,* these magazines target everyone with interests ranging from health to home to country, city, or coastal living to veganism.

The Transition from Magazines to Catalogs

In the fall of 1999, IKEA debuted a new lifestyle magazine, *Space*. It was part catalog, part magazine. Not only did it sell IKEA merchandise but it also had articles on health, travel, architecture, and design. Marty Marston, a spokeswoman for IKEA North America, said, "It goes beyond a catalog. We want to present IKEA as a lifestyle trendsetter, and that's why we are spotlighting our own products as part of a full range of merchandise" (Koenenn).

Catalogs became a major part of our lifestyle in the 1990s. A day does not go by that we do not receive at least one catalog in the mail. The catalogs are from manufacturers of lines of furniture, clothing, bed and bath products, home accessories, and office supplies, as well as from companies that represent product lines for a myriad of manufacturers. Pottery Barn, Design Within Reach, Martha Stewart's Catalog for Living, Williams-Sonoma, West Elm, Chicos, Victoria's Secret, J. Crew, L.L. Bean, and Lands' End are just a short list of catalogs that are published on a regular basis. If you are

FIG. 10.16 GE Kitchen of the Future. [Copyright © Bettmann/Corbis.] FIG. 10.17 Claire McCardell dress. [Reprinted with permission of Gibbs Smith, Publisher.] FIG. 10.18 Bonnie Cashin designs. [Courtesy, Fairchild Publications, Inc.]

10.19

decorating your home, accessorizing your kitchen, or dressing for play or success, there is a catalog for you (Figure 10.19).

Contemporary Consultants and Lifestyle Designers

Catalogs are not the only successful sales trend in branding and lifestyle; designers and manufacturers are also using consultants for the development of advertising, branding, and environmental concept packages. Designers who are associated with fashion, home furnishings, and other design disciplines are expanding their images and creating lifestyle brands.

KramerHutchison

Let's look at KramerHutchison, who they are, and what they do. KramerHutchison creates complete brand identities and environments for fashion companies. Robin Kramer listens to her designer clients, and then transforms their thoughts and wishes into a cohesive retail environment that "tells a story" and keeps the shopper coming back for more. Each project the firm undertakes varies according to the clients' needs. The consultant can reinvent a faltering corporate image, find the "personality" of another company, or design the real estate within a department store as it did for Tommy Hilfiger. Other clients include Donna Karan; Coach; Narciso Rodriguez; Barneys New York; and Jeffrey, a New York boutique. Along with partner Jeff Hutchison, an architect, Robin Kramer designs store interiors, including everything from the lighting, the flooring, and the fixtures on which clothing is displayed to the packaging. They are hired to "keep customers in stores buying things." Kramer was vice president of store planning and visual display for Calvin Klein before starting her own firm. Everything reflected the Calvin Klein image. "When you are in a Calvin environment, you know that you are in a Calvin environment," Kramer explained, "but you can't pin it on one thing" (as quoted in Bellafante) (Figure 10.20).

10.20

Ralph Lauren's Edwardian Lifestyle Image

Does that environmental concept conjure up other images? Take, for example, Ralph Lauren, a brand name we are very familiar with (see Chapter 9). What started with men's ties and shirts with Polo ponies has developed into a publicly held company with $2.2 billion in sales, employing more than 100 designers (Kaufman). Ralph Lauren is not responsible for a specific product, but according to Paul Goldberger, the architecture critic for the *New York*

does not design clothing; she designs a lifestyle. She can plan a menu, cook the food, and design the room and table on which it will be presented and served. Martha Stewart Living Omnimedia, which reported a $103.5 million gross profit in 2005, has a staff of more than 600. This media empire is responsible for *Martha Stewart Living, Everyday Food,* a TV show, a newspaper column, and the Martha Stewart Everyday line of home products. Her home product line includes the branding and design of paint, linens, china, and home and garden accessories. The Martha Stewart "brand" is available by mail-order catalog and online, while lower-price home products are available at K-mart. Martha's products have a more subtle approach to branding—they don't have a logo on them—but you know them when you see them. This is not as upscale an approach as Ralph Lauren's, but one that targets a broader audience and helps create a branded lifestyle image for the masses.

Even Martha Stewart's recent confinement for perjury about her insider information about the

Times, Lauren is "the ultimate producer of a completely packaged, perfect life, that has come to symbolize in this culture . . . something we might call the artifice business" (Troy p. 16). This packaged look is the brand for clothing, furniture, sheets, shoes, and upholstery. Ralph Lauren reflects a fantasy environment, carefully designed to project an Edwardian upper-class club (Figure 10.21) (Troy p. 16). This staged environment is created with the use of props such as leather luggage and satchels, wooden airplane propellers, horse-back riding paraphernalia, and the like that he and his staff locate in antique shops throughout Europe.

Martha Stewart

Martha Stewart has also created an empire, but it does not have the same old-money look. Stewart

10.21

FIG. 10.19 Assorted catalog covers. [Photo by Judith Griffin.] FIG. 10.20 Calvin Klein store interior. [Courtesy, Fairchild Publications, Inc.] FIG. 10.21 Ralph Lauren store display. [Courtesy, Fairchild Publications, Inc.]

stock market has failed to stop the Omnimedia juggernaut. Her partnership with K-mart is destined to expand her demographics as Sears progresses through its marketing of its K-mart chain.

Chris Casson Madden

You may not be as familiar with designer Chris Casson Madden, but along with Martha Stewart, she has created a lifestyle empire. For eight seasons Madden hosted *Interiors by Design* on the HGTV network, in which she focused on accessible and affordable residential design. She has also written many books on kitchen design and bed and bath design, guides to personalizing the home, and photo essays of designer showcase houses. Some of her titles include *A Room of Her Own: Women's Personal Spaces*, *Kitchens: Information and Inspiration for Making Kitchens the Heart of the Home*, and *Bedrooms: Creating the Stylish, Comfortable Room of Your Dreams*. Madden also writes for *Metropolitan Home*, *World of Interiors*, *Traditional Home*, and *Good Housekeeping*. Her approach to design takes a different path. Her philosophy is more of an inspirational and spiritual one, as indicated by the titles of her books, Madden takes a more sensitive approach to her design and lifestyle philosophy. She asks us to look within ourselves and assists us in coming up with something that is in our heart and dreams, "turning home into haven".

Mary Engelbreit

Mary Engelbreit, an illustrator, designs products such as greeting cards, calendars, dinnerware, and fabric, which are sold through thousands of retailers as well as her own retail and online store. Her

10.22

colorful graphic illustrations (Figure 10.22) and products have a whimsical, homey appeal that has generated over $1 billion in lifetime retail sales. The *Wall Street Journal* called her company "a vast empire of cuteness." Through her soft approach, Engelbreit has tapped into an enormous market that appeals to consumers in all stages of life. Engelbreit is also editor in chief of a bimonthly magazine, *Mary Engelbreit's Home Companion*. This creative lifestyle magazine includes articles on decorating, crafts, food preparation, family life, and antique collectibles.

Branding a City's Image

Branding is not limited to companies and individuals. New York has hired its first marketing official, Joseph M. Perello, who has the huge task of actually branding products to help New York make money. Mayor

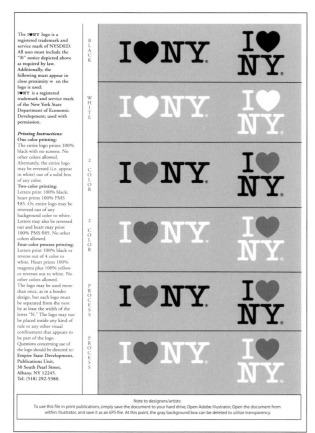

10.23a

10.23b

Michael R. Bloomberg says that the city "would approach this in a tasteful, albeit remunerative, manner." "Appropriate products," says Richard Kirshenbaum, the co-chairman of Kirshenbaum Bond & Partners, "would receive the official New York Seal of Approval." Similar to the *Good Housekeeping* Seal of Approval, it would assist in the sale of goods and services for the city (Kleinfield). This branding concept is still in the planning stages.

This is not New York's first attempt at branding. New York has had two successful advertising campaigns in the past. The "Big Apple" was first used to represent New York in 1907, when one guidebook included the comment, "Some may think the Apple

10.23c

FIG. 10.22 The banner on Mary Engelbreit's Web site and a PowerPoint slide about licensing for potential entrepreneurs. [Copyright © Mary Engelbreit.] FIG. 10.23 (a) "I Love NY" logo designed by Milton Glaser for New York State. (b) The logo in use on merchandise. (c) "I Love NY more than ever" poster designed by Milton Glaser after September 11, 2001. [(a-c) I [heart] New York is a registered trademark and service mark of the New York State Department of Economic Development. Reprinted with permission of the New York State Department of Economic Development and Milton Glaser. Photos by Judith Griffin.]

197

is losing some of its sap," referring to the upstate New York apple-growing region. "The Apple Marketing Board, alarmed by sharply declining sales, launched what some believe to be the earliest example of what would now be called a 'product positioning campaign'" (The Society for New York City History). The slogan, which represented not only the city, but the state, has remained a strong symbolic image.

Graphic designer Milton Glaser created the second and most imitated slogan and logo in 1977. It is the "I love NY" slogan, with a heart used as a symbol for the word *love*. The logo was designed for the New York State Department of Economic Development as an advertising campaign to stimulate tourism in New York State (Figure 10.23a). This popular logo is still used today (Figure 10.23b), and since the tragic events of September 11, 2001, it has symbolized the character and strength of New Yorkers (Figure 10.23c).

Military Branding

The military is a lifestyle choice for many people. Moreover, many see the military as a gateway to careers with companies whose images and advertising foster strongly patriotic characteristics. The armed forces have been looking toward new advertising strategies for their recruitment efforts. Their advertisements are targeting 18- to 24-year-olds. The military wants recruits to know that their patriotic efforts will create viable career options. The army, with its slogan "strength, character, will- power," is trying to show ambitious high school graduates the type of person they can become by joining this branch of the armed services (www.goarmy.com/findex.jsp). And

the marines' slogan, "America's elite fighting force," creates an image of exclusivity, challenging potential recruits to prove their worthiness of being accepted (www.usmarines.com/_html/default.asp). The military incorporates a complete branded lifestyle package including clothing, training, and education.

Military Styling in Private Sector Branding

For the majority of people, the military is not considered a preferred lifestyle. Nonetheless, the rigors of military life have not diminished consumers' appetite for all things military. Our kitchen appliances, our vehicles (Humvee), our clothing (boots and cargo pants), our laptops (ruggedized versions) appear to be built to "mil-spec" (military specifications).

Consider a Super Shark, a WindTunnel, an Orca Twister, or a Dyson. What are these "things"? They are part of a new and emerging product line that was once a simple vacuum cleaner. An object that was once purely utilitarian is now available in vibrant or metallic colors with sleek shapes that may remind us of small rocket ships or hard-shelled bugs. Instead of being hidden in closets or basements, the vacuum is now used in layouts in our lifestyle magazines (Figure 10.24). "'We set a stage for a vacuum to be seen as a luxury product,' said Lori Dolnick of Thacker & Frank Communica-

10.24

tions in New Jersey, which handles the image of the vacuum made by Miele Inc., a German appliance company founded in 1899" (quoted in Eastman p. F1).

In addition to appliances, clothing has borrowed an image from the military. Note the success of REI, North Face, or Patagonia; they are mountaineering stores that sell a lifestyle image. Their clothing, camping equipment, and supplies are rugged enough for military maneuvers. If you are planning a trip to Tibet or a hike in your local mountains, their well-equipped stores can outfit you and your troops with the best in military-style gear.

The Jeep is a classic example of how a military vehicle has transformed its image. The original Jeep was built for the military during World War II. It was built to be a tough, reliable vehicle that maneuvered in bad conditions and rough terrain. Jeep now targets its advertising to specific lifestyles. Young adults and single guys buy the "Wrangler" with its rugged interior; the "Cherokee Laredo" is popular with suburban moms; and the "Grand Cherokees," with their plush leather interiors, portray an upwardly mobile lifestyle image.

Jeep is not the only product line with different choices targeting different lifestage and lifestyle segments. Aside from his "clubby Edwardian" image, Ralph Lauren advertises yet another lifestyle image, one of the "rugged cowboy," using guns, saddles, and cowboy hats as props for his store displays and advertising campaigns. His approach is different, but his message is similar. If you wear this clothing, you will be admired for your outdoor ruggedness.

Architects and designers also take industrial approaches to their design projects. Dyed concrete floors and countertops, large wheels on tables and shelving, steel storefront windows and doors, and unfinished plywood sheathing are now integral parts of their designs. While this is not militaristic, it certainly differs from the "shabby chic" look.

Professional Sports Branding

Designers are also seeking out other outlets for their creative ideas. The recent emergence of professional sports branding has been remarkable, and sports organizations today begin the design process for their team logos, colors, uniforms, arenas, and stadiums years before they actually field teams. And why not, when immense revenue is derived from licensing fees for fashionable jerseys and hats? Interior design and architecture firms most important clients are the stadiums and arenas that seek to maximize their luxury suites' revenue by ensuring fresh environments that reflect team color schemes and images.

The Internet and Lifestyle

Cars, computers, cellular phones, clothing, sports jerseys, and vacuum cleaners, although very different products, must all be branded and advertised in the various media and now via the Internet. However, unlike magazine or TV advertising, advertising on computers is directly measurable. Advertisers know almost immediately whether their ads are successful. Advertising success on the Internet is measured by "clicks," "click-throughs," and purchases. Network servers that run ads on banners spread across computer screens are also capable of measuring the number of times the banners appear, the number of times the user hits a banner and clicks through to the advertisement

FIG. 10.24 Dyson DC07 vacuum cleaner. [Courtesy, Dyson.]

itself, and ultimately how many purchases are made. Never before have advertisers been able to immediately gauge their success or failure and make quick adjustments to their advertising campaigns. This is revolutionary.

The importance of e-advertising should not be underestimated. Computer users are spending over seven billion hours a month in front of their computers (*PC Magazine*). Search engines are regularly placing banner ads on virtually all their pages. Thus, advertisers are assured a captive audience of millions every day, every hour, and every minute. However, because of the transitory nature of Web-surfing, graphic designers must ensure that their clients' logos and icons are attractive and instantly recognizable.

It is equally important to understand the significance of lifestyle sites on the Internet. There are millions of such sites accessible to Web-surfers. The combination of e-advertising and the allure of these beautifully designed and consumer-friendly sites is an extremely powerful tool. Virtually every consumer product is represented on the Internet. Advertisers and designers are now able to track and, at times, influence trends. In turn, design forecasting has become more accurate and profitable. Thus, we've seen how brand and lifestyle imaging has evolved from the early days of Paul Poiret's boutique *Ateleirs Martine* in Paris to worldwide Internet campaigns that reach billions at the click of a mouse.

REFERENCES

CHAPTER ONE

Arnheim, Rudolph, *Visual Thinking*. Berkeley, Los Angeles, and London: University of California Press, 1969.

Evans, Caroline, "The Golden Dustman: A Critical Evaluation of the Work of Martin Margiela and a Review of *Martin Margiela: Exhibition (9/4/1615)*." *Fashion Theory* Volume 2, Issue 1, pp. 73–94.

Horyn, Cathy, "Reports of Couture's Death Were Exaggerated." *New York Times*, July 11, 2004, ST 5.

Küchler, Susanne, "Rethinking Textile: The Advent of the 'Smart' Fiber Surface." *Textile 1* No. 3, Autumn 2003, 262–72.

Laver, James, *Style in Costume*. London: Oxford University Press, 1949.

Little, William, H.W. Fowler, and J. Coulson, *The Shorter Oxford English Dictionary*. Third Edition, London: Oxford University Press, 1967.

Lupton, Ellen, *Skin: Surface Substance and Design*. Cooper-Hewitt National Design Museum, Smithsonian Institution. New York: Princeton Architectural Press, 2002.

Lupton, Ellen, Donald Albrecht, Susan Yelavich, and Mitchell Owens, *National Design Triennial: Inside Design Now*. Cooper-Hewitt National Design Museum, Smithsonian Institution. New York: Princeton Architectural Press, 2003.

Mazza, Samuele, *Cinderella's Revenge*. San Francisco: Chronicle Books, 1994.

Metz, Cade. "Smart Skin: A Sixth Sense, and a Seventh, and an Eighth. . . ." *PC Magazine*, July 2004, p. 111.

Ministry of Culture and Tourism, Korea, *Fashion Art from Korea*. Korea Foundation, 2000.

Muschamp, Herbert, "House of Games." *Los Angeles Times Magazine*. July 18, 2004, pp. 40–45.

Packer, William, *The Art of* Vogue: *Covers 1909–1940*. New York: Harmony Books, 1980.

Pevsner, Nikolaus, *Pioneers of Modern Design: From William Morris to Walter Gropius*. Middlesex: Penguin Books, 1975.

Raizman, David, *History of Modern Design*. Upper Saddle River, NJ: Prentice Hall Inc., 2004.

Rawsthorn, Alice, *Yves Saint Laurent: A Biography*. London: Harper Collins Publishers, 1997.

Trilling, James, *The Language of Ornament*. New York: Thames and Hudson Inc., 2001.

Vercelloni, Isa Tutino, ed., *Missonologia: The World of Missoni*. New York: Abbeville Publishing Group, 1995.

Wake, Warren K., *Design Paradigms: A Sourcebook for Creative Visualization*. New York: John Wiley and Sons, Inc., 2000.

CHAPTER TWO

Addressing the Century: 100 Years of Art and Fashion. London: Hayward Gallery, 1998.

Black, J. Anderson, and Madge Garland, *A History of Fashion*. London: Macdonald and Co., under the Black Cat Imprint, 1990.

Blakemore, Robbie G., *History of Interior Design Furniture: From Ancient Egypt to Nineteenth-Century Europe*. New York: John Wiley and Sons, 1997.

Boardman, John, ed., *The Oxford History of Classical Art*. New York: Oxford University Press, 1993.

Boucher, François, *20,000 Years of Fashion: The History of Costume and Personal Adornment*, expanded ed. New York: Harry N. Abrams, 1987.

Celant, Germano, ed., "Art/Fashion, Skira Editore, Biennale Di Firenze." New York: Guggenheim Museum Soho, March 12–June 8, 1997.

Conran, Terence, *Terence Conran on Design*. New York: The Overlook Press, 1996.

Damase, Jacques, *Sonia Delaunay Fashion and Fabrics*. London: Thames and Hudson, 1991.

Deslandres, Yvonne, *Poiret*. New York: Rizzoli, 1987.

Eidelberg, Martin, ed., *Designed for Delight: Alternative Aspects of Twentieth Century Decorative Arts*. Montreal Museum of Decorative Arts, Paris/New York: Flammarion, 1997.

Hardy, Anne, "Dressed for the Part." *House and Garden,* February, 1992.

Joyce, Carol, *Textile Design: The Complete Guide to Printed Textiles for Apparel and Home Furnishings*. New York: Watson-Guptill, 1993.

Larsen, Jack Lenor, *Material Wealth: Living with Luxurious Fabrics*. New York: Abbeville Press, 1989.

Mackrell, Alice, *Paul Poiret*. New York: Holmes and Meier, 1990.

Martin, Richard, *Fashion and Surrealism*. New York: Rizzoli, Fashion Institute of Technology, 1987.

Pile, John, *A History of Interior Design*. New York: John Wiley and Sons, 2000.

Tanaka, Ikko, and Kazuko Koike, *Japan Color*. San Francisco: Chronicle Books, 1982.

Tapert, Annette, *Swid Powell Objects by Architects*. New York: Rizzoli, 1990.

Twentieth Century Decorative Arts. Montreal Museum of Decorative Arts, Paris/New York: Flammarion, 1997.

Victor, Adam, *The Marilyn Encyclopedia*. New York: Overlook Press, 1999.

Weltge, Sidrid Wortmann, *Women's Work: Textile Art from the Bauhaus*. San Francisco: Chronicle Books, 1993.

Willett, C., and Phyllis Cunnington, *The History of Underclothes*. New York: Dover Publications, 1992.

CHAPTER THREE

Albers, Anni, *On Weaving*. Middletown, Connecticut: Wesleyan University Press, 1965.

Batterberry, Ariane, & Michael Batterberry, *Mirror Mirror: A Social History of Fashion*. New York: Holt, Rinehart & Winston, 1979.

Bevin, Marjorie Elliott, *Design Through Discovery*, Second Edition. New York: Holt, Rinehart and Winston, 1970.

Bunn, Austin, "Not Fade Away." *New York Times Magazine*, December 1, 2002, pp. 60–65.

Columbia, David Patrick, New York Social Diary.com. Available: http://newyorksocialdiary.com/archive/social-diary8.15.02.html.

Eisner, Lisa, and Román Alonso, "A Handmaiden's Tale," *New York Times Magazine*, October 31, 2004, pp. 54–59.

Freudenheim, Susan, "Defining Art: What If You Can Sit in It?" *Los Angeles Times Calendar*, March 16, 2003, E43. E52–53.

Freudenheim, Susan, "Design, Art, and Fun." *Los Angeles Times Calendar*, March 16, 2003, E53.

Fujiwara, Dai, and Issey Miyake, *A-POC Making*, Exhibition Catalog. Berlin: Vitra Design Museum, 2001.

Gill, John, *Essential Gaudí*. Bath, U.K.: Parragon, 2001.

Golbin, Pamela, *Fashion Designers*. New York: Watson-Guptill, 2001.

Grillo, Paul Jacques, *What Is Design?* Chicago: Paul Theobald and Company, 1960.

Grimberg, Salomon, *Frida Kahlo*. City?: JG Press, 1997. Reprint. North Dighton, MA: World Publications Group, 2002.

Hayward, Helena, ed., *World Furniture*. London: Paul Hamlyn, 1969.

Herman, Lloyd E., *The Woven and Graphic Art of Anni Albers*, Exhibition Catalog. Washington, D.C.: Smithsonian Institution Press, 1985.

Hirschberg, Lynn, "Knit Picking." *Fashions of the Times, New York Times*, Spring 2003.

Jaffé, Hans L.C., *Piet Mondrian*. New York: Harry N. Abrams Inc., 1985.

Jennings, Norman, "Jhane Barnes at IIDEX 1997." Available: http://www.mtarch.com/njbarnes.html.

Jouve, Marie Andrée, *Issey Miyake*. New York: Rizzoli, 1997.

Lehmann, Ulrich, "Fashion and the Cultural Fabric of Architecture," *Architectural Record*, April 2001, p. 61.

Leland, John, "How the Disposable Sofa Conquered America." *New York Times Magazine*, December 1, 200, pp. 86–96..

McCarter, Robert, *Falling Water: Frank Lloyd Wright*. London: Phaidon, 1994.

McDowell, Colin, *Jean Paul Gaultier*. New York: Penguin Putnam, 2000.

Mendes, Valerie, and Amy de la Haye, *Twentieth Century Fashion*. London: Thames and Hudson, 1999.

Milbank, Caroline Rennolds, *New York Fashion: The Evolution of American Style*. New York: Harry N. Abrams, 1989.

Moffitt, Peggy, *The Rudi Gernreich Book*. New York: Rizzoli, 1991.

Mulvagh, Jane, Vogue: *The History of Twentieth Century Fashion*. London: Bloomsbury Books. 1988.

Pickover, Clifford A., *Chaos in Wonderland: Visual Adventures in a Fractal World*. New York: St. Martin's Press, 1994.

Quintanilla, Michael, "A Grand Finale," *Los Angeles Times*, February 19, 2002, E1.

Scott, A.O., "Interior Life," *New York Times Magazine*, December 1, 2002.

Stevenson, Seth, "Gimme Temporary Shelter," *New York Times Magazine*, May 18, 2003, p. 26.

Theis, Tammy, "Frida Kahlo: Fashion's Favorite Rebel Muse." *Tallahassee Democrat*, December 1, 2002. Available: www.tallahassee.com.

Toledo, Ruben, *Style Dictionary*. New York: Abbeville Press, 1996.

Veillon, Dominique, *Fashion under the Occupation*. Translated by Miriam Kochan. Oxford, New York: Berg, 2002.

Wines, James, *Green Architecture*. Köln, Germany: Taschen, 2002.

Yasinskaya, I., *Revolutionary Textile Design*. New York: Viking Press, 1983.

Zerbst, Rainer, *Antoni Gaudí: The Complete Buildings*. Köln, Germany: Taschen, 2002.

CHAPTER FOUR

Birren, Faber, *Creative Color*. Atglen, Pennsylvania: Schiffer, 1987.

Brusatin, Manlio, *A History of Colors*. Translated by Robert H. Hopcke and Paul Schwartz. Boston and London: Shambhala, 1991.

Fehrman, Kenneth R., and Cherie Fehrman, *Color: The Secret Influence*. Upper Saddle River, NJ: Prentice-Hall, 2000.

Hampton, Mark, *Mark Hampton on Decorating*. New York: Random House, 1989.

Heeger, Susan, "Testing Ground: A Garden Is a Laboratory for a California Color Expert." *Martha Stewart Living*, September 2003, p. 168.

Heringa, Rens, and Harmen C. Veldhuisen, *Fabric of Enchantment: Batik from the North Coast of Java*. Los Angeles County Museum of Art and Weatherhill, 1996.

Holtzschue, Linda, *Understanding Color: An Introduction for Designers*. New York: John Wiley and Sons, 2002.

Itten, Johannes, *The Color Star*. New York: John Wiley and Sons, 1985.

Itten, Johannes, *Design and Form: The Basic Course at the Bauhaus and Later*, Revised Edition. New York: John Wiley and Sons, 1975.

Itten, Johannes, *The Elements of Color*. Translated by Ernst von Haagen. New York: John Wiley and Sons, 2001.

Jerstorp, Karin, and Eva Köhlmark, *The Textile Design Book: Understanding and Creating Patterns Using Texture, Shape, and Color*. Asheville, NC: Lark Books, 1986.

Jones, Owen, *The Grammar of Ornament: All 100 Color Plates from the Folio Edition of the Great Victorian Sourcebook of Historic Design*. New York: Dover, 1987.

Loe, Nancy E., *Hearst Castle: An Interpretive History of W.R. Hearst's San Simeon Estate*. Santa Barbara, CA: Companion Press, 1994.

McDowell, Colin, *Hats: Status, Style and Glamour*. London: Thames and Hudson, 1992.

McGuire, Barbara A., *Wire in Design*. Iola, WI: Krause, 2001.

Milbank, Carolyn Rennolds, *New York Fashion: The Evolution of American Style*, New York: Harry N. Abrams, 1996.

Ogawa, Yoko, Junko Yamamoto, and Ei Kondo, *Color in Fashion: A Guide to Coordinating Fashion Colors*, Rockport, MA: Rockport, 1990.

Wake, Warren K., *Design Paradigms: A Sourcebook for Creative Visualization*. New York: John Wiley and Sons, 2000.

Walch, Margaret, and Augustine Hope. *Living Colors: The Definitive Guide to Color Palettes through the Ages*. San Francisco: Chronicle, 1995.

Wong, Wucius, *Principles of Form and Design*. New York: John Wiley and Sons, 1993.

Zakia, Richard D., and Hollis N. Todd. *Color Primer I and II*. Dobbs Ferry, NY: Morgan and Morgan, 1974.

CHAPTER FIVE

Aav, Marianne, *Marimekko: Fabrics Fashion Architecture*. New Haven: Yale University Press, 2003.

Bayliss, Sarah, "The New Art Wallpaper: It Doesn't Just Hang There." *New York Times*, June 20, 2003, AR 28.

Boucher, François, *20,000 Years of Fashion: The History of Costume and Personal Adornments*. New York: Harry N. Abrams, 1983.

Chamberlin, Bob, "Holding the (Fake) Bag." *Los Angeles Times*, August 21, 2003, B4.

Chicago, Judy, *The Dinner Party: A Symbol of Our Heritage*. New York: Anchor Press, 1979.

Conran, Terence, *On Design*. New York: The Overlook Press, 5–23.

Cunningham, Bill, "Cat Spotting." *New York Times*, February 22, 2004, ST 4.

Fiell, Charlotte, and Peter Fiell, *William Morris*. Koln, Germany: Taschen, 1999.

Grape, Wolfgang, *The Bayeux Tapestry*. Munich, New York: Prestel, 1994.

Grushkin, Paul D., *The Art of Rock*. New York: Artabas, 1987.

Heringa, Rens, and Harmen C. Veldhuisen, *Fabric of Enchantment: Batik from the North Coast of Java*. The Los Angeles County Museum of Art, 1996.

Jackson, Lesley, *Twentieth-Century Pattern Design*. New York: Princeton Architectural Press, 2002.

Jean, Georges, *Writing: The Story of Alphabets and Scripts*. New York: Harry N. Abrams, 1992.

Joyce, Carol, *Textile Design: The Complete Guide to Printed Textiles for Apparel and Home Furnishing*. New York: Watson-Guptill Publications, 1993.

Kahn, Eve M., "Neither Fish nor Fowl, a Department Store Defies Definition." *New York Times*, September 4, 2004.

Kaiser, Amanda, "Gucci Expanding into Home." *Women's Wear Daily*, June 16, 2003, 2, 17.

Kilmer Rosemary, and W. Otie Kilmer, *Designing Interiors*. Orlando: Holt, Rinehart and Winston, 1992.

La Ferla, Ruth, "Front Row: Will Aztec Symbols Go for the Gold?" *New York Times*, August 5, 2003.

Larsen, Jack Lenor, *Material Wealth: Loving with Luxurious Fabrics*. New York: Abbeville Press, 1989.

Leland John, "The Guru of Goo (and Gels, Mesh, and Resin)." *New York Times*, March 14, 2002, B1, B12.

Mackintosh, Charles Rennie, *Designs for Fabrics*. California: Pomegranate Publications, 1992.

Macy's, "In Color." *Los Angeles Times*, March 1, 2004, A7.

McCully, Marilyn, *Picasso Painter and Sculptor in Clay*. London: Royal Academy of Dramatic Arts, 1998.

McHarg, Ian L., *Design with Nature*. Garden City, New York: Doubleday/Natural History Press, 1971.

Moore, Booth, "Pleas and Queues." *Los Angeles Times*, May 26, 2003, E1.

Moore, Rowan, "Space Ship Selfridges." *Metropolis*, March 2004, 82.

Myers, Diana K., and Susan S. Bean, *From the Land of the Thunder Dragon: Textile Arts of Bhutan*. London: Serindia Publications, 1994.

Nichols, Sarah, *Aluminum by Design*. Pittsburgh: Carnegie Museum of Art, 2000.

Oei, Loan, and Cecile De Kegel, *The Elements of Design*. New York: Thames and Hudson, 2002.

Pile, John F., *Interior Design*. Upper Saddle River, NJ: Prentice-Hall, 1995.

"Product Briefs." *Architectural Record*, September 2003, 201.

Regensteiner, Else, *The Art of Weaving*. New York: Van Nostrand Reinhold, 1970.

Shaw, Sarah, "Style Beat." *House Beautiful*, June 1995.

Straeten, Judith, *Toiles de Jouy*. Salt Lake City: Gibbs Smith, 2002.

Viladas, Pilar, "Hey Lady!" *New York Times*, February 22, 2004.

Weltge, Sigrid Wortmann, *Women's Work: Textile Art from the Bauhaus*. London: Thames and Hudson, 1993.

CHAPTER SIX

Anyara Aphorisms, "Fashion Quotes." Available: koti.mbnet.fl/neptunia/fashion0.htm.2001.

Artnet Worldwide Corporation Artists, "Jamel Shabazz." New York, 2005. Available: www.artnet.com/artist/162043/Jamel_Shabazz.html.

Asia Travel at Reservation Network PTE Ltd., A Subsidiary of Asiatravel.com Holdings Ltd. Available: www.asiatravel.com/singapore/1929/room.html.

Benton, Charlotte, Tim Benton, and Ghislaine Wood, *Art Deco 1910–1939*. London: V&A Publications, 2003.

Blakemore, Robbie G., *History of Interior Design: Furniture from Ancient Egypt to Nineteenth-Century Europe*. New York: John Wiley & Sons, 1997.

Boucher, François, *20,000 Years of Fashion: The History of Costume and Personal Adornment*, Expanded Edition. New York: Harry N. Abrams, 1987.

Chang, Jade, "Rococo A-Go-Go." *Metropolis*. June 2004, p. 46.

Chottai, Kal, "Heat of the Moment." *Surface*, Issue No. 31, pp. 130–131.

Codrington, Andrea, "Custom-Made Miracles." *Metropolis*. March 2002.

Conran, Terence, *Terence Conran on Design*. Woodstock, NY: Overlook Press, 1996.

Cunningham, Bill, "On the Street: Extra Starch." *New York Times*, May 2, 2004, ST4.

Cunningham, Bill, "On the Street: Gossamer Wings." *New York Times*, July 25, 2004, ST4.

Dal Co, Francesco, Kurt W. Forster, and Hadley Arnold, *Frank O. Gehry: The Complete Works*. Milan: Mondadori Electa Spa, 2003.

"Décor Doctor Is Very, Very In." *Los Angeles Times*, May 13, 2004, F1, 4.

Design 360, "Mary Quant." CNN Interview.

Fiell, Charlotte, and Peter Fiell, *William Morris*. Koln, Germany: Benedikt Taschen Verlag, 1999.

Gössel, Peter, and Gabriele Leuthäuser, *Architecture in the Twentieth Century*. Koln, Germany: Benedikt Taschen Verlag, 1991.

Hastreiter, Kim, "Mix Master: Karl Lagerfeld Looks Everywhere for Inspiration." *Papermag*, Available: papermag.com/magazine/mag_01/mag_sept01/karl_lagerfeld.

Knight, Christopher, "The Hall Mark." *Los Angeles Times*, July 28, 2004, E1,12.

Lampugnani, Vittorio Magnago, *Encyclopedia of 20th Century Architecture*. New York: Harry N. Abrams, 1986.

Lupton, Ellen, Donald Albrecht, Susan Yelavich, and Mitchell Owens, *Inside Design Now*. New York: Princeton Architectural Press, 2003.

Massey, Anne, *Interior Design of the 20th Century*. London: Thames and Hudson, 1990.

Moonan, Wendy, "Eames Chairs Are Bending the Market." *New York Times*, April 30, 1999.

Muschamp, Herbert, "The Library That Puts on Fishnets and Hits the Disco." *New York Times*, May 16, 2004, Section 2, pp. 1, 31.

Pile, John, *A History of Interior Design*. London: Calmann & King, 2000.

Pile, John F., *Interior Design*, Second Edition. Englewood Cliffs, NJ: Prentice-Hall, 1995.

Red Hen Press, "Swingin' Chicks of the '60s," Acme Web Sites Inc. Available: www.swinginchicks.com/mary_quant.htm.

Robinson, Julian, *The Golden Age of Style*, New York: Harcourt, 1976, p. 58.

Todd Oldham/Studio, Trademark of L-7 Designs Inc. Available: www.toddoldhamstudio.com/about.html.

Trebay, Guy, "On the Street: The Age of Street Fashion." *New York Times*, October 27, 2002, Section 9A.

Trocmé, Suzanne, *Influential Interiors: Shaping 20th Century Style through Key Interior Designers*. New York: Clarkson Potter, 1999.

Viladas, Pilar, David Farber, and Guido Barbagelata, "Design Language." *New York Times*, May 9, 2004, pp. 67–72.

Vogue.com, "Who's Who: Karl Lagerfeld." 2004. Available: www.vogue.co.uk/who's_who/Karl_Lagerfeld/default.htmlwww.designerhistory.com/historyoffashion/trigere.html.

CHAPTER SEVEN

Barber, Elizabeth Wayland, *The Mummies of Ürümchi*. New York, W.W. Norton and Company, 1999.

Bartholomew, Therese Tse, Patricia Berger, and Robert Warren Clark, *Tibet: Treasures from the Roof of the World*. Exhibition Catalog. Santa Ana, CA: Bowers Museum of Cultural Art, 2003.

Boucher, François, *20,000 Years of Fashion*. New York: Harry N. Abrams, 1987.

Celanese Acetate LLC, *Complete Textile Glossary*. New York, 2001.

Channing, Marion L., *The Textile Tools of Colonial Homes*. Marion, MA: Marion L. Channing, 1971.

Charney, Len, *Build a Yurt: The Low-Cost Mongolian Round House*. New York: Sterling Publishing Co., Inc., 1974.

Cheng, Scarlet, "A Long-Gone Culture's Timeless Textiles." *Los Angeles Times Calendar*, August 5, 2001, p. 58.

Colchester, Chloë, *The New Textiles: Trends + Traditions*. London: Thames and Hudson, Ltd., 1993.

De Koning-Stapel, Hanne Vibeke, *Silk Quilts: From the Silk Road to the Quilter's Studio*. Lincolnwood, IL: The Quilt Digest Press, NTC Contemporary Publishing Group, 2000.

D'Harcourt, Raoul, *Textiles of Ancient Peru and Their Techniques*. Seattle: University of Washington Press, 1962.

Dupont-Auberville, M., *Classic Textile Designs*. Originally published as *Ornamental Textile Fabrics*, London: Asher & Co., 1877. London: Random House UK, Ltd., 1989.

Guirand, Felix, *Greek Mythology*. London: Paul Hamlyn Ltd., 1965.

Hefford, Wendy, *The Victoria and Albert Museum's Textile Collection: Design for Printed Textiles in England from 1750 to 1850*. London: Victoria and Albert Museum, 1992.

Held, Shirley E., *Weaving: A Handbook of the Fiber Arts*. New York: Holt, Rinehart and Winston, 1978.

Herman-Cohen, Valli, "What's Good Enough for the Couch Is Good Enough for the Closet." *Los Angeles Times*, August 3, 2001, E 1–3.

Janson, H.W., *History of Art*. New York: Harry N. Abrams, 1991.

Joyce, Carol, *Textile Design: The Complete Guide to Printed Textiles for Apparel and Home Furnishing*. New York: Watson-Guptill Publications, 1993.

J. Paul Getty Museum, *Handbook of the Collections*. Los Angeles: J. Paul Getty Museum, 1997.

Kent, Kate Peck, *Navajo Weaving: Three Centuries of Change*. Santa Fe, NM: School of American Research Press, 1985.

Koda, Harold, *Goddess: The Classical Mode*. (Metropolitan Museum of Art Series), New Haven and London: Yale University Press, 2003.

Lebeau, Carolyn, *Fabrics: The Decorative Art of Textiles*. New York: Clarkson Potter Publishers, 1994.

Meller, Susan, and Joost Elffers, *Textile Designs: 200 Years of European and American Patterns for Printed Fabrics Organized by Style, Motif, Color, Layout, and Period*. New York: Harry N. Abrams, 1991.

Mendes, Valerie, *The Victoria and Albert Museum's Textile Collection: British Textiles from 1900 to 1937*. London: Victoria and Albert Museum, 1992.

Morant, Deborah, "Historic Ideas," *Traditional Home*, May 2003, 66–72.

Newman, Cathy, "Dreamweavers." *National Geographic*, January 2003, 51–73.

Nylander, Jane C., *Fabrics for Historic Buildings*. Washington, DC: The Preservation Press, 1990.

Paine, Melanie, *The Textile Art in Interior Design*. New York: Simon and Schuster, 1990.

Palmer, Michele, *Toile: The Storied Fabrics of Europe and America*. Atglen, PA: Schiffer Publishing, 2003.

Parry, Linda, *William Morris Textiles*. London: Weidenfeld and Nicholson, 1983.

Rhodes, Mary, *Small Woven Tapestries*. London: B.T. Batsford Limited, 1973.

Schoeser, Mary, *Fabrics and Wallpapers: Twentieth-Century Design*. New York: E.P. Dutton, 1986.

Schoeser, Mary, *World Textiles: A Concise History*. London: Thames and Hudson, 2003.

Strickler, Carol, *American Woven Coverlets*. Loveland, CO: Interweave Press, 1987.

Thomas, Michel, Christine Mainguy, and Sophie Pommier, *Textile Art*. Geneva: Editions d'Art Skira, New York: Rizzoli International Publications, 1985.

Trocmé, Suzanne, *Fabric*. London: Mitchell Beazley, Octopus Publishing Group Limited, 2002.

Wada, Yoshiko Iwamoto, *Memory on Cloth: Shibori Now*. Tokyo, Japan: Kodansha International, 2002.

Weissman, Judith Reiter, and Wendy Lavitt, *Labors of Love: America's Textiles and Needlework, 1650–1930*. New York: Random House Wings Books, 1994.

www.mastgeneralstore.com/msledger/february2005/productspotpatagonia.php3.

CHAPTER EIGHT

Abramovitch, Ingrid, "The Truth about Color." Photographed by Sang An and Francesco Mosto. *House & Garden*, March 2004, 85–95.

Alonso, Roman, "Big Chill." Photographs by Lisa Eisner. *New York Times Magazine Men's Fashions of the Times*, March 14, 2004, 93–96.

Arnold, Rebecca, *Fashion, Desire and Anxiety: Image and Morality in the 20th Century.* New Brunswick, NJ: Rutgers University Press, 2001. First published in Great Britain by I.B. Tauris, 2001.

Bahney, Anna, "New Way for Teenagers to See if They Bounce." *New York Times*, March 28, 2004, ST 1–2.

Barcott, Bruce, "Changing All the Rules." *New York Times Magazine*, April 4, 2004, p. 38.

Barthes, Roland, *The Fashion System.* Translated by Matthew Ward and Richard Howard. Berkeley and Los Angeles: The University of California Press, 1990. Originally published by Hill and Wang, 1983.

Bellafante, Ginia, "Art That Wears $780 Shoes." *New York Times*, April 11, 2002, AR 1, 29.

Bellafante, Ginia, "The Power of Adult Clothes in a Youth-Obsessed Culture." *New York Times*, Week in Review, March 28, 2004, p. 14.

Brannon, Evelyn L., *Fashion Forecasting.* New York: Fairchild Publications, 2000.

Brooks, David, "Our Sprawling, Supersize Utopia." *New York Times Magazine*, April 4, 2004, p. 46.

Cameron, Kristi, "Peep Shoe." *Metropolis*, July 2003, p. 40.

Carr, David, "Not for You, Mr. Trump." *New York Times*, Week in Review, May 9, 2004, p. 14.

Clines, Francis X., "The American Tribes Prepare Their National Showcase." *New York Times*, Week in Review, March 28, 2004, p. 12.

Cohen, Lizabeth, *A Consumers' Republic: The Politics of Mass Consumption in Postwar America.* New York: Vintage Books, Random House, 2003.

Crane, Diana, *Fashion and Its Social Agendas: Class, Gender, and Identity in Clothing.* Chicago and London: University of Chicago Press, 2000.

Critser, Greg, *Fat Land: How Americans Became the Fattest People in the World.* New York: Houghton Mifflin, 2004.

Davis, Fred, *Fashion, Culture and Identity.* Chicago: University of Chicago Press, 1992.

De La Haye, Amy, Cathie Dingwall, *Surfers Soulies Skinheads and Skaters: Subcultural Style from the Forties to the Nineties.* Woodstock, New York: The Overlook Press, 1996.

Dominus, Susan, "Life in the Age of Old, Old Age." *New York Times Magazine*, February 22, 2004, p. 26.

Estabrook, Barry, "In the Air, on the Cheap." *New York Times*, April 4, 2004, TR 9.

Forstenzer, Martin, "In Search of Fine Art Amid the Paper Towels." *New York Times*, February 22, 2004, BU 4.

Foster, Linda, "Ethical Consumerism." *Textile View*, Spring 2002, pp. 26–27.

Genocchio, Benjamin, "For Japanese Girls, Black Is Beautiful." *New York Times*, April 4, 2004, AR 36.

Gilster, Paul, *Digital Literacy.* New York: John Wiley & Sons, 1997.

Gladwell, Malcolm, *The Tipping Point: How Little Things Make a Big Difference.* New York: Little, Brown and Company, 2000.

Grimes, William, "Mocha Puffs and Berry Notes: An Ex Smoker Slips." *New York Times*, May 2, 2004, ST 8.

Grimes, William, "Supersize, We Knew Thee Too Well." *New York Times*, March 7, 2004, WK 2.

Harmon, Amy, "It's a Coddlin' Town." *New York Times*, April 11, 2004, TR 9.

Hine, Thomas, *I Want That! How We All Became Shoppers.* New York: Perennial, Harper Collins, 2003.

Hochman, David, "In Searching We Trust." *New York Times*, March 14, 2004, St 1–2.

Iovine, Julie V., "Petropolis: Cashing in on Being Cute." *New York Times*, January 20, 2002, BW 1, 4.

Ito, Robert, "Sewing Dignity." *Orion*, November/December 2003, pp. 16–17.

Kaiser, Amanda, "Gucci Expanding into Home." *Womens Wear Daily*, June 16, 2003, pp. 2, 17.

Kauf, Joyce, "Multi-generational Marketing Grows Up." *FGI Bulletin*, Issue 3, 2003, pp. 1–2.

Kuczynski, Alex, "A Lovelier You, with Off-the-Shelf Parts." *New York Times*, March 14, 2004, WK, 1, 12.

La Ferla, Ruth, "An Old Question for a New Crowd: 'Can We Talk?'" *New York Times*, May 2, 2004, ST 1, 9.

Levy, Ariel, "Shopping for Surgery." *Vogue*, June 2004, 180–82.

Marx, Patricia, "Absolutely Fatuous." Illustrations by Joe Eula. *New York Times, Fashions of the Times*, Spring 2003, p. 188.

Mechling, Lauren, "She's Wearing My Chair." *Wall Street Journal*, April 23, 2004, W1, 8.

Merkin, Daphne, "Keeping the Forces of Decrepitude at Bay." *New York Times Magazine*, May 2, 2004, p. 64.

Nakano, Craig, "Visionaries: A Photographic Memory." *Los Angeles Times*, March 3, 2005, F1, 10–11.

Norwich, William, "18th-Century Crib Notes." *New York Times Magazine*, April 25, 2004, p. 64.

Nova Marketing Inc., "The Multi-Generational Shopper." Available: www.novainc.com.

Nunberg, Geoffrey, "Geezers, Gerries and Golden Agers." *New York Times*, March 28, 2004, WK 7.

Perna, Rita, *Fashion Forecasting: A Mystery or a Method?* New York: Fairchild Publishing, 1987.

Pescovitz, David, "Body Tech." *One*, Premier Issue, 2000, pp. 130–135.

Popcorn, Faith, and Lys Marigold, *Clicking: Sixteen Trends to Future Fit Your Life*. New York: Harper Collins, 1996.

Quart, Alissa, *Branded: The Buying and Selling of Teenagers*. New York: Basic Books, Perseus Books Group, 2003.

Quintanilla, Michael, "Helping Men Cast Off Chains." *Los Angeles Times*, September 13, 2002, E1, 3.

Rendon, Jim, "Now, a Man's World Is at the Spa or Salon." *New York Times*, March 28, 2004, B3.

Rich, Frank, "The Joy of Gay Marriage." *New York Times*, February 29, 2004, AR Section 2, 1, 18.

Rozhon, Tracie, "Out to Retail Pasture? No, Just a New Track." *New York Times*, March 14, 2004, BU 10.

Samaty, Mark Alan, "Boox," *New York Times Book Review*, March 28, 2004, p. 19.

Sciolino, Elaine, "France, Seams under Pressure, Remeasures Itself." *New York Times International*, April 25, 2003, A4.

Shepherd, John, "Defining Moment: The Eye Popping Work of Takashi Murakami Brings New Airiness to Midtown Manhattan." Photographed by Thomas Loof. *House and Garden*, March 2004, p. 114.

Smith, Martin J., and Patrick J. Kiger, "The *Toink!* Heard 'Round the World." *Los Angeles Times Magazine*, March 28, 2004, p. 22.

Steingarten, Jeffrey, "Chain Game." *Vogue*, June 2004, pp. 250–253, 282–283.

Strasser, Susan, *Waste and Want: A Social History of Trash*. New York: Henry Holt and Company, 1999.

Tahmincioglu, Eve, "Cutting the Home Cord, Not the Home Number." *New York Times*, February 22, 2004, BU 9.

Tein, Ellen, "Pulse." *New York Times*, February 29, 2004, ST, 3.

Tung, Jennifer, "Things We Love." *House and Garden*, May 2004, p. 29.

Walker, Rob, "Sprite Remix." *New York Times Magazine*, March 28, 2004, p. 24.

Walker, Rob, "Unstained Masses." *New York Times Magazine*, May 2, 2004, p. 40.

Warner, Fara, "Yes, Women Spend (and Saw and Sand)." *New York Times*, February 29, 2004, BU 3.

Winters, Wendi, "FG Talk: Popeye's Girlfriend Would Be Thrilled." *FGI Bulletin*, Issue 1, 2004, p. 3.

Zernike, Kate, "First, Your Water Was Filtered. Now It's Your Life." *New York Times*, March 21, 2004, WK 4.

CHAPTER NINE

Avins, Mimi, "Material Girl." *Los Angeles Times*, August 2, 2001, E3.

Bell, Judith, and Kate Ternus, *Silent Selling: Best Practices and Effective Strategies in Visual Merchandising*, Second Edition. New York: Fairchild Publications, 2002.

Bell, Judith, *Silent Selling: The Complete Guide to Fashion Merchandise Presentation*. Cincinnati, Ohio: ST Publications, 1988.

Dean, Corinna, *Graphic Interiors: Spaces Designed by Graphic Artists*. Gloucester, MA: Rockport Publishers, 2000.

Diamond, Jay, and Ellen Diamond, *Contemporary Visual Merchandising*. Upper Saddle River, NJ: Prentice-Hall, 1999.

Diamond, Jay, and Ellen Diamond, *The World of Fashion*, Second Edition, Fairchild Publications, New York, 1997.

Diamond, Jay, and Sheri Litt, *Retailing in the New Millennium*. New York: Fairchild Publications, 2003.

Earnest, Leslie, "Bargain Hunters Stalk Aisles." *Los Angeles Times*, November 30, 2002, A1

Eastman, Janet, "A Welcoming Light." *Los Angeles Times*, August 1, 2002, E2.

Eastman, Janet, "Buying into a Trend." *Los Angeles Times*, November 1, 2002, E32.

Gladwell, Malcolm, "The Science of Shopping." *The New Yorker*, November 4, 1996, pp. 66–75.

Gladwell, Malcolm, *The Tipping Point: How Little Things Can Make a Big Difference*. New York: Little, Brown and Company, 2000.

Goldberger, Paul, "High-Tech Emporiums." *The New Yorker*, March 25, 2002, p. 100.

Kiger, Patrick J., "Living Ever Larger." *Los Angeles Times Magazine*, June 9, 2002.

Komaiko, Leslee, "It's a Mall World After All." *Los Angeles Times Calendar Weekend*, August 1, 2002, pp. 6–13.

McNamara, Mary, "Attention Shoppers: Kmart Wrote Its Epitaph." *Los Angeles Times*, January 25, 2002, E1.

McNamara, Mary, "See Page 32 to Order an Ideal Life." *Los Angeles Times*, December 20, 2001, E1.

Moore, Booth, "A Sweets Success Story." *Los Angeles Times*, October 3, 2002, E1.

Muhlhausen, John, "Wayfinding Is Not Signage." *Signs of the Times Magazine*. Available: www.signweb.com/ada/cont/wayfinding0800.html.

Muschamp, Herbert, "Forget the Shoes, Prada's New Store Stocks Ideas." Available: www.nytimes.com, December 16, 2001.

Pearlstein, Steven, "Stores Should Look Back to Find Future." *Washington Post*, March 2, 2005, E01.

Pegler, Martin, *Visual Merchandising and Display*, Third Edition. New York: Fairchild Publications, 1995.

Rosenbaum, Claudia, "Intrigue, Lust and Merchandising." *Los Angeles Times*, June 10, 2002, E2.

Schaffer, Carl, *Catalog of the International Retail Design Conference*, September 2002, p. 5.

Stone, Elaine, *The Dynamics of Fashion*, New York: Fairchild Publications, 1999.

Strasser, Susan, *Waste and Want: A Social History of Trash*. New York: Henry Holt and Company, 1999.

Twitchell, James, *Living It Up: Our Love Affair with Luxury*. New York: Columbia University Press, 2002.

Winfrey, Oprah, "Oprah Talks to Ralph Lauren." *O Magazine*, October 2002.

CHAPTER TEN

Adam, Peter, *Eileen Gray: Architect/Designer*. New York: Harry N. Abrams, 2000.

Albrecht, Donald, Robert Schonfeld, Lindsay Stamm Shapiro, *Russel Wright: Creating American Lifestyle*. New York: Harry N. Abrams, 2001.

American Memory, Today in History, "Good Housekeeping," April 22, 2003. Available: www.memory.loc.gov/ammem/today/may02.html.

Bellafante, Ginia, "Creating a Brand Image: The Mannequin Is the Message." *New York Times*, December 14, 1999, p. B16.

Colman, David, "The Gem in a Modern, Sleek Crown." *New York Times*. May 11, 2003, p. 8.

Eastman, Janet, "Equipped: The New Object of Desire? It's the Vacuum." *Los Angeles Times*, May 22, 2003, p. F1, 8.

Family Education Network, Inc., Meaning of Brandname, 2000–2003. Available: www.print.infoplease.com/spot/trademarks1html.

Fashion Group International, *Hit or Miss? Frontliners Event*. New York: FGI. Issue 2, 2002.

Filler, Martin, "Ruhlmann Rules." *House Beautiful*, pp. 96–101.

Food Network, "Martha Stewart: Biography," June 4, 2003. Available: www.staging.foodtv.com/celebrities/stewart-bio/0,3405,,00.html.

General Electric Theater, "U.S. Anthology," June 29, 2003. Available: www.museum.tv/archives/etv/G/htmlG/generalelect/generalelect.htm.

Gobé, Marc, *Emotional Branding: The New Paradigm for Connecting Brands to People*. New York: Allworth Press, 2001.

Hanks, Kurt, Larry Belliston, and Dave Edwards, *Design Yourself!* Los Altos, CA: William Kaufmann, 1978.

Home and Garden Television: "Interiors by Designs," June 4, 2003. Available: www.hgtv.com/hgtv/shows_ibd/article/0,1805,HGTV_3858_1388249,00.html.

Johnson, David, "Trademarks: A History of a Billion Dollar Business." infoplease.com/spot/trademarks, 2003.

Kaufman, Leslie, "Après Yeves, Le Deluge?" *New York Times*, January 20, 2002, Section 9, p. 1, 2.

Keiser, Sandra J., and Myrna B. Garner, *Beyond Design: The Synergy of Apparel Product Development*. New York: Fairchild Publications, 2003.

Kleinfield, N. R., "The Lincoln Tunnel? Maybe Not, But New York Is Open to Branding Possibilities." *New York Times*, April 6, 2003, p. A20.

Koberg, Don, and Jim Bagnall, *The Universal Traveler: A Soft-Systems Guide to: Creativity, Problem-Solving and the process of Reaching Goals*. Los Altos, CA: William Kaufmann, 1976.

Koenenn, Connie, "IKEA Exploring Home Décor in Space." *Los Angeles Times*, October 7, 1999, p. E3.

Laermer, Richard, *Trend Spotting: Think Forward, Get Ahead, and Cash in on the Future*. New York: Berkley Publishing Group, 2002.

Massey, Anne, *Interior Design of the 20th Century*. London: Thames and Hudson, 1990.

New York State Emblems – "I (Love) NY," June 20, 2003. Available: www.nysl.nysed.gov/emblems/iluvny.htm.

Online with Mary Engelbreit, "Meet Mary," June 4, 2004. Available: www.maryengelbreit.com/MeetMary/Meet-Mary.htm.

Pile, John, *A History of Interior Design*. London: Calmann & King, 2000.

A Short History of Bonnie Cashin, June 29, 2003. Available: www.swankvintage.com/cashin.html.

A Short History of Claire McCardell, June 29, 2003. Available: www.swankvingage.com/mccardell.

Sischy, Ingrid, "The Designer Coco Chanel," June 29, 2003. Available: www.time.com/time/time100/artists/profile/chanel.html.

Smith, Jane S., *Elsie de Wolfe: A Life in the High Style*. New York: Atheneum, 1982.

Society for New York City History.

Temporal, Paul, *Branding in Asia: The Creation, Development, and Management of Asian Brands for the Global Market*. New York: John Wiley & Sons, 1999.

Troy, Nancy J., *Couture Culture: A Study in Modern Art and Fashion*. Cambridge, MA: Massachusetts Institute of Technology, 2003.

Twitchell, James B., *Lead Us into Temptation: The Triumph of American Materialism*. New York: Columbia University Press, 1999.

Twitchell, James B., *Living It Up: Our Love Affair with Luxury*. New York: Columbia University Press, 2002.

INDEX